T0128021

From Ouisconsin to Caughnawaga

Or

Tales of the Great Lakes First Nations

David D Plain

Order this book online at www.trafford.com
or email orders@trafford.com

Most Trafford titles are also available at major online book retailers.

Printed in the United States of America.

ISBN: 978-1-4669-8479-0 (sc)
ISBN: 978-1-4669-8684-8 (e)

Trafford rev. 09/10/2013

www.trafford.com

North America & international
toll-free: 1 888 232 4444 (USA & Canada)
fax: 812 355 4082

Also By David D Plain

The Plains of Aamjiwnaang

Ways of Our Grandfathers

1300 Moons

Contents

To The First Nations of the Great Lakes

Preface

From *Ouisconsin to Caughnawaga* is a collection of historical tales of the indigenous peoples of the Great Lakes region. Although they are histories and they are non-fiction they are first and foremost a compendium of short stories and should be read for entertainment. Sources for the stories range from historical letters and reports to works by nineteenth and twentieth century historians. Much use was made of historical societies such as Wisconsin, Michigan, Ohio and New York as well as University archives. Some of the content also contains First Nation oral stories. A few of these stories can be found in my other books however, these are for the most part more fully expanded.

For those readers who don't understand the French language Ouisconsin is how the Territory of Wisconsin was spelled in the historical record during the French regime in North America. The spelling for Caughnawaga is also taken from those same records and was a Mohawk community at the confluence of the Ottawa and St. Lawrence Rivers in Quebec. It still exists today as a Mohawk reserve at Montreal and is commonly spelled Kahnawake.

The reader will also notice dates inserted below the sub-titles. From *Ouisconsin to Caughnawaga* is actually a collection of blog postings I did over a three year period. These dates represent the dates the various stories were posted to the official Books by David D Plain Blog. I left them in so you might be able to see how the blog postings actually went. Notice at the end of each post the next sub-title is given as NEXT WEEK. Also notice I didn't often meet that target. You might also observe a great gap between November 2011 and September 2012. During this time I was experiencing one of those infamous "writer's blocks". The postings have undergone very little editing. Titles and subtitles were edited somewhat in order to collect the postings into individual short stories. Also comments referencing certain images have been edited out as there are no images in the book so they made no sense.

The book is laid out in two sections; ALLIES WITH THE FRENCH and ALLIES WITH THE BRITISH. It flows chronologically and begins with the story of the Sauk War which happened c 1618. It ends with the story of an "Indian Council" in 1818. As you read through the short stories you will encounter many historical events and people you recognize; events such as the establishment of Detroit, the fall of Fort William Henry, and the Battle of Moraviantown. You will also recognize such famous characters as Cadillac, Montcalm and Wolfe, George Washington, Daniel Boone and Isaac Brock. The period covered was one of tumultuous upheaval as First Nations tried their best to stem the tide of much more dominant societies. It only takes a quick perusal of the Contents to see that they continually lurched from conflict to conflict.

The first Europeans into the area were the French. They had a policy of exploiting the resources, mostly furs, and taking them back France. There was little desire for land and no great influx of colonists. This arrangement of trade of pelts for European goods worked well for both and there was no warring against the French.

However, when the French was supplanted by the British the situation changed. The British also engaged in the fur trade but they had a colonial policy of providing land for their colonists as well. Of course this land had to be taken from First Nations and was done so either by treaty or by settler squatting. After the American Revolution First Nations had to deal with the Americans and were constantly fighting their surge ever westward. First Nations looked upon the Americans as a Windigo with an insatiable appetite for more land. From *Ouisconsin to Caughnawaga* tells the story of this struggle through the telling of its fourteen short stories.

Allies with the French

The Sauk War

A War of Expulsion

October 21, 2009

I'm going to post a weekly blog on the history of the Great Lakes Basin. It shall be a series of historical snippets garnered from a variety of sources. These include professional and amateur historical publications as well as traditional stories passed down for generations among the native peoples of the area. I will not be citing any sources but will be telling these stories as if speaking to a group in the grand lodge. The following is my first installment and I sincerely hope that you enjoy it and will want to come back for more.

Long ago, before the great Iroquois War, even before the white man set his eyes on the lower Lake Huron and St. Clair River districts, they were occupied by the Sauk Nation. Their lodges were pitched in the Saginaw watershed and they used the St. Clair region as their hunting grounds. About the year 1618 the Petun or Tobacco Nation who lived in the Bruce Peninsula area of Ontario wanted to expand their hunting grounds, so they asked their allies and trading partners, the Ottawa, if they would join them in a war on the Sauk. The Ottawa agreed and reported their intentions to the Chippewa and Potawatomi because all three nations made up the Three Fires Confederacy.

Now the Sauk was a powerful nation who had been belligerent and antagonistic toward their neighbors. They had continually made war on the Chippewa who lived to their north and the Potawatomi to their southeast. The Three Fires in a grand council held at Mackinaw Island determined they should join in and make it a war of expulsion.

The Petun and Ottawa moved down the eastern shore of Lake Huron and attacked various Sauk parties in the St. Clair district. At the same time the Chippewa and Potawatomi made their way down the western shoreline of Lake Huron to Saginaw Bay where they camped until nightfall. Under the cover of darkness they stealthily made their way up both sides of the Saginaw River until they came upon a large ridge where the Sauk had made one of their main villages. The warriors on the western side of the river waited until dawn then attacked with such ferocity that most were massacred. Some survivors fled up river to a village located near present day Bay City, Michigan. The eastern division of the invading warriors attacked it with the same ferocity and it suffered the same fate.

Survivors fled to a small island about a quarter mile up the river. They had a measure of security there because the invaders had no canoes to reach them. A siege was put in place until the next morning. The river had frozen over the night before enabling both parties to attack, one from each side. All the Sauk were killed except 12 women who were taken prisoner.

NEXT WEEK: Flight to Wisconsin

Flight to Wisconsin

October 28, 2009

We left the story at that small island on the Saginaw River where the invading warriors had exterminated the Sauk garrison.

The Chippewa/Potawatomi force moved up the Saginaw to the confluence of the Cass, Shiawassee and Tittabawassee rivers where the main force divided sending a group up each of those rivers. The band that moved up the Shiawassee divided again sending warriors up the Flint River. There were many small villages on these rivers and each one was overpowered and many were slain. A few from each battle escaped always fleeing upstream.

There were three particularly large Sauk towns on the Saginaw tributaries. One was located on the bluffs of the Flint River near the present-day town of Flushing, another just a few miles up the Tittabawassee. The third was located on the Cass River at the bend where Bridgeport now stands. The Sauk that were killed at their town on the Tittabawassee were buried in a mass grave on the banks of that river creating a large burial mound.

After each battle some Sauk survivors escaped always fleeing west. They gathered on the eastern shore of Lake Michigan where they fled across the lake to Wisconsin. This left a large expanse of territory in central Michigan empty. The victors returned to Mackinaw Island with the twelve women captives. They were the only prisoners taken.

A grand council was held to determine what to do with the twelve and to consider the appropriation of the territory gained. The elders decided to send the twelve women west to be put under the protection of the Sioux. This angered many of the young men because they wanted to put them to death by torture. The territory on the east side of Lake Huron and the St. Clair River district was given to the Ottawa and Petun as new hunting grounds.

The Saginaw watershed was shared by the Chippewa and Potawatomi as a neutral hunting ground. However, as they ventured into the new territory some unfortunate occurrence seemed to happen to each hunting party. After some time they began to surmise that some Sauk warriors were still there lurking about seeking their revenge. Others thought the territory haunted with the spirits of the slain Sauk warriors. Eventually the territory was avoided and only used as a place of exile for members who had committed serious crimes.

NEXT WEEK: The Jesuits Arrive in Huronia.

Life in Huronia

The Jesuits Arrive in Huronia

November 4, 2009

This week I'm starting a post on Huronia and the great change it had undergone by the middle of the seventeenth century. Indeed, the whole of Southern Ontario had undergone tumultuous upheaval. But first let me describe the first contact between the Iroquoian speaking peoples of Southern Ontario and the Europeans.

In the first half of the century the Huron Nation were living between Georgian Bay and Lake Ontario. The Tobacco Nation was living just west of them in the area of the Bruce Peninsula with the Neutral Nation occupying the territory north of Lake Erie. But the first to see the bearded, pale skinned men were the Huron.

Samuel D. Champlain made his way to Huronia via the Ottawa River. A sharp left at the Mattawa River, a short portage to Lake Nipissing and down the French River to Georgian Bay brought him to the outskirts of Huronia. This would quickly become the preferred trade route to Montreal and far superior French trade goods.

Never slow at recognizing an opportunity to save lost souls the Church sent its most ardent evangelists, the Jesuits, back to Huronia to show these poor devils the way to Paradise. And they didn't mind the arduous, month-long trip either. In 1637 Father

Jean de Brebeuf wrote in his instructions for arriving Jesuits that they had to try to eat at daybreak because the day was long and the "barbarians" only ate at sunrise and sunset. He also said of his own journey there that he was on the road for thirty days of continual hard work with only one day of rest. Not a trip for the faint of heart!

Huronia, he tells us, was a thriving country of about twenty towns with a population of 30,000. At first the outlook for the new relationship between these very different peoples looked bright. Trade was good and this pleased the Governor who represented the state. Conversions were being made pleasing the Bishop who represented the Church in New France. But all was not well in the land of the Huron. There was a foreboding sentence at the end of his very first letter that foreshadowed a calamity to come.

Smallpox and measles! These were dreaded diseases in the seventeenth century, even more so for the poor Huron. The Europeans had struggled with these maladies for centuries and had built up some immunity, but not the peoples of the New World. They had no immunity.

The Jesuits believed their immunity to be a gift of God and blamed the sickness on the "deviltry" practiced by the Huron. They continued to tend to the sick and reported back to their superiors that the sickness had grown more general and widespread. Father Francois Joseph Mercier reported in 1639 that of the 300 conversions at his post that year 122 people were sick!

All this sickness produced another critical problem for them, famine. There weren't enough healthy people to tend the fields or go on the hunt to produce the amount of food required to support the population. So, only a few short years after meeting their saviors from the east the mighty Huron Nation was languishing in sickness and famine. Two calamities had befallen them. Would there be a third? Stay tuned next week to find out!

NEXT WEEK: Huronia in the 1640's

Huronia in the 1640's

November 11, 2009

Hi Everyone! Well another Wednesday is here and it's time to find out how our poor Huron people are going to fare. We left them last week languishing in sickness and famine.

One of the difficulties the Black Robes brought to their new mission field was division. The coming schism in the Nation would set one Huron against another. This would only serve to weaken a once proud and powerful people.

The Church considered a Christian to be anyone partaking in the sacrament of Baptism. Not all were so inclined. Many preferred to remain true to their father's religion thus exasperating the good Fathers. In history these obstinate ones were referred to as traditionalists.

However, the Jesuits at the time were not so kind to them either in name or in deed. Father Peron cried out to his superiors back in Quebec that their holy men were the devil's religious, their traditional practices no more than deviltries. Their medical practitioners he labeled as sorcerers and their instruments charms. Their staunch belief in dreams he called idolatry, master of their lives and the god of the country. Needless to say the traditionalists were looked down upon.

On the other hand those who converted were given preferential treatment. The Father's duty was to look after the Christian Huron, to heal their diseases both of soul and body all to the great advancement of Christianity. According to Father Ragueneau the new converts all seriously attended to their soul's salvation and this clearly banished vice. Virtue ruled in the new Church at Huronia and it was seen as the home of holiness. To the Church it became a black and white issue. The convert was in the Kingdom of God and the rejectionist the Kingdom of Satan!

Preferential treatment was not limited to the Church. The state also indulged in the practice. Trade practices influenced by the Society of Jesus gave converts preferential prices for their pelts. Much worse was French trade policy regarding firearms. Guns were not traded to the Huron except in extraordinary circumstances. If a convert proved he was sincere over a long period of time he could procure a gun upon his priest's recommendation. Needless to say there weren't many muskets the fair land of Huronia.

Not so in the land of the Five Nation League of Iroquois. They had been trading furs for guns for a long time with the Dutch without restrictions. This of course gave them quite an advantage over their neighbors to the north. Father Barthelemy Vimont wrote the bishop that the Mohawks had about 300 guns and were making incursions into the country to north. The Huron, who were going to Montreal for trade and not for war, had not one gun. So when met by a party of Iroquois their only defense was to abandon their pelts and flee.

The French blamed the Dutch accusing them of putting the Mohawks up to these raids. They thought that it was the Dutch's design to have the French harassed by the Iroquois to the point of giving up and abandoning all. The French misunderstood. What they didn't know was the Iroquois trapping grounds south of Lake Ontario were becoming depleted. Years of trade had taken its toll and new beaver grounds had to be found. Up to now these raids were only designed to rob the Huron of their peltry in order to continue trading with the Dutch. All of these things, the sickness, the famine and the schism causing the lack of firearms were coming together to make the perfect storm. The last of the calamities is about to visit the Iroquois' cousins to the north.

NEXT WEEK: Can the Huron Survive?

Can the Huron Survive?

November 18, 2009

You will recall that last week we left Huronia being continually raided by the Iroquois. The Tobacco Nation lived to the west and the Neutrals the southwest. Although these three outnumbered the Iroquois four-to-one firearms gave the latter such a tremendous advantage that the former had no chance.

This tactic of raiding the Iroquoian speaking peoples of Southern Ontario and stealing their pelts to trade with the Dutch continued for a few years. Father Jerome Lalemant complained in 1647 that each year the ambushes of the Iroquois had resulted in the massacre of a considerable number of "savages" allied to the French. Finally the Five Nation Iroquois decided to take the rich beaver grounds of Southern Ontario for themselves by force of war.

In 1648 the mission of St. Joseph suffered a surprise attack. The Christian converts were celebrating mass and the traditionalists were in their cabins. The Huron resisted as best they could but were soon overcome. The Iroquois set fire to the village and massacred the helpless; men, women and children alike. Father Daniel, who was in charge of the mission, saw that all was lost so he ran to the longhouses baptizing all he could. He believed that if their lives were lost at least their souls would be saved.

When the Iroquois reached the church the good Father went out to meet them. This gave the inhabitants still alive a chance to escape, which many did. Many more were killed, especially young mothers slowed down by the burden of their infants.

Father Daniel was quickly overcome by gun shots and his naked corpse was thrown into the flames which were consuming the church. About 700 Huron were massacred at St. Joseph that day. Many more escaped and most fled to St. Marie. Many of the other missions suffered similar fates that year.

In the fall of 1648 the Jesuits were maintaining eight missions in the country of the Huron. Some reinforcements had arrived from Montreal and this served to give the Fathers new courage. But just when they thought things would turn around the other shoe dropped!

In the spring of 1649 the Iroquois were back with 1200 well-armed warriors. They made a sudden attack at daybreak on the mission of St. Ignace. This was only about ten miles from the main mission of St. Marie. St. Ignace was taken almost without a fight. Most of the inhabitants were sleeping so most were slain or captured.

The victors quickly moved on to the mission of St. Louis which was on the road to St. Marie. The few warriors defending St. Louis were quickly overcome and the village burned. The Iroquois cast all they could not take with them as prisoners into the flames. Again, this included the old, the sick, and the wounded and little children. It was here that two of the more famous martyrdoms of the war occurred.

Fathers Jean de Brebeuf and Gabriel Lalemant refused to abandon their charges. They were captured along with most of the converts and their captors vented their full rage on these two. They were tortured beyond all others suffering several excruciating torments over a long period of time until they finally succumbed.

The Iroquois planned to advance to St. Marie but their advance guard suffered a partial defeat so they decided to abandon that plan and return home. They had taken too many captives so they kept as many as they could and the rest were burned to death.

Due to the relentless attacks of the Iroquois, the worst famine in fifty years and the sickness that filled the land, Huronia was filled with consternation. Fifteen villages had been abandoned and the survivors had fled northward. In less than a year St. Marie had taken on 6,000 refugees. In the spring of 1649 the Black Robes decided to abandon that mission. Most fled to the north to seek refuge with their Ottawa friends on Manitoulin Island. About 900 went to the Island of St. Joseph, which today is Christian Island, with the Jesuits.

They had planned to set up a new mission called St. Marie II, but the island could not support that many refugees so the plan was abandoned. The Christian Huron returned to Quebec with the Jesuits and the traditionalists joined the other refugees at Manitoulin. They would later move to Michilimackinac and become known as the Wyandotte. The French had called them Huron from an old French word meaning ruffian. Wyandotte is a corruption Ouendat, the name the Huron called themselves.

NEXT WEEK: New Policies, New Allies

New Policies, New Allies

November 25, 2009

You will recall in my last post the remnants of the Huron, Tobacco Nation and Neutrals joined and fled north to Michilimackinac and became known as the Wyandotte. France changed their governor and the Church changed its bishop. These two new administrators of New France also changed the policy of "no guns to the Indians". Still enemies with the Iroquois they needed to find new allies and trading partners. They looked northward to the Ojibwa.

The Ojibwa held the richest trapping grounds on the continent. We were also the largest military power on the continent. The French established a trading post at Michilimackinac. The Church established their main mission on the St. Mary's River near present-day Sault Ste. Marie.

Now for a change of pace: This week and maybe the next two I want to describe the culture and some of the traditions held by France's native allies. More of how we lived than what we did. The Ojibwa were Algonquian-speaking people and we had a far different lifestyle than the Iroquoian-speaking people we have been learning about.

The Iroquoian-speaking people were agrarian people. They produced excess farm products particularly squash, beans and corn. Their towns were considerable in size with one to two thousand or more people living there. They constructed double palisades around the town. Inside the palisades they constructed long houses about 100 feet long and 30 feet high. On the insides they sectioned off double bunks where whole families would sleep in each of the sections. Communal fires were placed every 30 feet or so for cooking.

Outside the palisades they farmed large tracts of land. They understood the principle of crop rotation but practiced it differently than Europeans. Their towns were not as permanent as those built by the Europeans so they rotated the entire town approximately every ten years. They would move to a previously used site, build a whole new town and let the fields at the old site go fallow. They usually had two or three town sites they would rotate.

This agrarian lifestyle made the Huron good candidates as trading partners for the Algonquin speaking peoples. The Ojibwa and Ottawa were hunters and fishers and their lifestyle produced an excess of meat and fish products.

The economic system of the native peoples was totally unlike the economic system of Europe. For example, in Europe if there was a nation of fishers on the coast and a nation of farmers on a plain they would trade by bargaining. One may offer a bushel of wheat for three barrels of fish. The other would counter offer a barrel of fish for a bushel of wheat. They may come to an agreement of two barrels of fish for a bushel of wheat. Or they may not be able to come to an agreement. If they could not they would let the excess produce rot.

Not so with the aboriginals of North America. They had no monetary system and their worldview would not allow them to waste their extra produce. The Europeans' Judeo-Christian teachings said that humanity was God's crowning achievement and they were to dominate and subdue the world. The product of their work was theirs to do with as they wished.

On the other hand native peoples saw humanity at the bottom of a hierarchy and the weakest of God's creatures. Naked and vulnerable our teachings said that the Great Mystery asked mother earth to sustain us. That included the animals, fish and birds giving up their lives for our sustenance. They agreed so everything that we had including life itself was a gift from the Creator. It would be an affront to mother earth who sustained us and to the Master of Life who ordained it to let the Great Spirit's gifts go to waste.

There was no haggling over excesses. We would give to each other freely. If one suffered a drought and crops failed the other trading partner would give up all their excess meat and fish knowing that what goes around comes around. The Ojibwa word for this type of trading was "daawed". Here is a hint. This word is going to come up much later so this type of trade is important to remember.

NEXT WEEK: Lifestyle and Worldview of the Ojibwa.

The Ojibwa

Lifestyle and Worldview of the Ojibwa

December 2, 2009

Well, another week has just flown by. Thanksgiving has come and gone and now we're looking at Christmas. Happy holidays everyone! I'm going to continue for this week and next describing the Ojibwa's lifestyle and traditions then we'll get back to the history of the Great Lakes region.

The Ojibwa had larger territories than the Iroquoian speaking peoples. This was due to different lifestyles. Ojibwa villages were smaller and more temporary. Each territory had one or more main villages consisting of family lodges called wigwams. These villages had from a few hundred to 1,000 inhabitants. There were no palisades and the villages were often moved to different locations but in the same general area. Village members would congregate at the villages in the summer months. Summer was a time of rest and relaxation. Time was spent tending small gardens, gathering fruits and berries as they ripened and trading with our allies. It was a time for festivals called gatherings or powwows. Many would come from other territories to participate in the drumming, dancing, singing and feasting. There was great competition in the games played with much wagering on the athletes. Each evening the village storyteller would mesmerize children and adults alike with his repertoire of traditional stories told around a huge community fire.

When the leaves began to turn color we would strike the main village and break up into small groups of two or three families. Each would head out to the winter hunting camps which were located throughout our territory. We would spend the winter there, hunting and trapping. The men would do the hunting and manage the trapping lines and the women and children would dry the meat and stretch the skins. The long winter nights were spent in our lodges repeating traditional stories around a small campfire.

In mid-February we would leave the hunting camps and gather in larger groups of five or six families at the sugar bushes. For two or three weeks while the sap rose in the maple trees we would produce our sugar products. The men would tend the lines and the women and children would run the sugar lodges. They were larger lodges than wigwams being 30 or 40 feet long by 12 or 15 feet wide. Three or four very hot fires were continually tended to boil down the sap to syrup. If the weather was conducive the boiling was done outside the lodge. It took 30 to 40 gallons of sap to get one gallon of syrup. In March when the sap stopped running utensils were stored in small tepees to be used again the following year.

Carrying our meat and sugar products with us each group would move on to the fishing camps. These camps were made up of much larger groups and were often located at the mouths of rivers and streams or at rapids where the fishing was good. The spring runs produced the huge quantities of fish that were caught in our nets or weirs. Whitefish was a staple of the Ojibwa diet and there were huge runs on the St. Mary's, St. Clair and Niagara Rivers. Ojibwa men would go out into the rapids in canoes, float downstream and while standing scoop large quantities of fish into the canoes with long poles that had nets attached to the ends of them. Needless to say we had an uncanny sense of balance and were excellent canoeists. The men did the fishing and the women and children dried or powdered the fish. When the fish runs were over we all moved back to the main village for another summer of leisure. Such was the lifestyle of the Ojibwa. It was a good life and we were a happy and contented people.

NEXT WEEK: Ojibwa Systems and Beliefs

Ojibwa Systems and Beliefs

December 9, 2009

Greetings once again, I spent this morning fixing my crashed satellite system. Now that I'm online once again we can continue with the social aspects of the Ojibwa people.

Our traditional political system was extremely flat or another way to describe it is it had very little hierarchy. Each village had a council made up of elders. This council held the only coercive power in the community. Certain elders were asked by the council to serve by sitting on the council as a member. Of course these would be people who showed they used the wisdom earned by a lifetime of experiences wisely. Not a bad idea to marry political power to the wisdom of the community.

There were two kinds of chiefs, a war chief and a civil chief. They were asked to serve by the council. These chiefs had charismatic power only. If a war chief wanted to raise a war party then he had to convince the warriors of his village to follow him into battle using his charisma. The civil chief was chosen to serve because he displayed good negotiating skills and was a good orator. However, he only had the power to commit to what the council had already instructed him to do. It was the council that made the important decisions for the village. Each village was autonomous making decisions based on what they thought was best for the village so there was in effect no central government. There was an alliance called the Three Fires Confederacy which was mainly a military alliance between the Ojibwa, Ottawa and Potawatomi nations. However, they held no power over individual villages.

If there was no central government what held the nation together? It was held together by a common language and family. The family was the most important social structure in the nation. Each family had a family mark called an odem or totem. They were usually animals, birds, fish, amphibians or reptiles but sometimes they were other objects. For example my totem is oak. The rules for the family structure were fairly simple. No two people with the same family mark could get married. This of course was designed to prevent intermarriage. There were no distant relatives. Everyone with the same totem was considered a close relative such as brother, sister, aunt or uncle. Even if a stranger having the same totem passed through the village from a distant part of the territory and he was by western standards a third cousin once removed, he could not marry one with the same family mark. The family of the village was also expected to treat him with the respect due to a visiting brother. They were to provide him with shelter, food and gifts even though they may not know him. It was this understanding of closeness of family that was the glue that held the Ojibwa nation together.

The traditional Ojibwa person did not have a personal relationship with God. He was called the Great Mystery and remained transcendental and mysterious. The Ojibwa's worldview was very spiritual. It was one filled with spirit beings called muneedoog or manitous. These manitous interacted with the people. Some of these spirits were helpers and some were mischievous and a few were evil. They had human-like qualities in that they could change depending on the circumstances.

Our understanding of the cosmos was that life was an illusion, a sort of imitation of the real world which was the spiritual realm. There were certain portals to the real world through which messages or directions could be transferred. Seers used chants and ceremonies such as the shaking tent ceremony to communicate with the manitous. Healers also used drumming, chanting to get direction from their spirit guides on how to release the spiritual power contained in certain herbs and medicines. The most important portal for the common person was dreams. This is why dreams were held in such high regard and used extensively to guide each on their journey through life.

When an individual died the cross over into the real world was not instantaneous. It was a journey. The body would be placed in the grave facing west. That is the direction which we believed the afterlife existed. All that person's utensils were placed with them as they would need them on their four-day journey. A small bark house about two feet high was built over the grave. It had a small door on the west end to allow the person's soul to escape when they started on their spirit journey. When they reached their final destination they would be in a place of bliss and happiness enjoying the company of loved ones that had made the journey before them.

I've just touched on the culture and traditions of the Ojibwa in order to give you a flavor of their practices and lifestyle. For a much fuller description see my book *Ways of Our Grandfathers.* When reading about the history of a people I believe some knowledge of the culture helps to understand why they did the things they did.

NEXT WEEK: The First Ojibwa/French Military Alliance

The First Ojibwa/French Military Alliance

December 17, 2009

Good morning everyone! Well, at least it's morning as I write this. I had some problems with my blog this past week. It was suspended for suspicion of violating the terms of service. It was a mistake and as you can see I'm back on-line. Sometimes I long for the 'good old days'. Now, back to some Great Lakes history!

You will recall that the French had moved their endeavors north to Superior country. The Iroquois had moved into the rich beaver hunting grounds of Southern Ontario. The military advantage the Dutch had given them made their ego soar with arrogance. The British had taken over the Dutch colony and changed the name of the main post from Orange to Albany. They also continued to supply the Iroquois with firearms. The Iroquois continued to harass their neighbors and were continually making war on the French. Such was the situation when we pick up our story in the year 1686.

The Governor of New France, Monsieur Le Marquis de Nonville, ordered the explorer Du Lhut to build a military post at de troit. This was the name the French called the waterways between Lake Huron and Lake Erie. It means the strait. The main purpose of a military fort at the lower end of Lake Huron was to keep the British out of the upper Great Lakes. He chose a spot where the St. Clair River was the narrowest and established Fort St. Joseph. That site is located in what is now Pinegrove Park in downtown Port Huron, Michigan.

In 1687 de Nonville decided to have a war of extermination of the Seneca. They had embarrassed the French by slaughtering many colonists in constant raids and had totally defeated the Miami and the Illinois who had put themselves under the protection of the French. To this end he gathered an army of 1,500 French regulars and 500 praying Indians from Quebec. These were mostly Iroquois the French had converted to Christianity. He also ordered Du Lhut to gather a force of Far Indians to join the expedition.

Du Lhut convinced some of the war chiefs to follow him in this venture and some 500 Potawatomi, Ottawa, Wyandotte and Ojibwa warriors began gathering at Fort St. Joseph. However, most of them were Saulteux Ojibwa from the St. Mary's River district. My great, great, great-grandfather, Kioscance or Young Gull was a war chief of the Saulteux at the time and was in all likelihood leading this group of warriors. When they had all arrived they left to meet de Nonville's forces at Irondequoit on the southern shore of Lake Ontario.

The French forces left Montreal and part of them moved along the north shore of Lake Ontario and part of them moved along the south shore. They did this in case the weather presented any strong winds that would prevent either one of the groups from reaching the rendezvous place the other group would make it there on time. However the weather was fine and all three forces met at Irondequoit Bay on the same day.

De Nonville first sent scouts up the Genesee River to survey any Seneca towns and their strengths. The Seneca knew they had arrived so they sent their women, children and old people further into Seneca country for protection. They gathered a force of 500 warriors and lay in wait hiding themselves in the underbrush waiting for the ambush. The French scouts passed them, found the first town they encountered burned and deserted. They found two more towns further upstream in the same condition so they returned to make a report to the governor. All the time they were unaware of the 500 Seneca warriors who watched them from their hiding places.

The French governor decided to move the French regulars upstream to the three Seneca towns. As they were passing the hidden Seneca they sprung their ambush. The French soldiers were taken completely by surprise and panicked. Some fled east and some west and they began firing back on each other. The Seneca had bested them but the Three Fires warriors arrived and they were much more adept at forest warfare. The tide turned and the Seneca retreated back up the river.

When de Nonville arrived at the towns he stopped. He was quite shaken by the disarray of his soldiers. After all they were regulars and the best the French had. He ordered the fields burned, which took several days while the native allies looked on in disbelief. They knew the enemy was in full retreat and they thought the best course of action was to pursue and finish the job. As the soldiers cut down the corn and beans and gathered the squash the Ojibwa and their Three Fires brothers fumed. De Nonville then ordered a retreat saying the Seneca had been taught a good lesson. The Ojibwa and their allies accused de Nonville of doing nothing but warring on the cornfields and left in a huff. It would be a long time before they would again join the French in any military campaigns.

NEXT WEEK: A Dish Best Not Served!

The Iroquois War

A Dish Best Not Served!

December 23, 2009

Wow, one day left till Christmas! Guess I better get shopping. I've been posting to this blog since September and we've moved through a half century of history and learned a little bit about First Nation culture. Now let's get back to some more history.

We are now approaching the end of the 1600's. For the latter half of the 17th century the Iroquois Five Nations was flexing their muscles by expanding their territory and annoying their neighbors. This was especially true of the Seneca and Mohawk nations. They had moved into Southern Ontario and at first used it only as beaver trapping grounds, but after a couple of decades they began establishing several towns.

The Mohawk nation had pushed at the Three Fires Confederacy's territory making many raids waylaying trading expeditions to Montreal and stealing their pelts. Threats were made; peace agreements were agreed to and then broken. The Ojibwa's patience was running out. They had taken the brunt of the Iroquois raids so they threatened to bring the whole weight of the Three Fires Confederacy to bear. A peace conference was scheduled to take place at a major Mohawk town at the mouth of the Saugeen River.

According to a traditional story told to me by my grandmother who came from Saugeen a delegation left Superior country for the peace conference. While they were on their way a Mohawk raiding party attacked an Ojibwa village and kidnapped the Ojibwa chief's young son. They returned to the Saugeen by a different route and making double time arriving there before the Three Fires delegation. The young boy's father was among the delegates.

When they arrived they received the royal treatment. A huge feast was put on for them and there was one particular dish not recognized, however the meat was delicious. A new agreement was quickly reached and the Algonquian speaking delegates left for home not realizing their antagonists had cooked and fed the son they had captured to his own father!

The news spread and the Ojibwa were outraged. A Three Fire's Grand Council was called and many of the council members called for a war of expulsion. There was little or no opposition. They devised a stratagem where they would leave the next spring with four divisions of warriors. They would only travel at night and when all were in place would attack simultaneously on the new moon.

The eastern division was made up of the largest of the Ojibwa tribes, the Mississauga, and was led by their war chief Bald Eagle. They were to use the trade route to Montreal. That would have been up the French River and across Lake Nipissing, portage to the Mattawa River and halfway down the Ottawa River. They then turned inland to confront the Iroquois towns from the east.

There were two divisions that moved in unison southward from Bawitig which today is called Sault Ste. Marie. The division that was made up of Amikouai or Beaver tribe warriors was led by White Cloud. They made their way to the Saugeen (Bruce) Peninsula to lay in wait for the new moon.

The other division that was to attack directly south was made up of Ottawa warriors led by their great war chief Sahgimah. They arrived at the Penetanguishene Peninsula where they lay in wait.

My forefather Young Gull had by this time become a major Ojibwa war chief and he led the western division. They were made up of Ojibwa, Potawatomi and Wyandotte warriors and they made their way down the Lower Peninsula of Michigan to

Round Lake (Lake St. Clair) where they would attack from the west. According to Young Gull's son, my great-great grandfather, Animikeence or Little Thunder the western division consisted of 400 war canoes each manned by eight warriors. They stretched out the entire length of the St. Clair River from its mouth at Lake Huron to Bkejwanong or Walpole Island. When all were in place and the new moon arrived they attacked. This time the Iroquois adversaries had 50 years of trading with the French for guns so they were equally well-armed. However, population tipped the balance of power to the Three Fires. They outnumbered the Iroquois by four to one!

NEXT WEEK: The New Moon Arrives!

The New Moon Arrives

December 29, 2009

Well, Christmas is over. I hope everyone had a fine holiday. I enjoyed three Christmas dinners but I'm paying for it. I now have a few extra pounds to work off! My last post had the Three Fires warriors stealthily move into place for an all-out attack on the Iroquois in Southern Ontario.

When the new moon arrived all four divisions went on the offensive. The western division had been camping along the western shore of Lake St. Clair and when the time arrived we moved around the top of the lake to the eastern shore and up the Horn River. We called it the Horn because it took the shape of an antler. The French would later call it Riviere La Trenche but today it is known as the Thames.

About 12 miles up the Thames, just west of the current city of Chatham, Ontario there was a very large Seneca town. Young Gull and his warriors put it under siege. During the first offensive against the well-fortified town some Seneca warriors escaped fleeing back to their homeland in up-state New York for reinforcements. Young Gull sent a large force of Wyandotte in hot pursuit.

The siege lasted a few days before Young Gull's forces finally burned their way through the double palisade. There was little the town's 400 warriors could do. The western division was there with all its might, 3,200 warriors minus the Wyandotte pursuing the escapees. A tide of fierce Ojibwa and Potawatomi warriors surged into the town massacring everyone in sight. None survived. The end was furious but mercifully it came quick.

All of the bodies of the slain were desecrated. They were decapitated and all the heads piled in a large pyramid. Later this pyramid of skulls would serve as a warning to all of the fierce power the Three Fires Confederacy. The remainder of the bodies were dismembered and scattered. This was our practice and would prevent the enemy from entering the afterlife.

The warriors of the western division that fell in battle were buried in a mass grave with all funeral rites afforded the brave and loyal. They were buried with all of their weapons and daily utensils. This would provide them with the necessary items to make their four-day journey to the land of souls as easy as possible. The mass grave created a huge burial mound. It was still there some 115 years later when recorded on a British Naval Surveyor's Map of the River Thames c 1815. The note on this map reads, "In the side of this knoll there are great quantities of human bones. A battle is said to have been fought between the Chippewas and Senekies contending for the dominion of this country, when the latter were put to flight with great slaughter and driven across the river at Niagara."

The Seneca reinforcements never arrived. Young Gull's Wyandotte warriors returned from Niagara to lay in wait at Long Point on Lake Erie. A huge force of Seneca came skirting along the north shore of the lake headed pell-mell for their town on the Thames. When they arrived at Long Point they were ambushed. The Iroquois typically used dugout canoes which were much heavier and more cumbersome than bark canoes. The Seneca were easily out maneuvered and all were killed on the lake. This is one of the few Native American naval battles to have occurred.

The victorious pursuers rejoined the main body of Young Gull's warriors. They moved up the St. Clair river and then northward along the eastern shoreline of Lake Huron. Meanwhile, the other three divisions moved on their targets with equal devastation.

NEXT WEEK: A Four Pronged Attack!

A Four Pronged Attack!

January 6, 2010

Here we are, another New Year. Best wishes to everyone and may this be your special year, full of good health, good times and prosperity! Last week the new moon had arrived and the four pronged attack on the Iroquois had begun. At the same time Young Gull was annihilating the Seneca town on the Thames White Cloud's force landed at the tip of the Bruce Peninsula at what today is Cabot Head.

White Cloud was the leading war chief of the Amikouai Ojibwa or Beaver People from the north shore of Georgian Bay. His division consisted of Ojibwa warriors and their first encounter was with a small force of Mohawks as soon as they landed. The battle continued to Griffith Island where this small band of Mohawks was finished off.

At the same time Young Gulls forces arrived at Saugeen where there was a Mohawk town. A great battle was fought there on the flats of the Saugeen River near the mouth. Evidence of this battle was still visible some 150 years later when the artist Paul Kane visited there. He wrote in his memoirs that he saw great burial mounds with many human bones protruding out of them. This battle is still known today as the Battle of Skull Mound.

Some of the other encounters in the area with the Mohawks were the Fishing Islands at Red Bay just north of the Saugeen. The bay was given its name for the condition of the waters after the battle that occurred there. Three hundred Mohawk warriors were defeated where they had entrenched themselves on White Cloud Island in Copley's Bay. The island of course was named after the victorious Ojibwa chief. There were other skirmishes at Skull Island in Georgian Bay so named because of the large quantities of human skulls left there. The Iroquois also suffered defeats at the Clay Banks near present-day Walkerton, Ontario, at Indian Hill near the Teeswater River and at Wadiweediwon or Owen Sound, Ontario.

Young Gull joined White Cloud at Owen Sound and both divisions moved east to Nottawasaga Bay where they encountered a body of 1,000 Iroquois warriors who had moved down the Nottawasaga River. They met at the mouth of this river where the Iroquois were overwhelmed by the far superior numbers of the Three Fires. The Ojibwa called the Iroquois people Naudoway meaning serpents and saugeeng means a coming out place. So the meaning of both the Nottawasaga River and Bay is the coming out place of the Naudoway.

Sahgimah's Ottawa had made landfall on the Penetanguishene Peninsula where they vanquished a force of about 1,200 Iroquois who had arrived via the Lake Simcoe route. They moved south from there to Lake Couchiching where they fought another battle just north of present-day Orillia, Ontario.

Meanwhile, Bald Eagle and his eastern division of Mississauga met a force of Iroquois along the Mattawa River. Human bones have been found there attesting to this battle as late as the 20th century. Following the victory there Bald Eagle encountered the Iroquois at the Otonabee River near Lakefield, the Moira River near Madoc and at Rice Lake. He then pushed west to destroy towns at the mouths of the Rouge River and the Humber River on Lake Ontario. There was also an Iroquois town at Burlington Bay where the Iroquois put up a stiff resistance. However, the Mississauga Ojibwa were just too numerous and they succumbed.

There was an old Indian Trail that ran between Burlington Bay and the Grand River. Halfway along this trail was another Iroquois town which also capitulated to Bald Eagle.

Two major chiefs of the Five Nations approached the Earl of Bellomont, Governor of New England at Albany for help. He promised that if the British would help them in their war with the Three Fires they would have no further dealings with the French. But the British were neither in the position nor were they interested in helping their First Nation allies. They were mostly interested in the fur trade so the Governor's advice to the two Iroquois sachems was to make peace seeing they were vastly outnumbered and further war would only end in their destruction.

The French were also only interested in the fur trade and with all this warring going on there was little trade being done. The French had much influence with the First Nations of the Upper Country so the Governor General of New France, Louis-Hector de Callieres, brokered a peace not only between the Three Fires Confederacy and the Five Nation Iroquois League but several other First Nations who were also fighting amongst themselves at this time. This peace conference at Montreal culminated in the Great Peace Treaty of 1701. The Iroquois War was over and the Five Nations had been dispersed to their original homeland of upstate New York. This left Southern Ontario a great vacuum.

NEXT WEEK: Great Changes and Expansions

Fort Ponchartrain

Great Changes and Expansions

January 10, 2010

I've got some excellent feedback on my posts so I'd like to thank those who have made comments. It gives me encouragement to carry on realizing that people are profiting from my work.

There was another great change that took place besides the general peace brought on by the Great Peace Treaty. The French closed their trading post at Michilimackinac and governor Callieres ordered Antoine de Lamothe Cadillac to establish a new one at de troit. The Company of the Colony was formed in 1700 as an association to secure the monopoly of the western fur trade and Cadillac was one of its directors. By the way The Company became insolvent in 1705 and the monopoly was handed over to Cadillac. The French were worried about British trade incursions into the upper country and this new fort was also designed to block them. Cadillac had the idea that if he invited all the nations from the far country to establish themselves around his new post this would not only enhance trade but also firm up military alliances. However, his plan had some wrinkles in it.

For one thing it had its detractors. Although the Church's superiors in Montreal were on board the Jesuit missionaries at Michilimackinac harbored secret resentments. They were jealous of their mission and saw de troit as a detriment to all their hard work in the upper country.

Callieres wrote to the Fathers at Michilimackinac asking them to go with the Ottawa and Wyandotte to de troit and both Fathers Etienne de Carheil and Joseph Marest wrote supporting letters back to their superiors but Cadillac accused them of working against the project by dividing their First Nation charges with lies about the new post and by uttering threats if they moved there.

Cadillac was right. At a council held at Fort Ponchartrain on October 3, 1701 the First Nations betrayed the Jesuits real intentions. Ontonagan spoke for all the Ottawa. He was a major chief and was also known as Jean Le Blanc. He informed Cadillac that the missionaries had shown them a letter from him supposedly sent by three Iroquois that he had met on Lake St. Clair. Cadillac was supposed to have said in this letter that the Ottawa should not go to de troit because the Iroquois there will betray them and they would all become dead men.

Cadillac denied he wrote any such letter. He told Ontonagan that although the Black Robes and the Grey Robes (the Jesuits and Recollects) were the rulers of religion and never lied about such matters as for other matters he could not speak for them.

Koussildouer, the oldest Ottawa chief relayed a message to Cadillac from Ouilemek, chief of the Potawatomi. He informed him that next spring Ouilemek would take the Potawatomi to live near the Miami on the St. Joseph River. He would then come to trade at the new post and if the prices were good he would come often, otherwise he would trade with the British at Albany.

Cadillac's response to this was that Ouilemek was welcome at Fort Ponchartrain but if he wished to trade elsewhere he could do as he saw fit and it would not bother Cadillac.

The Wyandotte spoke at the council next. Alleyooue and Quarante-Sous agreed with what Ontonagan had said. He said that although Father de Carheil had told the Wyandotte the same things they did not believe him because Onontio or the Governor had told them in Montreal to go and encamp near Fort Ponchartrain. Father de Carheil had invited them to go and encamp near the Miami but to return to Michilimackinac the following year. Alleyooue said that they had granted him what he asked but only to get rid of him. Their real desire was to move to de troit near the new fort.

Alleyooue also said that Father de Carheil told them at their last council with him that Cadillac was not establishing a new post at de troit but was only going there to trade after which he would return to Montreal.

The Wyandotte informed Father de Carheil that they would tell Cadillac all that was said in their councils with him and he forbade them to do so. Not only did they disobey the missionary but asked Cadillac for land near the new post where they could establish themselves.

Cadillac commended them and suggested that Father de Carheil was probably just mistaken in his belief that he was only going to de troit to trade. He pointed out the new fort already built and lands cleared that it would be a permanent post. He then promised them land to settle on as soon as they arrived.

On the other hand the Ojibwa preferred to keep themselves at arm's length from the French. Although they needed the trade for European goods they liked to keep their distance. This attitude dovetailed with Young Gull's wish to move to St. Clair country. He had fallen in love with the place when he stayed at Fort St. Joseph in 1686. So he led a large group of Saulteux Ojibwa south from the St. Mary's River district and established villages on the Black River and Swan Creek in present-day Michigan.

The Mississauga expanded in the eastern part of Southern Ontario taking up residence between the Grand and Gananoque Rivers. They established themselves on the Grand, at the mouth of the Credit River, at Lake Scugog and Rice Lake. However, they did set up a village just north of the new post at de troit.

The Amikouai Ojibwa expanded across Georgian Bay to its south shore with villages at present-day Cold Water, Owen Sound and at the mouth of the Saugeen River.

NEXT WEEK: More Intrigues at Detroit

More Intrigues at Detroit

January 20, 2010

Hi everyone! Another week has gone by with some major things happening in the world. A major earthquake in Haiti which is a catastrophe the likes of which we have not seen. They need so much help and I urge everyone to give to a registered charity. Also there was a big election in Massachusetts yesterday that's going to bring big changes in U.S. politics.

Now to get back to the story of the founding of Detroit not only was Cadillac having trouble with the Jesuits discouraging the First Nations from settling around the new Fort Ponchartrain but the various First Nations were reluctant themselves. The Miami and Potawatomi were settled along the St. Joseph River in southwestern Michigan. A group of about thirty Wyandotte families were living near them.

Michipichy, called by the French Quarante-Sous, was the head chief of the Wyandotte at the St. Joseph. The governor asked him in Montreal to go back to the St. Joseph and bring his people who were there to de troit, which he did. He also obtained a promise from the Miami that were there that they would also move to de troit after they collected the bones of their dead and set them in order.

Cadillac claimed they would all be there if the missionaries had not dissuaded them. They encouraged them to settle at the St. Joseph because they had a small mission already there and they wanted to expand it. He also claimed that the real reason they wanted to do this was to make de troit fail because he had brought a Grey Robe or Recollect priest there. The Augustinian Recollects and Jesuits were competing missionaries.

Another strange thing had happened. The governor, de Callieres, had told the head chief of the Miami in Montreal to settle on the St. Joseph after instructing Cadillac to invite all the First Nations to settle at de troit. This only served to confuse the Miami as well as the Wyandotte. So Michipichy went to Michilimackinac to see Sastaresty the head chief there. They were under the impression that the governor did not want them to go to Detroit. They decided to send their elders to Montreal to see the governor to settle the dispute and to do whatever de Callieres wanted.

All this confusion made its way back to France even all the way to the King. Louis XIV sent a letter back to the Canadian officials detailing his wishes. His Majesty reported that on the one hand Sieur de la Mothe Cadillac is adamant that de troit will produce all the effects expected of it.

On the other hand others have reported that the land there is no good and will not produce the food required to support the population expected there. There is only the poor fishing available and the hunting grounds are 30 to 40 leagues away. There is also the fear of attack by the Iroquois and because the colony lacked the means to defend the newly established fort the result would be that war would recommence. Also, the Company of the Colony were reporting that the cost of establishing this new venture was so exorbitant that it was impossible to sustain. It seems Cadillac had a host of opponents all with their own agendas.

So the King ordered through Governor de Callieres and Intendant Beauharnais that Cadillac and the most important of the French settlers at de troit meet and discuss the pros and cons of establishing the new settlement and outline them in a document. Also, all present at the deliberations were to sign the document. His Majesty would then be able to make an informed decision whether to continue augmenting that post, or to leave it as a trading post only or to abandon it altogether.

NEXT WEEK: And the Winner Is . . .

And the Winner is . . .

January 27, 2010

Last week we left Cadillac struggling with various opponents to his dream of monopolizing the fur trade at de troit. Fathers Carheil and Marest were doing their best to keep their First Nation charges at Michilimackinac. The Jesuits had also established a mission at the St. Joseph to destroy de troit, or so he thought. Now even more problems appeared.

Governor de Callieres died and his replacement was Philippe de Rigault, Marquis de Vaudreuil. The new governor was visited in Montreal by a delegation of Ottawa representing about eighty people left at Michilimackinac. They told him that they wished to die in their villages and refused to move to de troit.

Vaudreuil had also received word that the Miami and Wyandotte that had moved to de troit had met in council with the Seneca Iroquois about safe passage through their territory. They wished to explore trade with the British at Albany. Quarante Sols, the Wyandotte chief of de troit confirmed this and Vaudreuil forbade it. The Company of the Colony was also complaining loudly about the cost of establishing the new post.

All this led de Vaudreuil to send a report to France. Count Ponchartrain, Minister in charge of the Colony, was informed that he and Indendant Beauharnois had decided to send Father Marest back to his mission because the Ottawa and Wyandotte there refused to move. He also stated that if trade between their First Nation allies and the British was ever established it would be because of de troit. It was burdensome to the Colony as well because of the exorbitant costs of enticing the First Nations to give up their villages and move to lands around Fort Ponchartrain. He advised that de troit be abandoned.

Cadillac fought back. He appealed in a letter directly to the King. The job of getting all the nations around to move to de troit was all but complete. He reported that there had been to date 2,000 First Nations people living around the new fort. They had 400 men under arms, ample protection from attack by the Iroquois. These 2,000 souls included a village of mixed Saulteux and Mississauga Ojibwa, a Miami village of about thirty families, all the Wyandotte except 30 who remained a Michilimackinac. Also all the Ottawa were there except eighty who also remained at Michilimackinac. There were some Nipissing that joined the Ottawa as well and a village of Delaware Loup. Trade was being done and at no cost to France's treasury.

Cadillac also informed the King of the bickering that was going on in the far country of the Colony. The Sioux had attacked and killed some Miami and it had escalated to a war between the Sioux and eight of France's First Nation allies. Cadillac took credit for brokering a peace but implored the King to augment the new fort with French regulars and settlers not abandoned it. He said the reason the peace was so hard to keep was because of the lack of a French presence in the far country. Cadillac won out. The newly established Fort Ponchartrain would not only survive but would be expanded.

Cadillac was an imposing presence, well-liked by the First Nations and could manage the affairs of the new post quite well. However, the one area he had problems with was trade. The Miami and the Wyandotte did secure safe passage to Albany. So did the Saulteux and Mississauga Ojibwa. At the same time the Great Peace Treaty was being negotiated in Montreal a number of Ojibwa chiefs travelled to Albany with some French fur traders to explore the idea of trade with the British.

Towasquaye a Wyandotte trader visited Albany a couple of years later and found he was treated well. He returned with a delegation sent by the chiefs of de troit to visit the governor Lord Cornbury. Tehonwahonkarachqua, a Miami and son-in-law of Michipichy the principle Wyandotte sachem and Rughkiwahaddi a Wyandotte spoke for their chiefs. They found not only were they well received but the goods were cheaper and of better quality than French goods.

This would lead to competition driving the price of European goods down to the benefit of the First Nations, but that would be in the future. Monopolizing trade would not be the only problem the French would have to deal with. Much larger problems loomed on the horizon!

NEXT WEEK: Trouble in Paradise . . . 1706

Trouble in Paradise . . . 1706

February 4, 2010

Let me apologise for this week's post being late. We had friends we hadn't seen in nine years visit. It's funny how time just slips by. Anyway we are all caught up with the news in each other's lives. Hope it's not another nine years.

Last week we left Cadillac seeming to get his way. In 1706 Fort Ponchartrain was being reinforced with French soldiers, settlers and a Recollect missionary. Cadillac had also been successful in attracting First Nations to settle around the newly constructed fort. However, it would take a strong hand to manage the peace as some of these nations were traditional antagonists. Cadillac had that quality in abundance but Vaudreuil had another plan to thwart de troit's success.

He had Cadillac called to Montreal and arrested on a trumped-up charge brought forth by the Company of the Colony. He was put on trial but found innocent by the Indendant. While he was away Sieur de Bougmont was left in command. He was a capable military man but didn't have the strong hand that Cadillac had. Unfortunately, trouble broke out between the Nations at de troit.

A disagreement arose between the Mississauga and Miami and de Bougmont intervened thinking he had in had brought the matter to a successful conclusion. But the matter still simmered with the Ottawa taking sides with the Mississauga. To make matters worse a Potawatomi who was married to a Miami warned the Ottawa that the Wyandotte chief Michipichy or Quarante Sols conspired with the Miami in private to destroy the Ottawa.

The Ottawa had planned to go to war against the Sioux. Quarante Sols' plan was to wait until they left and after three days attack their villages and eat their women and children. Eat was a euphemism for kill. When they heard the news of the Wyandotte and Miami plan they hastily called a council of the three Ottawa Nations that were at de troit. Le Pesant or the Heavy Man and Outoutagan or Jean Le Blanc, their two head chiefs were at the council.

Le Pesant, who was a bit of a hot head, became enraged when he heard what they were planning. He said that since the Miami were determined to kill them and boil them they should prevent them from doing so by striking first. Outoutagan counselled against it but couldn't prevail because of Le Pesant's great influence and the fury that his harangue caused in their young warriors.

The Ottawa then went to the fort and informed commandant de Bougmont of what they had heard. In order to return to their own fort they had to pass by the Wyandotte's stockade where they came across eight Miami chiefs going there for a feast. Le Pesant gave a great cry and said the chiefs of the one's who would kill them were in front of them and they should put an end to it then and there. He gave another loud shout and the Ottawa began firing on the Miami chiefs. They killed seven of the eight with only Pacamkon escaping to the French fort.

Then the Ottawa rushed to the Miami village to kill the rest of them in their lodges but none were there. They had all gone into the French fort. The enraged warriors rushed to Fort Ponchartrain determined to burn it but Outoutagan's brother chief Miscouaki threw himself into the midst of them, snatching their flaming arrows and imploring them not to do any harm to the French. Chief Outoutagan saw that there was a grey robe and a soldier trapped outside the fort so he warned them to go to their fort quickly and tell the commandant not to fire upon the Ottawa nor give the Miami any powder. Unfortunately, they did not make it. The young Ottawa warriors killed them right at the gates of the French fort because they were furious at the killing of two of their chiefs.

The next day Outoutagan went to the French fort with a flag that the Governor had given his brother. He was told that as long as he carried that flag he would be safe. When he arrived at the gates of the fort the warriors with him had their arms all turned down. He asked to speak to de Bougmont to explain their reasons for attacking the Miami. Commandant de Bougmont told him that he had nothing to say to him and that he should wait until Sieur de la Forest returned in the early spring, which was another six months. He could then explain to him.

Since the commandant would not speak to them they returned to their fort. When the young men heard of this they determined again to burn the French fort. The elders wanted to cool things down so they sat in council for three days where Outoutagan said to Le Pesant that it was his entire fault. How foolish it was to attack the Miami at the gates of the French fort. Now they were all dead and they had killed themselves!

NEXT WEEK: Wyandotte Treachery

Wyandotte Treachery

February 10, 2010

First, congratulations to the New Orleans Saints for winning the Super Bowl! It not only lifted and renewed the city's spirits but inspired the nation.

Last week we left Jean Leblanc trying to make peace by talking to the French. But Commandant de Bourmont refused to parlay and instead made the threatening gesture of putting swords on the end their poles. This caused great mistrust of the French among the Ottawa.

So the Ottawa went to the Wyandotte thinking they were their allies. Quarante Sols gave them a belt that signified that they were allies with the nations around them including the Ottawa, Chippewa, Mississauga and Potawatomi. They told Jean Leblanc they would share the French words with them on the Ottawa's feast day and so they would not fear meeting in their lodges they would meet in a clearing where they would plant a French flag.

The next day the Wyandotte planted a French flag in open grassland just as they said they would. The French came and spread out large blankets on the ground near the flag and put large quantities of grain on them. The Wyandotte women did the same. But the Ottawa were very distrustful so the sent out scouts to survey the sounding area. They reported back that they had seen trails leading to the deep woods that encircled the open grassland.

The following day was their feast day. The Ottawa suspected a trap so they remained in their fort. The Miami and Wyandotte had some of their warriors hidden in the glades around the clearing but most of them were hidden in the deep woods surrounding the Ottawa fort. They had two bands. One came along the water and destroyed their canoes thinking it would prevent their escape. Then both rushed the fort to massacre all the women and children. They assumed the Ottawa had gone to meet at the clearing.

The Ottawa opened fire from their fort surprising the enemy. The Ottawa only lost one young man but the Miami and Wyandotte lost many. They retreated but returned that night. On their way they met Katalibou and his brother. They killed and scalped them.

The next day the Wyandotte joined the Miami outside the Ottawa fort. Cletart, Quarante Sols' brother, called out insults calling the Ottawa warriors women and saying that Onontio, the French Governor had long ago abandoned them. This riled the young Ottawa warriors and they rushed out of their fort to attack them. The Wyandotte held their ground but the Miami fled even though they had 400 men under arms. The next day they returned and attacked the Ottawa fort again but it was of little consequence. Before they left they shot a prisoner who was an ally of the Ottawa.

The same day some of the Ottawa's young men along with two Mississauga returned to de troit from fighting the Flathead. The Wyandotte captured and bound them. They took the Ottawa warriors to the French fort but kept the two Mississauga men at the Wyandotte fort where they later released them.

The Miami released one of the young men with a message. The Miami did not wish to kill the other prisoners but wanted the Ottawa to cover the Miami dead with presents thereby ending the hostilities. This was according to native custom.

The Ottawa collected all that they had to secure the release of the prisoners. They offered two packs of beaver pelts, ten pieces of porcelain beads, twenty kettles and various other small gifts. They took them unarmed to the appointed place in front of the French gates where Quarante Sols offered Jean Leblanc his hand. Just as he took it a shot rang out from the French fort and grazed Jean Leblanc's shoulder. The Miami shot seven more killing two. The Ottawa fled with the Wyandotte and Miami in hot pursuit. The Ottawa warriors who had stayed at their fort rushed out to help their fleeing brothers.

During one of the Miami sorties they captured a young Ottawa woman and whisked her off to the French fort. Some of the Ottawa pursued them but arrived at the French fort only to hear the young woman's screams as the Miami burned her alive! They spent the rest of the day fighting.

In fact all this fighting went on for almost two months. The Ottawa tired and were short of ball and shot so they chose Onabemamtou, one of their chiefs, to approach the Miami. He had danced the calumet peace dance with them in earlier times. He was successful at brokering a peace with them and reported back that they had laid all the blame at the feet of the Wyandotte and the French. They agreed to withdraw to their homeland on the St. Joseph and the Ottawa withdrew to Michilimackinac.

Cadillac returned to Fort Ponchartrain livid. He was upset with de Bourmont for not taking charge in the beginning. He chastised him for taking sides and not threatening each with the power of the French Governor. Now it was up to him to restore things and secure restitution for the killing of one of his soldiers and the Grey Robe.

NEXT WEEK: Reparation Granted

Reparation Granted

February 20, 2010

Tax season is upon us. I do tax returns hence the late post. It probably will be this way through April. Also the Winter Olympics are on distracting my attention. Oh well, what's a blogger to do?

We left de troit and New France in a quandary. The Ottawa had withdrawn to Michilimackinac and the Miami to the St. Joseph and Wabash Rivers. The Delaware Loup had also withdrawn from the new French post. This not what Cadillac had envisioned.

The disturbances at de troit made things even dicier for Governor Vaudreuil. The Ottawa had let it be known that they neither wanted war with the French nor did they fear it. There were eight or ten nations spread around the lakes that were their allies and they were indignant at the Wyandotte and Miami for what they had done. Vaudreuil feared the British would supply the upper nations from their posts on Hudson Bay. And a war with the Three Fires Confederacy and their allies would do irreparable harm to the fur trade.

There was also the fact that two of their own had been killed, one being the Recollect Priest Constantine. This had to be dealt with in the sternest of terms, blood for blood. However, it looked like an impossible task to get the Ottawa to turn over any of their own for French execution.

The governor also had people at Michilimackinac whose safety he was ultimately responsible for. They tried to withdraw back to Montreal but were prevented from doing so by the Ottawa. Vaudreuil did not know if they were being held hostage or did they meet an even worse fate.

On the other hand things were not going well for the Ottawa either. When they withdrew from de troit it was late August and their corn at de troit had been ravaged. It was far too late for a new planting at Michilimackinac. They had no food to get them through the winter other than what their kinsmen could share with them. The winter of 1706-07 was going to be long and hard.

They did make it through although they ended up eating grass, tree bark and boiled moccasins. They decided to go to Montreal and sue for peace. They sent a delegation of four chiefs of each of three of their nations, the Ottawa Kiskakoua, Sinago and La Fourche. Jean Le Blanc spoke for them all.

He laid the blame for all the trouble at the feet of Le Pesant. He said that he understood that their way of making reparation for a death with goods was not enough. He understood that the death of the two Frenchmen must be paid the French way, with blood. So they offered up two former prisoners that they had adopted into their nation to the governor to do with what he wished.

Vaudreuil refused. He wanted the head of Le Pesant and this is what he told Le Blanc. The Ottawa refused to give up one of their most prominent chiefs saying that he was a 'great bear' with much influence among all the nations of the lakes. They could not promise that they could pay the reparation that the governor demanded. So the council in Montreal ended in failure.

The governor-general was stymied. He had no idea how to defuse the situation so he did what all good politicians do when they find themselves in a situation such as this. He passed the buck. He had been informed that Cadillac had sent word to Le Blanc to come to de troit so he referred the matter to him with orders to find a way to make peace with all the nations.

Cadillac took charge. He was no Bourmont, the unfortunate young ensign assigned to look after the post when all the trouble started. He demanded in the sternest possible voice that they bring him Le Pesant and if he refused to come then they should kill him on the spot. If they didn't do what he asked then it would be war meaning the death of their young men and hardship for their wives and children. He also demanded their answer a little before sundown.

The Ottawa caved in. They decided to capitulate to Cadillac's demands and hand over Le Pesant or slay him themselves if he refused. The Wyandotte and Miami did not believe the Ottawa would do what they said they would do but agreed to accept anything that Cadillac did in regard to the matter and would abide by the peace.

The Ottawa returned with Le Pesant and handed him over to Cadillac to do with as he pleased. However, they did beg the commandant to spare him. After humiliating and incarcerating him Le Pesant escaped over the stockade walls and fled into the woods. Knowing that his countrymen had abandoned him and his influence was depleted Cadillac made the wise choice of not pursuing him. This would make for better relations with all the upper nations and the Wyandotte and Miami had already agreed to abide with any decision he made.

The peace was restored and the nations began to return to de troit, but there was still trouble ahead for both Cadillac and de troit.

NEXT WEEK: Now it's the Fox's Turn!

Now it's the Fox's Turn!

March 3, 2010

The Olympics are over but tax season is just getting underway. I'm still finding it hard to find the time to post here but I'll do my best.

Cadillac had managed to smooth things over by 1708 but Vaudreuil came up with another plan to rid himself of the thorn in his side. He couldn't seem to discredit Cadillac to the powers that be back in France so he thought a promotion might do the trick. In 1711 he recommended to the King and Minister Ponchartrain that Cadillac be named to the vacant position of Governor of Louisiana. He was and ordered to leave for his new post immediately.

Monsieur Jacque Charles Dubuisson was appointed new commandant of Fort Ponchartrain at de troit. He was an able administrator but no Cadillac. He commanded neither the strength of resolve when dealing with the First Nations nor the respect they had for the former commander. He was there but a year when crisis broke out again. This time it was with the Fox and Mascoutin nations and would spiral into all-out war ending in disaster.

Before Cadillac left for Louisiana he invited the Fox and Mascoutin to settle at de troit. About 1,000 came from Wisconsin along with a few Sauk. They settled on land assigned to them but built a fort of their own within a pistol's shot of the French Fort. The next summer a disagreement arose between them and the French. Dubuisson accused them of conspiring under British influence to destroy Fort Ponchartrain but the Fox said it was the French that started the war for reasons unknown to them.

Apparently Dubuisson complained about the nearness of the Fox fort and ordered them to remove themselves. Some of the Fox's young men under their great chiefs Lamima and Pemoussa shouted out insults to the French saying they were the owners of all the surrounding country. Actually they were the owners a century earlier.

Dubuisson was in a precarious position. The Wyandotte and Ottawa warriors had not returned from their winter hunt and Dubuisson had only about thirty Frenchmen at the fort. So he had to endure all of the escalating aggravation from the Fox and Mascoutin. He sent word to his allies at their hunting grounds to return as soon as possible.

The Fox were awaiting the arrival of their allies the Kickapoo when they received alarming news. The great Ottawa war chief Sahgimah had gone off in pursuit of a band of Mascoutin. He had the Potawatomi war chief Makisabi with him and about 100 warriors. Some the Mascoutin men had insulted Sahgimah by calling him a coward so they were out to avenge the insult. They came upon the Mascoutin wintering on the St. Joseph River where they attacked and killed 200. About fifty survivors fled to their kinsmen at de troit for protection. When they heard the news they immediately determined to burn an Ottawa lodge. Then they pillaged the crops growing outside the French fort. A Fox spy named Joseph had warned Dubuisson of their plans so he had time to save most of their wheat by bringing it into the fort.

Dubuisson was bracing himself for disaster when the Wyandotte and the Ottawa arrived from their hunting grounds. The Wyandotte met with Monsieur de Vincennes at their fort and insisted that the Fox and Mascoutin be annihilated according to the governor's wishes. They claimed to know this from a previous council in Montreal.

Two hours later Sahgimah and Makisabi arrived. Not only their own warriors with them but also some Missouri, Illinois, Osage and other more remote nations that Dubuisson did not recognize. They picked up these other warriors as they returned from the St. Joseph and now had about 600 with them. They were in a highly agitated state. To make thing worse they discovered that the Fox had taken some hostages and among them was Sahgimah's wife!

This multitude of nations let out a loud war cry and the Fox returned in kind. Then they rushed the Fox fort with the Wyandotte and Ottawa at their head. About forty Fox and Mascoutin warriors rushed out to meet them but immediately retreated back into their fort. Dubuisson's allies requested permission to enter the French fort, which they did and he gave them supplies including ball and shot. After speeches from their war chiefs and harangues from their old men they all raised the war cry. Guns discharged from both sides and balls flew like hail. The war had begun!

NEXT WEEK: The Fox Parlay for Peace

The Fox Wars

The Fox Parlay for Peace

March 20, 2010

The weather is great as I sit to write this week's post. The sun is shining and it's warming up. However, it still could get a little warmer . . . no, a lot warmer! I am so looking forward to summer.

We last left the Fox and Mascoutin hunkered down in their fort surrounded by hostile First Nations less than 100 yards from the French fort. The French erected two twenty foot scaffolds in order to shoot down on their villages. All Dubuisson's allies left Fort Ponchartrain and fanned out to the edge of the forest surrounding the settlement. They had the Fox pinned down and they couldn't go out for food or water. This siege lasted nineteen days.

During this time the French fired upon the Fox fort continually night and day. Their allies kept returning to the fort with prisoners they had captured in the woods. These were Fox and Mascoutin kinsmen coming to join them not knowing they were besieged. Their sport was to kill them with arrows and then burn them. Meanwhile the Fox in their fort were becoming exhausted with thirst and hunger. They hoisted twelve red flags in their villages and called out to the French they had no father but the English and called out to the Ottawa and their allies they would do better to change sides. Their attempt at intimidation failed.

Finally, the Potawatomi war chief Makisabie mounted one of the French scaffolds and called out to the Fox. He entered into a long harangue chastising them and their British "masters". He didn't get too far along when Dubuisson broke in stopping him. The Fox had asked for this interlude only so they could sneak out for water. The French recommenced their firing killing thirty Fox including some women who had gone for water. The fox returned fire killing twelve Frenchmen.

The Fox had taken a French house that was outside their fort and it had a mound of earth on the gabled side of it. They erected a scaffold behind it on which to stand and fire upon the French. The French bullets would not penetrate this defence so they hauled one of their small cannons up on their scaffold, aimed it at the Fox scaffold and fired. Upon the first two discharges the Fox scaffold fell killing some of them. They were so fearful they called out for a meeting with the French and their allies.

Dubuisson held a council with all the war chiefs and they decided to hear them out thinking they may still be able to extract the three women prisoners the Fox had taken including Sahgimah's wife.

The next morning the Fox war chief Pemoussa came out of his fort with two others and a white flag. They also had with them two captives who had been living with them for a long time. Dubuisson sent an armed escort to bring him to the fort and also to protect him from the insults of some of the young warriors. The council was held in the parade grounds of Fort Ponchartrain with the Fox delegation surrounded by enemy war chiefs.

Pemoussa asked for a two-day cease-fire so their elders could determine in council a way to turn aside their enemy's wrath. He also offered up the two captives as partial payment for the blood they had spilt.

Dubuisson told Pemoussa that if his heart was right he would have brought the three women hostages instead of the two strangers they offered. If they really wanted peace they could begin by bringing the three women otherwise the war would continue. All the war chiefs concurred saying they had nothing to say to

Pemoussa and that if he wanted to live let him turn over the three women. Pemoussa and his delegation including the two strange captives were escorted back to their fort.

Two hours later a Fox chief along with two Mascoutin chiefs returned to the French fort under a white flag. They had the three women with them. The three chiefs spoke to Dubuisson and all the war chiefs asking that the Ottawa, Potawatomi and others retire and the French cease firing for two days in order that they may go for food and water. They explained their people were dying inside their fort for lack of provisions. Dubuisson deferred their answer to the war chiefs.

They chose the Illinois war chief Makouandeby to be their speaker. He then told the Fox and Mascoutin chiefs that they were not to be trusted. They knew of their commitment to the British to kill the French and burn their fort. Because of their bad hearts they would not retire leaving the French alone to be killed and as soon as the Fox and Mascoutin chiefs re-entered their fort they would be fired upon and the war would recommence.

NEXT WEEK: The Fox's Demise

The Fox's Demise

March 18, 2010

Ah, the weather is so fine . . . just like summer! I do so want it to continue. But, alas I heard rumblings about a chance of wet flurries next week. Oh well, back to reality and back to our story.

We left the Fox and Mascoutin chiefs being escorted back to their fort after their First Nation adversaries rejected their peace plan. When they were returned safely the firing recommenced. For four days they fired upon each other without a word being spoken.

The Fox shot flaming arrows at the French fort hoping it would catch fire and burn down. Sometimes these flaming missiles flew three or four hundred at a time. It was a good plan because the buildings inside Fort Ponchartrain had thatched roofs. Some of them did catch fire and the French panicked but Dubuisson reassured them. They replaced the thatch with bear and deer skins, filled large pirogues with water and fashioned large poles with mops on the ends to extinguish any skins that might start to smolder. This sufficed in handling the matter.

Now Dubuisson had another problem. He heard rumours that some of his First Nation allies want to quit the fight and leave. Others heard the same rumours and again the Frenchmen began to panic. They told Dubuisson they thought they should retire to Michilimackinac as quickly as possible. He rejected that idea immediately and called the plan cowardly. Then he called a council with the war chiefs.

When they were all gathered he started a harangue to encourage them to remain and fight to the end. But in the middle of his discourse the chiefs interrupted him. They told him they never would quit the fight and that some liar had started these bad rumours. They got so riled up that they all sang the war song, did the war dance then with a loud war cry rushed out of the fort to attack the Fox.

Every day a few Sauk who were with the Fox would abandon them and come over to the French side. They brought intelligence with them on the condition of the enemy. By this point in the war they reported that the Fox were in very poor condition. They said that over eighty women and children had died from lack of food and water. They were unable to intern them along with the warriors being killed daily because of being continually fired upon. This in turn caused disease to break out in their fort. They were indeed in bad shape, so bad that they had no other choice but to try again to sue for peace.

They demanded permission to speak to their adversaries and permission was granted. The Fox's two greatest chiefs, Pemoussa the war chief and Allamina the civil chief came along with Kuit and Onabimaniton the two greatest Mascoutin chiefs. Pemoussa was dressed in his finest carrying wampum belts and painted green. He was supported by seven female captives who were also painted, adorned with their finest beadwork and carrying wampum belts. Pemoussa led the procession.

The other three chiefs each carried a chickikoue, a small drum used to enlist spiritual assistance. They preceded into the French fort in single file the three chiefs beating their chickikouies and all singing the song of it. When they had entered the fort they ceased the song and Pemoussa spoke.

Pemoussa conceded defeat and offered the seven women captives as payment for his life. He said he was not afraid to die but conceded for the lives of their women and children. He offered six wampum belts to tie the Fox and Mascoutin to the French and their allies in friendship and asked for a good word with which he could return to his village. Dubuisson again acquiesced to the war chiefs to give the Fox an answer.

The chiefs and their warriors were so enraged at the Fox they refused to give them any answer but instead asked to speak with Dubuisson in private. They wanted to kill the four head chiefs on the spot so the Fox would be leaderless and surrender without condition. Dubuisson dismissed this idea out of hand. Besides, if he agreed to such a dishonorable plan the Governor General would not forgive him. The chiefs agreed and the Fox delegation was returned to their fort safely but without a treaty.

The firing recommenced once again and on the nineteenth day of the siege the Fox and Mascoutin decamped about midnight and their escape was not discovered until the next morning. The Ottawa, Wyandotte and the rest of their allies went off in hot pursuit. De Vincennes and a few Frenchmen went with them.

The Fox and their Mascoutin allies knew they would be pursued so they stopped at what today is Grosse Pointe, Michigan on Lake St. Clair and made an entrenchment there. They built very good ramparts which enabled them to kill twenty of the pursuers. Another siege ensued that lasted four days.

Dubuisson had sent word to the Ojibwa on the St. Clair River and the Mississauga on Lake St. Clair to come to their aid when the war first broke out. They couldn't because all their young men were gone on their winter hunt. But now they had returned and they began to show up at the rate of 100 canoes a day for the four days. Then they stormed the Fox entrenchment and slaughtered all but 100. Then they returned to Fort Ponchartrain with their 100 captives which they killed about five a day until they were all dead.

The Fox and Mascoutin who were invited to de troit were totally annihilated. They lost 1,000 men, women and children in the war. The Ottawa, Wyandotte and their allies, including twenty-five Iroquois from Fond du Lac, suffered sixty men killed and wounded and the French had one killed and several wounded. This tragedy at de troit would commence a period of about twenty-five years known in history as the Fox Wars.

NEXT WEEK: The French Instigate the War

The French Instigate the War

April 11, 2010

Greetings All! Well I'm back from my hiatus. I gave a presentation on Aamjiwnaang history and culture at a Native American Celebration Day at the St. Clair County Community College, Port Huron, MI last week. So, I let everything slide beforehand to prepare. But now back to the early 1700's in the Great Lakes.

In the last post we left about 1,000 Fox and Mascoutin men, women and children being massacred at Grosse Point, MI on Lake St. Clair. Back in their main villages the Fox, Mascoutin and their Kickapoo allies heard about the disaster at de troit. This made them extremely agitated so they began sending out war parties everywhere to exact revenge. They sent them to Green Bay and de troit attacking all who were not allied with them. This made the routes of travel totally unsafe.

In the spring of 1713 they killed a Frenchman named l'Epine at Green Bay. They then attacked de troit killing three Frenchmen and five Wyandotte people. So the Wyandotte along with the Miami sent a delegation to Quebec to ask the French to join them in an expedition against the Fox and their allies in order to seek satisfaction.

Governor Vaudreuil agreed thinking the Fox had become so unruly that if the French did nothing they would be looked upon with contempt by all the far nations. But, he didn't want the expense of any expedition to be charge to the King's treasury so he hatched a plan to pay for it by using the colony's commerce.

There was in the upper country about a hundred coureurs de bois who were French fur traders that had gone rogue. They had been ordered to cease their trading activities but they refused the direct order from the King. Many were even dealing with the English for trade goods. They were now considered outlaws. But, Vaudreuil reasoned, if the King were to pardon them he could issue them new licences, supply them with trading goods if they would promise to congregate at Michilimackinac and join in the war against the Fox. The profits from the trade goods could in turn pay for the expedition.

In 1714 Claude de Ramsey became acting governor while de Vaudreuil was in France. For two years the French did nothing but in the spring of 1715 they sent presents to the Miami and Illinois in order to arrange a peace between the two. They were both very large nations and both were common enemies of the Fox.

Meanwhile de Vaudreuil returned, asking Sieur de Louvigny, a military man with some import with the First Nations, to go to Michilimackinac. He was to take with him twenty men, munitions for the garrison and trade goods. He also had orders to accomplish three things.

First he was to ascertain if a general peace was even a possibility. Depending on the attitude of the far nations toward the Fox and their allies he would know if there was anything acceptable to them to "cover their dead" and if the Fox were to agree to the terms. Second, he was to encourage the Sioux to break the peace they had arranged with the Fox and not to give them safe haven once the expedition commenced. Third, he was to offer the King's amnesty to the coureurs de bois if they all came to Michilimackinac and agreed to participate. However, de Louvigny got sick and could not go until the following spring.

Finally he arrived at Michilimackinac and ascertained that a general peace was not possible. However, when he arrived he found the situation rife with problems. The Sauk were fighting with the Puants and Sauteurs. The coureurs de bois were a lawless group trading with everyone including the Fox. This upset all the far nations allied against the Fox. He also discovered that they were getting their trade goods from unscrupulous merchants in Montreal. To top things off the goods and munitions to supply the expedition didn't arrive until late August, too late to do anything that year!

NEXT WEEK: Louvigny's Expedition

Louvigny's Expedition

April 21, 2010

After two years of trying to get his war off the ground the French's First Nation allies got tired of waiting. A party of Iroquois from Sault Ste. Louis along with the Wyandotte and Potawatomi from de troit met with the northern nations at Chicago. They determined to go to le Rocher, a village in Illinois country, to see the sons of de Ramezay and de Longueuil. Their plan was to get them to raise a French force to join them on a march against the Fox's allies.

When they arrived in Illinois territory they found both Frenchmen very sick at Kaskaskia. However, they ordered a Frenchmen named Bizaillon who was on the Illinois River to raise as many Illinois warriors as he could to join the expedition. After raising some Illinois he and a Frenchman named Pachot joined the campaign.

They found seventy wigwams belonging to the Mascoutin and Kickapoo who were hunting along a river. They attacked so their enemy dug in on a steep rock and after a long siege their fortress gave way. The Iroquois and allies killed more than 100 and took 47 prisoners not counting women and children. In order to make tracking them difficult they moved down the river a distance of 75 miles but after eleven days they were overtaken by 400 warriors who were the elite of the Fox Nation.

The Fox attacked at dawn. The Iroquois, Wyandotte, Potawatomi and Illinois had only eighty warriors left in their party and fifty of them defended the redoubt where the wounded and prisoners were being kept. The battle raged until three o'clock in the afternoon when the Fox finally retreated after losing many warriors. The Iroquois etc. pursued them for several hours killing even more.

When they returned to Illinois country they took a count reporting twenty-six killed and eighteen wounded. This expedition took place in November 1715 and the two stunning defeats served both to bolster the spirits of the French First Nation allies and demoralize the spirits of the Fox and their allies. Both the Mascoutin and Kickapoo nations surrendered themselves to the governor Vaudreuil swearing that if the Fox refused to capitulate as well they would turn on their former ally.

The following spring de Louvigny left Montreal with 225 Frenchmen and another 200 from de troit and Michilimackinac joined him. Another 400 First Nation allies also joined the campaign. They had all the munitions needed for the war including two pieces of cannon and a grenade mortar. They found 500 Fox warriors and 3,000 women congregated on their river in a fortress with three palisades.

The attack began in earnest but the bullets from their firearms were of no effect. However, they kept the heavy artillery firing constantly night and day. This constant barrage quickly damaged the palisades and the Fox feared they would be breached by the third night. They also had expected another 300 warriors to arrive as reinforcements but they didn't materialize. Things looked bad for the Fox so they called out for a parlay to talk peace.

The French and allies ignored the Fox's first overture and kept on firing. They also covertly placed two bombs underneath the gates of the fort and were ready to blow the gates off when the Fox called out again. This time Louvigny submitted the call to surrender to his First Nation allies. The First Nations imposed such stringent conditions that they thought the Fox would never agree to them. They were of the mind to utterly destroy the Fox Nation.

First, they had to agree to make peace with all the First Nations around them. Second, they had to bring their allies, the Mascoutin and Kickapoo on board, even if it be by force. Third, they must return all prisoners they held to their respective nations. Fourth, they must go to war in distant lands to get prisoners to replace all those killed by them during the war. Fifth, they must cover the costs of the war by goods procured through the hunt. Sixth, they must give up six chiefs or children of chiefs to be taken to Vaudreuil as and held as guarantees for the articles of the treaty. Much to everyone's surprise the Fox agreed to these conditions!

Sieur de Louvigny's campaign against the Fox was a great success but this would not be the last of their belligerence nor the end of the Fox Wars.

NEXT WEEK: The Fox Return To their Old Ways.

The Fox Return to their Old Ways

May 6, 2010

Greetings to all! So nice to get back to my posts and I'm glad they're appreciated.

After the 1716 peace agreement with the French the Fox followed through by sending three of their chiefs to Montreal. They were about to send more when smallpox broke out in the city. Two of the three chiefs died including their great war chief

Pemousa. Needless to say they were not happy about this turn of events so they held back the other hostages.

Meanwhile war raged on between the Illinois and the Mascoutins along with their allies the Kickapoo. But the Fox who were traditional allies with the Mascoutins and the Kickapoo kept out of it. That is until Minchilay, a nephew of Ouashala, who was a major Fox chief, undertook an ill-fated attack on the Illinois. He was captured and most cruelly burned to death.

Minchilay's death so angered his uncle that he set off in a rage to avenge his nephew's death. His brother, Navangounik was with him as they led a large war party of young warriors. They put the Illinois village responsible for Minchilay's death under siege. The village began to run out of food and water so they asked for a parlay.

The young men wanted nothing to do with a parlay for peace but only wanted to burn the village leaving none alive. But Ouashala and Navangounik were more level-headed and insisted on listening to the Illinois chiefs. Three of them came out of their village with three prisoners of their wars with the Fox allies offering them for their lives. The young men were still intent on destroying the village but their two chiefs prevailed and a peace was reached.

The two Fox chiefs along with the son of another chief named Elecavas went to a council held at Monsieur de Montigny's house. Elecavas was too sick to travel so he sent his son to speak for him. There was also a French missionary in attendance. They went there to explain their actions against the Illinois.

The two chiefs who took action against the Illinois village explained themselves by saying that although it was wrong of Minchilay to attack a nation that they were not at war with it was also wrong of them to so cruelly burn him to death. This was an act that needed to be avenged. But they pulled back from totally destroying that village and followed de Louvigny's example toward them in 1716 by letting them live. They also promised to return to the terms of the peace and keep them if the French would forgive them and not call all their allies to make war on them.

Elecavas brought his father's words which were less conciliatory than Ouashala's. He said he wanted de Montigny to say to Governor Vaudreuil that it had been two years since they had seen any trade goods and it appeared that the Governor still harbored the desire to totally destroy the Fox nation. They still waited for French goods but when they absolutely need to they would trade with the English. If Vaudreuil still wanted to annihilate them they could find them still at their fort and they would all die together.

De Montigny ignored Elecavas' words but answered Ouashala. He generally agreed with him and reiterated that if the Fox returned to the path of peace he would not bring down all of their First Nation allies upon them. The last thing the French wanted was another war with the Fox and their allies. They were continually trying to settle disputes among the far nations which distracted their ability to maximize profits from the fur industry.

The Fox tried their best to keep the peace even after being attacked by the Saulteux Chippewa from Michigan's Upper Peninsula. Four times they were attacked and four times they gave no response. But after being assaulted by the Ottawa from Saginaw they went on the offence. This escalated to a full-blown war with the Saulteux. This only hindered the French's plans to cultivate trade with the Sioux because to get to their country they had to go through Fox country and the Fox, who were friends with the Sioux, were now killing any Frenchmen they came across. Vaudreuil called upon Sieur de Lignery, commandant at Michilimackinac, to affect a peace between them.

De Lignery arrived at Green Bay in 1724 and managed to quell all the warring nations except the Fox and the Illinois and their allies. Apparently the Illinois did not live up to the last peace agreement in 1716 because they still had not returned their prisoners.

To make matters worse the English stepped up their intrigues with all the nations of the upper lakes. Over the next three years they secretly sent collars, which were peace offerings, to them all encouraging the enemies of the French become their allies and trading partners. At the same time they encouraged the allies of the French to destroy all the French posts among them and to slaughter all the Frenchmen in their territories. The French's response was to plan a war of extermination on the Fox!

NEXT WEEK: The Fox Wars Escalate

The Fox Wars Escalate

May 14, 2010

The Fox Nation only wanted their prisoners of war back from the Illinois. This was according to the peace agreement of 1716. A decade later and they were still waiting. The French had tried to facilitate them but the Illinois were still being obstinate. So the Fox escalated their hostilities against the French. No Frenchmen was safe travelling through their country.

The French were trying to expand their posts westward into Sioux territory. The Sioux had asked for a post with a few Frenchmen to live among them. However, they were allies of the Fox. After a small expedition to their country the Frenchmen decided to return to Montreal by heading south skirting Fox territory making their way to Detroit. To accomplish this they had to travel through the Fox's ally's country. They were captured by the Mascoutins and Kickapoo and held prisoner.

When the Fox heard of this they sent a delegation to their allies demanding they hand over the French prisoners to them. The Mascoutins and Kickapoo refused. They sent a second delegation even more arrogantly expressing their demands. Again they were refused. This so incensed the Fox that on the way home they came across a small camp with two lodges. They found a Mascoutin hunter in one and a Kickapoo in the other. They killed them both. This breached the alliance they had with their two most important allies.

Meanwhile, The King of France after hearing of all the perceived trouble the Fox were continually causing among the other First Nations determined that a war of extermination was called for. So he issued the order. The French began by giving presents to the Sioux, Winnebago and the Iowa in order to induce them not to give refuse to the Fox should they ask for it. In the east the Iroquois had made friendly overtures to the Fox allowing them to trade with the English and could offer them asylum if they needed it. To prevent this they used the Potawatomi and the French Fort at the St. Joseph River to block them. They seemingly had the Fox penned up in their own country.

Monsieur de Lignery was chosen to lead the expedition. He arrived at Michilimackinac in August of 1728 where he found waiting there about 100 Menominee warriors along with the nations of Detroit, the Lake Huron Saulteux and the Ottawa of Michilimackinac. His army was composed of 1,200 First Nations warriors and 450 Frenchmen. They immediately struck out for Green Bay.

When they arrived at la Baye a few Sauk warriors joined them. The First Nations camped on one side of the river and the French on the other. The Sauk warriors brought one Fox and three Winnebago captives to de Lignery. After questioning them he turned them over his allies on the other side of the river. They put them to death the next day.

They continued their march toward Fox country but lost some time and most of their canoes due to the great rapids of the Fox River. Finally they came upon a Winnebago village. But the Winnebago had abandoned it two or three days before de Lignery arrived.

They continued their march arriving in Fox country that evening. Because it was too late to engage them they camped between two Fox villages. The next morning de Lignery sent out scouts who returned with a Fox woman and girl who told them their countrymen had left the village in great haste moving upstream about three days earlier. Another scouting party returned from the other Fox village with an old man they had captured. He told them the same thing the two female captives had told them. All but 600 of the First Nation force moved on to the third village. It was empty also so de Lignery returned to the middle village where they came across an old woman who had been a captive of the Fox.

Ouilemek, the great Potawatomi war chief, questioned her and she told him that the Fox had left four days earlier. She said that they had 100 canoes in which they placed all of their elders, women and children and the warriors had followed them along the banks on foot in order to protect them.

A council was called and de Lignery asked his First Nation allies to follow the Fox. They asked for two hundred Frenchmen but they were in such poor condition a forced march would have killed them. The expedition was a hard one and most had lost their shoes and had no food except some corn they had scavenged from the Fox's fields. At this point de Lignery decided to halt the expedition. He ordered four villages burned as well as all the lodges scatter round about the countryside. They harvested the Fox's crops, which were abundant, leaving the Fox with no food. Then they began the retreat to Michilimackinac. So went de Lignery's war on the Fox, which he considered a success because he estimated that half the population of those villages would starve to death over the winter!

NEXT WEEK: Relentless Attacks

Relentless Attacks

May 22, 2010

The Fox came under attack from various enemies over the next three years. In 1729 the Mascoutins and the Kickapoo made several raids on their villages. They were seeking revenge for the killing of their two hunters. The next year they were attacked by a force of 150 Frenchmen, from both Canada and Louisiana, and 900 First Nation warriors. The Fox had constructed a fort on a plain situated between the Wabash and Illinois rivers about 180 miles south of Chicago and southeast of present day Peoria, Illinois. They blockaded them in their fort finally forcing them out by starvation. They chased them down killing 200 warriors and 200 women and children. Another four or five hundred women and children were taken captive and distributed among the various First Nations.

The year after their defeat in Illinois the nation of the same name attacked the Fox once again at a Fox village somewhere between le Rocher on the Illinois River and Miami country. When the Kickapoo, Mascoutins and Potawatomi heard this they went there immediately. When they arrived the Illinois withdrew and six Potawatomi were wounded and a seventh one was killed. Two Mascoutin were also killed as well as a few of the Fox warriors. They traded insults with the Fox calling out that they would make their supper off the Potawatomi, Mascoutin and Kickapoo. The great Potawatomie war chief, Madouche replied it was the Fox that would make food for all the nations. Then the Illinois returned to join the fight and sometime later the Fox withdrew.

In the summer of 1732 the Wyandotte, Ottawa and Potawatomi from Detroit made a sortie into Fox country. They split into two groups. The first group contained all the Wyandotte and about ten Ottawa warriors. They were the first to arrive on the shores of Lake Marameek where the Fox had constructed a fort on a tongue of land between the shore and an impassable wetland. Lake Marameek is undetermined but there is a Maramee River about 20 miles south of St. Louis, Missouri.

They held back until the next day when, at daybreak, they sent a party of five or six to scout near the palisade. A woman came out and they killed her. When the Fox saw this they sortied out of their fort but were ambushed by the larger force. They had four warriors killed and a few more wounded so they retreated back into their fort.

The next day the rest of the Ottawa and Potawatomi arrived and they brought the le Rocher Illinois with them. The Fox came out to meet them again and three Wyandotte were killed and a few of their allies were wounded. The Fox retreated again into their fort.

The Wyandotte called a council and it was decided to parlay with the Fox. They determined that a Potawatomi chief should go into the fort and propose that the Fox surrender and they would spare their lives. When he delivered this proposal the Fox told him they did not trust them to keep their word. Instead they proposed that the war party from Detroit should withdraw and the Fox would stay quiet in their fort until the following spring at which time they would come to Detroit or the St. Joseph River to settle up for the lives lost. This is how the whole affair ended. However, the Wyandotte sent their greatest chief La Forest to Montreal to ask the Wyandotte of Lorette and the Iroquois of the Lake of Two Mountains to join them in a war on the Fox to settle the matter.

The Fox had lost their allies and were being refused asylum by their once friendly neighbors the Sioux and the Winnebago. The French were attacking them as well as all the nations around them. By 1732 they were in poor shape indeed.

NEXT WEEK: The Iroquois' Foray into Fox Territory

The Iroquois' Foray into Fox Territory

June 5, 2010

First let me apologize for being late with this post. The weather has been so fine I took advantage to work on my nature trails. I put in a bridge over a small stream that flows into the first pond. The wetlands are really taking shape.

We last left our story with the Detroit Wyandotte sending their chief La Forest to Quebec to invite the Quebec Wyandotte and Iroquois to join them in a war upon the Fox. Wouldn't you know forty-seven Praying Indians from Lake of Two Mountains showed up at Detroit in October! Nobody went off to war with winter about to set in, nobody but the Iroquois that is. The Mission Iroquois from the mission at the widening of the Ottawa River near Montreal were called Praying Indians.

When they arrived they found that nearly all of the young men of the Ottawa and Potawatomi had already left for their winter hunting grounds. The Detroit First Nations gave the Wyandotte collars to persuade them to wait until spring when they promised all their warriors would join them but the Iroquois said it was impossible for them to wait. They procured arms and ammunition from the French commandant with directions as to the best route to follow to engage the Fox and off they went. They left on the 17th of October 1732 with a war party composed of seventy-four Wyandotte, forty-six Iroquois and four Ottawa warriors.

They arrived at the St. Joseph River after a few days and found that all the Potawatomi there had also left for the winter hunt so they pushed on to Chicago. Some Potawatomi chiefs came to them there and proposed they wait until spring when they would also join them but they refused. From there they pushed into Kickapoo country. The Kickapoo were very frightened at first to see this small army of the fiercest of warriors in their territory but when they were told why they were there they offered to join them. However, they said they also had to wait until spring. But the war party refused and moved on.

They entered the country of the Mascoutins next and the results were the same. The Mascoutin's territory bordered on Fox country, so they asked them for ten men to act as guides. The Mascoutins provided them but said they didn't think they could overcome the Fox because they were so numerous. The guides took them as far as the Fox border in Wisconsin, pointed them in the right direction to engage the Fox then returned to their village.

Meanwhile the first of the winter snows arrived with blizzard like conditions blanketing the ground in heavy snow. The hardy warriors donned their snowshoes and marched for several more days. Some of them became sick and the older ones fatigued so they held a council to determine what to do. Some of the old men counselled a return home but the young men would not hear of it. One even said he would rather die than return home without killing some men. Two of the great Wyandotte chiefs said that although they were old they still felt strong enough to continue so the camp broke up with most of the older warriors making their way back to Chicago and the younger men marching forward. Now there were forty Wyandotte and thirty Iroquois left.

They followed the route that led to the Wisconsin River and after a few days they saw three men coming toward them across a prairie. When the three Fox men saw them they turned and fled. Thinking they were from a small village of four or five lodges the Mascoutin guides had told them about they followed them over a large hill. When they reached the top of the hill they discovered much to their surprise the principal village of the Fox, forty-six lodges in all, lay stretched out on the banks of the Wisconsin River. The three warriors who had fled upon first sight of their enemy had arrived in time to warn the large village. When the Fox saw the Iroquois and Wyandotte on the top of the hill ninety well-armed Fox warriors came out to meet them. The battle was on!

NEXT WEEK: The Iroquois Do It Right!

The Iroquois Do It Right!

June 12, 2010

The Fox sent a volley of bullets toward the top of the hill. The Iroquois and Wyandotte return the fire with two quick volleys of their own. The chiefs told them not to amuse themselves with gunfire but instead to lay down their firearms. They wanted to deal with the Fox by hand to hand combat in the deep snow because they were well experienced in manoeuvring on snowshoes and the Fox were not.

The Iroquois and Wyandotte rushed their enemy before they could reload. They each had a tomahawk in one hand and a knife in the other. The Fox were outmaneuvered and forced back into their fort but not without great carnage. There were seventy Fox warriors killed on the spot and fourteen taken prisoner. They pursued the fleeing warriors into the fort where they killed eighty women and children and took 140 prisoners. Ten warriors escaped but were not dressed for the cold winter air. They later died of exposure. The Wyandotte had five killed and several wounded with the Iroquois having no casualties.

After the attack they dressed the wounded leg of a Fox chief and released him and six women. They were to carry a message to their nation. They were to say that the Iroquois and Wyandotte had just eaten up their main village and they would be staying there for two days. After that if they wished to follow them they could, however as soon as they were spotted they would begin by breaking the heads of all the women and children. They would then make a rampart of their bodies and afterward pile the remainder of the Fox Nation upon them.

The Fox chief arrived at a small fort of nine lodges on the banks of the Mississippi River. When they heard of the attack they sent word to a group of three lodges nearby. Sieur Dorval and two other Frenchmen were wintering there. They had left Montreal with Monsieur de Linetot for Sioux country but were unable to make it. The Monsieur had built a fort on the Mississippi at a place called the Mountain Whose Foot is Bathed by the Water. This is now Mount Trempealeau, near the village of Trempealeau, Wisconsin about ninety miles above the mouth of the Wisconsin River. De Linetot found himself short of provisions so he sent some of his party out to winter with the Fox. Dorval and his two compatriots were some of these.

One Fox chief said to Dorval that it was Onontio, the French Governor that had caused them to be killed because neither the Iroquois nor the Wyandotte rise from their mats unless commanded to do so by the governor. Dorval replied that the Wyandotte were from Detroit and no doubt the expedition started from there without Onontio's knowledge. He didn't know that Governor Beauharnois had told them that although he couldn't give them permission because he had promised the Fox their lives he would not interfere in any disputes the First Nations might have amongst themselves.

The Fox chief said that if the French had nothing to do with the attack then Dorval should make them return his three children whom they were taking away. Dorval accepted the errand and the chief gave him a robe and seventeen beaver pelts as a ransom.

The Fox disarmed the Frenchmen, took them to their main village where the attack had taken place then led them to the spot where the victors had lit their last fire. Then he was told to return when he had ransomed the three children. Dorval quickly overtook the Wyandotte and Iroquois but instead of completing his errand for the Fox chief he returned to Detroit with the Iroquois and Wyandotte.

The Fox lost over 300 people killed or captured in this incident. The Wyandotte returned to Detroit with less than 100 prisoners. They killed thirteen women and two men trying to escape on the way back to Detroit. They killed another fifty-six on the journey home because of the difficulty of leading such a large group of prisoners and the fear that many could escape. They were of the opinion that there were only about thirty Fox left living on the Mississippi and that their enemies, the Puants or others, would destroy them as well.

The only ally the Fox had at this point was the Sauk and they quickly abandoned them when they saw all the surrounding nations lifting the tomahawk against them. Most of the Sauk returned to their home at Green Bay but a few went to settle at the St. Joseph River. After over twenty years of warfare the great Fox Nation had been reduced to a mere shadow of its former self; thus ended the so-called Fox Wars.

NEXT WEEK: The Affair of the Wyandotte of Detroit

Upheaval at Detroit

The Affair of the Wyandotte of Detroit

June 19, 2010

If you have been following my posts you will recall that after the catastrophic war with the Iroquois in 1649 the remnants of the Huron, Petun and Neutrals who had not converted to Christianity made their way to Michilimackinac to live near the Ottawa. There they became known as the Wyandotte, a corruption of what the Huron called themselves, Ouendat. The Jesuits cut back their mission work in North America to mainly Lower Canada, but did keep a presence at Michilimackinac and Illinois as well as Michigan. They also set up a mission called The Mission of l'assomption Among the Huron at Detroit which, for nearly forty years bore no fruit.

Father Armand de la Richardie arrived at Detroit in 1728 and labored among the Wyandotte for many years with no conversions. He finally gained one convert, an old Wyandotte chief named Hoosien. His family quickly followed but it wasn't long after his conversion that he died. Thinking that after the old chief had gone his family would quickly revert to their traditional beliefs Father Richardie, who was in ill-health, thought of giving up and returning to Quebec. To his surprise his mission kept growing and within 3 years of the death of his first convert all the Detroit Wyandotte had embraced Roman Catholicism.

In 1738 the Wyandotte and the Ottawa of Detroit had a falling out. The Jesuits thought the Ottawa were 'more brutal and superstitious' than the Wyandotte. Sastaresty, the title of the principle Wyandotte chief, sent word to the Governor General as well as to their brothers, the Iroquois of Sault St. Louis or Caughnawaga and the Huron of Lorette near Quebec City. He reported that the Ottawa had raised the hatchet to them and had asked the other Algonquian speaking nations there to join them in exterminating them. This of course would be referring to the Saulteux Ojibwa, Potawatomi and Mississauga.

The Governor General sent presents to them asking, through the Commandant of Detroit Monsieur de Noyelle to settle the peace and keep the Wyandotte at Detroit. The Wyandotte agreed to heed the Governor but said at the first alarm they would either go to the Seneca or else beyond the Belle Riviere. This was the name the French had given to the Ohio River.

That winter the First Nations of Detroit lived in apprehension of each other. The Wyandotte wintered in the interior which was not their custom to do so. In the spring the principle chief of the Wyandotte, Orontony, whose baptismal name was Nicolas, sent branches of porcelain to the Governor begging him to allow the Detroit Wyandotte to move to Quebec. They asked for a tract of land near him to settle on and a French officer to escort them as protection from attack.

Meanwhile, they made peace with the Flathead to the south. This was a nation that continuously skirmished with the Nations of Detroit. They made threats to move south among them but reconsidered after receiving harsh words from Entatsogo, chief of the Sault. Now they begged the Governor to forgive them for not sending their elders to Montreal as asked to do so because they were alarmed by the Praying Indians of Sault St. Louis. They also sent word to the Governor that it was not the custom of the Wyandotte to ask for protection or asylum but that it was the duty of one who had compassion on them to come and console them or to lead them to a new place where they would be safe.

In June of that year Father Richardie wrote to the governor that he had done all he could to influence their minds but they would not let go of their fears and apprehensions. They had been talking to both the English and their allies the Iroquois of Upstate New York and that those two nations had been taking advantage of the Wyandotte's alarm and trying to induce them toward their side. The Father suggested the Governor allow the move to Quebec and even send his nephew to escort them rather than see his charges go over to the other side. The good Father stated that if the move was made the Wyandotte would not be missed at Detroit because there was some Saulteux Ojibwa from the St. Clair willing to move to Detroit to take their place not to mention the Shawanee.

NEXT WEEK: More Upheaval at Detroit!

More Upheaval at Detroit!

June 27, 2010

Greetings to everyone! It's powwow weekend here at Aamjiwnaang. The weather is not looking so great however. It's cloudy and rain is in the forecast. I hope they're wrong.

When we last left Detroit in the fall of 1738 the nations were in great turmoil. The Ottawa of both Detroit and Saginaw and their allies the Potawatomi, also of Detroit, and the Saulteux Ojibwa of the St. Clair and Au Sable Rivers were threatening to destroy the Wyandotte of Detroit. The Wyandotte were afraid for their women and children so were determined to move out of the area. Their preference was to be allowed to move to Quebec to be with their Iroquoian speaking brothers. The Mohawk and Huron of Quebec were all Jesuit converts. They were also considering moving to Upstate New York to live among the Five Nation Iroquois. They were allies but the Five Nation still held the faith of their fathers.

The French were desperately trying to make peace between them because the Wyandotte were allies with the Iroquois and the Ottawa were allies with all the other Nations of the Upper Great Lakes. If the Wyandotte located among the Five Nations then they would lose them to the British. They wanted to avoid this at all costs. A larger problem was that this situation could have easily gotten out of hand and turned into a full-blown war with the French in the middle.

So, how did things come to this? To understand we have to return to the following spring. The Wyandotte had called a council at Sieur de Noyelle's house. He was the commandant of Detroit. The chiefs or their representatives of all of the above mentioned nations were there. They presented a belt to the Ottawa saying that by that belt they wished all to know that they had made peace with the Flathead and they now considered them brothers. They wished all would follow in order to make peace reign in the whole land. Then they issued a warning saying that if any of the other Detroit nations sent war parties against the Flathead it would assure that some of their young men would go ahead and warn them that they were coming to devour them. The Flathead were also called Choctaw and got their name from their practice of artificially flattening their foreheads when very young.

The Ottawa refused the belt asking the Wyandotte who they thought they were to dictate law to them. They accused the Wyandotte of considering bad actions and then take refuse with the Flathead. They took the belt and gave it to de Noyelle saying that it was him who represented Onontio, the governor, and that if the governor accepted it then they would honor his wishes.

The Ottawa also said the Wyandotte should remember that at the last general peace Onontio gave all the nations the Flathead to devour because they had become friendly with the British; that their blood was shed on the trails of the Flathead and on their mats. Their bones were still in the lodges of their enemy with their scalps hanging over them and that the frames on which they were burned were still spread out with the steaks still standing. Moreover, they said, if the Flathead Nation wanted peace with them they would have approached them and then they would consider peace or not.

The Wyandotte gave also gave a belt to the Potawatomi but were given a similar reply. They gave a third to the Saulteux who said because they were young men they would take it to their elders who would decide what to do. Then the council broke up.

Sometime soon after this the Ottawa, Potawatomi and Ojibwa raised a war party of seventeen men and set out for Flathead country. Two parties of Wyandotte joined them on the trail but did not continue on with them. When the war party reached their destination they found themselves surrounded by warriors in the forest all making the call of the raven. This was a common thing done before an attack signifying they were looking for blood. This surprised the Ottawa because this was not a custom of the Flathead so they suspected Wyandotte treachery.

Suddenly they found themselves attacked in the front by the Flathead and in the rear by the Wyandotte. One of the Ottawa recognized one of the Wyandotte and he killed him. Only three escaped the ambush including the Ottawa who had recognized the Wyandotte warrior. Five others were made prisoner and nine were killed.

NEXT WEEK: The Detroit Ottawa Are Furious!

The Detroit Ottawa Are Furious!

July 5, 2010

When the three escapees arrived back at the Ottawa village they uttered the cries for the dead. The Wyandotte came to the village when they heard the wailing and those who had survived the ambush said it was the Wyandotte that had killed them. The Wyandotte denied having any part of it saying they were allies to the Ottawa and could not slay their brothers. The warrior who had recognized and killed the Wyandotte warrior at the ambush accused the Wyandotte of not only being capable of killing their brothers but their father as well! He said the only reason they have not done so is there were so few of them. He told of hearing of the cries of the raven just before the attack explaining that he had been on several sorties against the Flathead and they never used this cry. It was a Wyandotte's tradition. He then announced the killing of the Wyandotte warrior from Detroit that he recognized and said if it were untrue let them produce that man as he was missing from the Wyandotte congregation. After these accusations the Wyandotte returned to their village and fortified themselves from attack.

The Jesuit fathers returned to the safety of the French fort and the Ottawa congregated around the Wyandotte fort. They called out to those inside their fortification saying that it seemed they were afraid walling themselves up in their stronghold daring not to come out while the Ottawa were out in the open. They accused the Wyandotte of fearing an attack but said they were mistaken. They allow them to go to their cornfields unmolested but when they did decide to attack them they would declare it as they were incapable of any treachery.

The Ottawa sent three sticks of porcelain to the Five Nations meeting them at Niagara. They presented them to their representatives with the request that they remain neutral in the dispute but if their intentions were to take the Wyandotte's side they should declare it first. The Iroquoian envoys said they could not provide an answer but would take the strings to their towns.

The Wyandotte requested assistance from the French by appealing directly to Governor Beauharnois at Montreal. They also sent belts to the Christian Mohawk at Lake of the Two Mountains and St. Louis Falls asking them to take their side and provide asylum for them in Quebec.

The French realized they had a full-fledged crisis on their hands. De Noyelle issued orders that no Frenchman should sell any powder, lead or guns to either side of the dispute. They were afraid this could cause the other side to accuse the French of providing the means of one side destroying the other. Beauharnois sent a great number of presents to Detroit with instructions to de Noyelle to settle things down.

However, dissention persisted for the next two years with the Ottawa, Ojibwa and Potawatomi threatening the Wyandotte with extermination and the Wyandotte men fearing for their families. In the fall of 1738 they formally asked the governor for asylum. They sent word to Beauharnois that they had met with an emissary at Michilimackinac sent by their brothers from Sault St. Louis. They were invited by them to settle with them because they were currently living amongst a multitude of nations that liked them not.

However, they recalled an invitation given them by the former Governor Vaudreuil to come live near him where they would have asylum, a Father and a protector. This was the option they preferred most and if it was not repeated by Beauharnois they said they preferred to withdraw somewhere else to die, but if he did grant their request they asked to be sent a military man to guide them safely through the nations who were intent on destroying them.

In June of 1739 they sent the words of Sastaresty Taatchatin and Orontony to Beauharnois. They asked the governor again to provide asylum near him. They said this was always their only wish and that would never change. They also issued warnings saying that if they were not allowed to settle in Quebec they would be forced to do something the governor would not like but did not say what. Probably this was a veiled reference to going over to the English side. They also said that they could never be strong in their new religion unless remove from among so many nations that were not Christian.

The Wyandotte were desperate. They implored de Noyelle along with the three Black Gowns at the Mission of l'assomption Among the Huron to write to the governor on their behalf recommending so strongly their request that the governor would be sure to grant it. In the summer of 1740 he wrote to the governor saying that after desperately trying to bring peace he now thought it impossible. Although it was the wish of the governor that they stay at Detroit he thought it would either bring on their destruction or they would ally themselves with the Iroquois and the British. Like Father de la Richardie he also felt that their move to Montreal would be no loss because the Shawnee were ready to take their place at Detroit. Would Beauharnois finally consent?

NEXT WEEK: The Saga Continues

The Saga Continues

July 20, 2010

It's been two weeks since I last wrote a post. Summer always seems to be so busy with outdoor projects that my writing seems to suffer. However, I also seem to get a lot of 'other things' done so the guilty feelings about my neglect is tempered somewhat.

In the last post the year of 1740 was one of tension and mistrust among the nations of Detroit. Seventeen forty-one was no different. In one instance a Wyandotte woman was working in their cornfield when a party of Saulteux happened along. They threatened the woman with death and killed her dog in front of her. This frightened her very badly and set the whole Wyandotte village on edge.

In another incident an Ottawa man in a state of intoxication accused the Wyandotte of killing his brother. This story spread throughout the Ottawa and their allies' villages. De Noyan had to get involved in order to prevent things from getting out of hand. He implored the Ottawa not to act on the word of a drunken man so they took his advice. It proved to be a good thing too as the rumour turned out to be false.

De Noyan came up with a plan to make peace. He advised the Wyandotte to break their peace with the Choctaw and attack them taking as many prisoners as possible. Then they could offer the prisoners to the Ottawa as payment for the blood shed at the original ambush. They could also reclaim their ally status because they had attacked the enemy of the Ottawa.

However, the plan was thwarted by a few who did not want to break their peace with the Flathead. They had secretly sent a collar to them warning of the plan. Not only did this foul up De Noyan's plan but they also warned them of an impending Ottawa attack. A large party had left Detroit to make a raid on the Flathead but when they arrived in their country they only found two abandoned villages.

Finally the Governor decided to allow them to move to Quebec. He sent his nephew to present his words to the Ottawa, Saulteux, Potawatomi and Mississauga of Detroit. He had to say it was his idea that the Wyandotte should be removed and not the Wyandotte's desire due to fear. He didn't like this but after four years of prodding by Detroit's commandant and the Black Robes he gave in.

Unfortunately by this time the Wyandotte had broken into three factions. The majority still wanted to remove to Quebec as did Sastaresty Taatchatin. This group had moved to the little Lake. This is what the French called what today is Rondeau Bay on the north shore of Lake Erie. Orontony or Nicholas and his followers set up a village at Sandusky Bay in Ohio and Angouirot, the third Wyandotte chief, had a smaller following that wanted to set up a new village about three leagues from Detroit on Grand Isle in the Detroit River.

This fracture of the Wyandotte Nation gave Governor Beauharnois cause to reconsider his offer. He had always wanted the Wyandotte to stay at Detroit and for peace among the nations there to be the norm. Three Wyandotte chiefs had gone to Montreal in 1742 to pick out the land they thought they would be allowed to move to but Beauharnois gave them a new message to take back to Detroit.

He sent word back to the Wyandotte elders that he understood that they had left the decision-making on the matter of moving to their young men and that they had all decided to move to

Grosse Isle. This contravened what the elders had begged him to do and although he did not understand what had caused misunderstandings among them he was pleased that all the unpleasantries at Detroit had apparently been smoothed over. Therefore, he could not place them anywhere because he had no information regarding the decisions taken by the Wyandotte Nation. All he could do was be pleased that they had decided to move nearby Detroit and he wished that they would live in peace at whatever place they chose to settle.

Governor Beauharnois also had a new ally for peace that only served to reinforce his decision. The great Ottawa chief Mekinac had moved to Detroit from Michilimackinac. He was one of the signees of the Great Peace Treaty of 1701 and was highly influential among his nation. He had visited Beauharnois that same year in Montreal along with chief Kinousakis. They led the two factions of the Detroit Ottawa. Both expressed their great desire for peace and promised to work with the French commandant toward that end. So Beauharnois had reason to believe that all would eventually be worked out. The Wyandotte never did move to Quebec but would instead remain in the Detroit area for another 150 years.

NEXT WEEK: First Nations of the Upper Country Revolt

First Nations of the Upper Country Revolt

August 8, 2010

In the 1740's the British were doing all they could to disrupt the alliance between the French and their First Nation allies. In the spring of 1745 a group of the French's Wyandotte allies returned to Detroit from visiting Chouaquin or Fort Oswego.

They reported to the French that many of their allies attended a council where the British told them that they should consider them the only source of trade because the British navy was going to put to sea to take Canada and become the absolute masters in North America. Therefore, trade goods would be scarce or unavailable at the French trading posts.

This news produced so much consternation among the villages around Detroit that native traders would leave for British trading posts without saying a word. This of course was contrary to the wishes of the governor of New France. The French tried to rally their allies to attack the British and several parties of Ottawa and Saulteaux struck out for the Carolinas that summer but it was a half-hearted effort and they returned without striking a blow.

Meanwhile goods did become very scarce at the French posts. This drove the prices up and lowered the value of pelts considerably. French traders needed a licence to trade, which they normally purchased but these economic conditions forced the commandants at the various trading posts to provide trading licences for free. All this made trading with the British all the more attractive, so much so that many were ignoring the direct orders of the governor not to trade with them.

The Wyandotte war chief Nicholas moved his followers to Sandusky on the south side of Lake Erie. That spring some of his young warriors killed five Frenchmen and stole their furs. They were returning from the French post on the White River, a tributary of the Wabash. The news was brought to Chevalier de Longueuil, the commandant of Detroit by a Wyandotte woman whose loyalties were still attached to the French. She also informed him that all the neighboring nations had formed a plan to annihilate all the French of Detroit on one of the holidays of Pentecost, but the brash young warriors had struck too soon.

Nicholas decided to press on with the plan to destroy Detroit. He attacked and destroyed the mission and villages on Bois Blanc Island in the Detroit River and the Black Robes fled to the safety of the fort.

The commandant called a council of the First Nations that were allied to the French at Detroit. The Ottawa professed their loyalty as did Sasteradzy, the principal chief of the Detroit Wyandotte. The Wyandotte chief Taychatin confirmed his allegiance as well. They all claimed to have had no involvement in the treachery committed by Nicholas' people that spring.

The following spring Nicholas burned his village on the Sandusky River and moved his band to the White River in Indiana. He died that autumn in an outbreak at Kuskusky while visiting the Iroquois. Kuskusky was a First Nation town in the Beaver River Valley near the present-day New Castle, Pennsylvania.

Of course the French blamed the English accusing them of sending secret belts to all the nations in the territory encouraging them to attack and destroy the French. They were probably right. Although in 1747 their allies confirmed their loyalties the future would bring even more turmoil.

NEXT WEEK: More of France's Allies Revolt!

More of France's Allies Revolt!

August 22, 2010

While Nicholas' warriors were harassing Detroit the Saulteaux Ojibwa from the St. Clair joined in. They had killed and carried off some of the local farmers' cattle and some of the farms were attacked by "unknown Indians". This was the work of some of the more brazen young men who were disregarding their chief's disapproval. All this upheaval made it impossible for the French to get the fall harvest in putting the post in jeopardy.

A party of chiefs and warriors arrived at Montreal to visit the Governor General. Among them were eight Ottawa chiefs and eight other warriors including two Seneca. Also some Wyandotte from Lorette came who had accompanied Sieur Beleatre to Detroit the year before. Four Wyandotte chiefs were also with them including Sasteradzy, the principal chief and Taychatin another main chief.

In the council with the governor they professed their loyalty and the Wyandotte, who had converted to Christianity, asked for Father La Richardie to return to Detroit to minister to their needs. He was their former missionary and they had the utmost confidence and respect for him. The French saw this as an opportunity to assist in settling things down at Detroit so they jumped at the chance. The governor quickly gave his approval, the priest consented and the deal was done.

Things were bad at Detroit with some of the young warriors getting out of control but they were worse at Michilimackinac. There was total confusion at that post. The Ottawa, Saulteaux Ojibwa and Mississauga were ill-disposed toward the French. The Ottawa of Saginaw had already struck a blow by killing three Frenchmen who were on their way from Detroit to Michilimackinac. The Saulteaux attacked two French canoes at La Cloche, an island in Georgian Bay between present day Little Current and Birch Island. One of the canoes escaped by discarding their cargo and fleeing to Michilimackinac. The other was totally defeated. Another Frenchman was stabbed by the Saulteaux just two leagues from the post at La Grosse Isle.

The post itself was on high alert. Various warriors had killed all the horses and cattle they could not catch and were continuously hurling insults and threats at the fort. Only a few at a time were allowed inside the post and only under the strictest control. A council was held but ended in recrimination when it was discovered that some of the young warriors had come armed with knives. The French were in a very precarious position as they only had 28 men manning the post. They were relieved a few days later when de Noyelle and a contingent of Frenchmen arrived from Point Chagouamigon on Lake Superior.

At the same time an Ottawa name Nequionamin arrived with alarming news. He reported to the commandant that the Iroquois, the Wyandotte and the Flathead had reached an agreement with the English to attack and destroy all French everywhere. He also reported that the Nations of Detroit were in on the plot. The Ottawa led the revolt; the Potawatomi would cooperate as well as the Mississauga and the Saulteaux of St. Clair. He said the Ottawa of Saginaw had already struck referring to the three they had killed on Lake Huron. They also had sent seventy men to council with the Ottawa of Michilimackinac but they were reluctant because they had a contingent of their village visiting Montreal. He advised the commandant not to let anyone leave the fort and to keep a strict watch. The French needed to gain some control!

NEXT WEEK: St. Pierre to the Rescue!

St. Pierre to the Rescue!

August 29, 2010

Things had truly gotten out-of-hand at the upper posts. This was especially true of Michilimackinac. So the governor had the voyageurs called in and ordered to trade only from that post. This had the effect of increasing the manpower to over 100 which seemed to be an adequate defence for the fort. But to keep them there over the winter he had to provide them with food and supplies. To this end he ordered ten cargo canoes loaded with 30,000 lbs. of goods to make the trip from Montreal to Michilimackinac.

The governor also commissioned a Lieutenant St. Pierre to take charge of twelve well-armed canoes and settle the peace in the upper country. He was to operate out of Michilimackinac travelling to the post at Green Bay with presents in order to sound out the First Nations there. They had seemed favourable to the French but if they were not then he was to do all in his power to win them over.

When St. Pierre arrived at Michilimackinac a council was called. He advised the chiefs at this council the object of his mission which was to restore the peace which they had so unworthily broken. He also demanded that they bring the murderers of the Frenchmen to him for his disposal. If they did not deliver these murderers to him then he would go and look for them himself!

The next day several chiefs who were at the council came to him and said they would turn the men responsible over to him but asked that he spare their lives. He said he could not say what their fate would be as this was up to the governor alone to determine.

Meanwhile, the Ottawa contingent that had gone to Montreal in the spring was led by a chief named Pindalouan. They were now anxious to return home because of the lateness of the season. The governor informed them of the sad state of affairs at Michilimackinac and they were genuinely surprised. This made them even more anxious explaining they would put things in order when they arrived home.

Monsieur de Vercheres and the thirty cargo canoes arrived at Michilimackinac in October and they had with them a prisoner they had captured along the way. Vercheres reported that they came across five canoes they thought had been the ones that attacked the French and pursued them. They beached their canoes and fled into the woods but the Frenchmen caught one. He had on him some French goods and a scalp so they asked him where he had gotten them. He replied that he was given them as a present by some warriors at Green Bay. He consistently claimed he was not guilty of attacking the French. Two Ottawa canoes arrived from Montreal and claimed this prisoner saying that he was of the family of Koquois, a chief very loyal to the French and a friend of de Vercheres. So de Vercheres released him to the Ottawa stressing the great favour he was doing them.

By October the nations around Michilimackinac had become very quiet. The two Saulteaux warriors who had joined in on the attack on the French earlier returned their portion of the booty to prove their innocence. They still claimed that upon seeing their people firing on a canoe they had joined in to help not knowing the circumstances. The commandant accepted this explanation.

Back at Detroit the commandant de Longueuil was extremely anxious. Nicholas had been in communication with the Saulteaux and Ottawa and they were about to attack the fort. If that happened then Mekinac, an Ottawa chief from Saginaw, would also declare against them. The Potawatomi were waiting as well to join in the fray. The only people to remain faithful to the French were those under the Ottawa chief Quinousaki. Almost all the cattle had been lost and if help didn't soon arrive they would not be able to get the harvest in and they would perish.

But help was on the way. Sieur Dubuisson arrived at Niagara with the convoy from Montreal. While there some of men of the guard got drunk and ill-treated the Grand Chief of the Seneca. He left for Seneca country very dissatisfied and the commandant, Monsieur Duplessis, had to send Sieur Chabert to his town at the Little Rapid with presents to appease him. The convoy spent little time at Niagara choosing instead to press on to Detroit.

The Ottawa and Potawatomi were supposed to attack the French village on Bois Blanc Island just south of Detroit. If they took this village they would effectively be able to block help from arriving. However, 100 men mostly traders from Illinois and other posts to the west arrived and prevented them from doing so. Dubuisson arrived at Detroit unheeded to find de Longueuil engaged in bringing in the harvest and all the nations around that post also began to settle down. Peace was being restored to the upper country.

NEXT WEEK: A Rising Star among the Ojibwa

Prelude to War!

A Rising Star among the Ojibwa

September 10, 2010

By 1750 the Saulteaux Ojibwa living in the St. Clair region had expanded. The Ojibwa from Swan Creek expanded across Lake St. Clair and up the Thames River. They had established a village near present day London and one at the mouth of Kettle Creek on Lake Erie.

The Ojibwa living at the mouth of the Black River, at the foot of Lake Huron, had expanded both east and west. They had established villages on Bear Creek as well as the mouth of the Au Sable River in Ontario. They also expanded west establishing villages at Nepessing Lake and along the Flint River in Michigan. Animikeence or Little Thunder was their leading war chief at this time.

Under the Treaty of Utrecht the English claimed they had gained the right to trade with the First Nation allies of the French from the upper lakes. Although the French contested this point it was a certain fact that it did not give them the right to set up trading posts in Ohio country. However, they did just that.

British traders moved into the Ohio Valley setting up posts along it as well as its tributaries. They did this under the pretense that it was Iroquois land and as sovereign over the Iroquois they had the right to expand into this new territory. The French claimed it as part of New France, discovered by La Salle and there had been a French presence there for decades.

None of this was really true. Ohio country was First Nations lands belonging to the Miami, Delaware and Shawnee nations. The French didn't really discover the territory as it was never lost nor were the British ever the Iroquois' sovereigns. Be this as it may the French forged ahead with a plan to oust the English.

Monsieur Celoron, major commandant at Detroit was to take a detachment of French soldiers supported by a large force of First Nation allies and clear the region of English traders. The idea was to arrest the traders, confiscate their goods and make the Miami understand that although they could go to Albany to trade with the English under no certain terms could they allow the English to establish themselves in French territory.

The plan failed miserably. The Saulteaux refused to endorse it saying that because of the close proximity of the Miami many had intermarried and they would have no part in a war against their relatives. Little Thunder also refused to allow French allies from further north to pass through their territory to support Celoron.

Celoron pushed ahead entering Miami territory with a few French regulars and a few First Nation warriors. They had a little success in removing a few English traders and their goods but in the process killed two Miami people. These murders only served to stir up the First Nations who were trading with the English and setting them against the French.

Meanwhile, Monsieur de Lajonquiere, Governor of Canada, had instructions from France to encourage the Five Nations to destroy the English post at Oswego. He was to convince them that an English post on their territory was an affront to their sovereignty. To accomplish this he went too far by giving the impression that France accepted the Onondaga's contention that Ohio belonged to the Iroquois and that the French should not establish themselves there without their permission. He did this at solemn council which also included the Christian Iroquois from Quebec as well as the Abenaki of St. Francis and the Ottawa of Michilimackinac.

In 1752 de Lajonquiere was replaced by Ange du Quesne as Governor. The French minister wrote to du Quesne with orders from the king. He was to make sure the territory was cleared of English traders and their goods confiscated without causing a war with any of the First Nations, no easy feat with Little Thunder and the Saulteaux standing in the way. He was also ordered to do all in his power to destroy the impression of First Nations sovereignty over land and to prevent any consequences that might arise due to de Lajonquiere's error in judgement.

NEXT WEEK: Langlade Captures Pickawillany

Langlade Captures Pickawillany

September 17, 2010

In the 1720's Augustin Mouet de Langlade, a French trader living at Michilimackinac married Domitilde, an Ottawa woman who was a sister of an important chief named Nissowaquet. The French called Nissowaquet La Fourche meaning The Fork. They had a son who was baptized Charles Michel Mouet de Langlade in May of 1729.

Because of a dream Nissowaquet believed his young nephew had a protecting spirit so he convinced his parents to let ten year-old Charles accompany him to Tennessee on a war party against the Chickasaw. On two previous raids they were repelled by their foes. They were successful on this particular sortie in that a treaty was made between the two when the confrontation ended in a stalemate. This adventure earned him the name Aukewingeketawso meaning Defender of his Country. So Charles Langlade became enthralled with military service at a very young age.

Sixteen years later Augustin Langlade purchased a position for his son in the French colonial regulars as a cadet. He was 21 years old. Although he served in the French military he wore the dress of an Ottawa warrior. Over the next two years he gained much influence with the Ottawa side of his heritage.

In 1752 he was visiting the village of Memeskia an important Miami chief on the Great Miami or Rocky River. It was situated at the mouth of Laramie Creek and had the considerable population of 8,000 and was a hub of English trading activity. The French called Memeskia la Demoiselle or Your Lady but the English called him Old Britain.

Memeskia was pro-British and held the French in great disdain. What Langlade was doing in Ohio country is not known but probably he was spying for the French. At any rate Old Britain insulted him in some way and Langlade left the country in a huff. When he got to Detroit he angrily related the incident to his friend Pontiac an important Detroit Ottawa war chief. Both became enraged so they convinced Little Thunder and his Saulteux Ojibwa to allow Langlade passage through their territory to exact his revenge.

Detroit commandant Celoron couldn't be happier. At last his First Nation allies were on board to help him fulfill his orders to clear the English traders out French territory and return the Miami to the French fold. Langlade returned from Michilimackinac with 250 Ottawa and Ojibwa warriors bent on restoring his good name. However, he could not convince Little Thunder and the St. Clair Ojibwa to join them so they carried on alone picking up a contingent of French regulars at Detroit.

On the morning of June 21st they arrived at Pickawillany, the name the English called Memeskia's village. Most of the warriors there were away on their summer hunt but the women were in the cornfields and eight traders were in the outbuildings.

The Ottawa and their allies came upon them suddenly. They surprised the women taking them prisoner. Three traders were besieged in a house and they surrendered immediately but the Miami warriors fought on. A truce was called in the afternoon with all but two traders being handed over. The Miami kept these two hidden. The women were released. Memeskia's widow and son had escaped; however, la Demoiselle's fate was an Ottawa cooking pot. They partook in the old custom of eating a defeated foe whose qualities of leadership and bravery could be had by literal consumption. They also killed one of the traders who was wounded and ate his heart. When the expedition returned to Detroit they had plunder worth 3,000 British pounds Sterling and five English traders who were arrested and put in prison.

Governor du Quesne was elated. Although the French officially denounced the above mentioned custom as an atrocity du Quesne wrote to the French minister in Paris asking for an annual pension of 200 livres for Langlade saying that he would be highly pleased with it and it would have great effect in the country. He also reported that the Miami had come back to the French alliance greatly diminishing the English influence in French territory.

NEXT WEEK: The British Eye the Ohio Valley

The British Eye the Ohio Valley

October 11, 2010

By the mid-18th century the Ohio valley was a hotbed of activity. The population was made up of many First Nation villages and towns. They included many Delaware, Shawnee, Miami and Wyandotte communities with a few roaming Ottawa and Iroquois bands. The English called the Iroquois in the area Mingo. British traders had set up trading houses at the larger First Nations' towns. But the English had more in mind than just trade with the First Nations. They wanted their land for settlement.

They had signed the Treaty of Albany with the Iroquois in 1722 that marked out a line dividing their territory with the colony of Virginia. That line basically followed the Blue Ridge Mountains. However, Virginian settlers soon began crossing the Blue Ridge and squatting on First Nations' territory. Many paid with their lives and by the 1740's the Iroquois were so frustrated with their allies, the British, that they were ready to declare all-out war on Virginia. In 1743 the British paid the Iroquois 100 pounds Sterling for any territory claimed by them in the Shenandoah Valley. The following year under the treaty of Lancaster the Iroquois sold the British all of the Shenandoah Valley for 200 pounds of gold. At the Treaty of Logstown in 1752 the Iroquois recognized English trading rights in all of their territory southeast of the Ohio River.

The French saw the Ohio River Valley as French territory by way of discovery by La Salle and by way of French presence in the territory for a hundred years previous. They saw all this British activity as a violation of the treaty of Utrecht, which at best gave the British only the right to trade with First Nations in their own territory. The British crown complained to the French court in Paris, but this was a long process.

Lieutenant-Governor Dinwiddie of Virginia believed the Ohio Territory belonged to the Colonies under Virginia's original charter. The boundaries in the charter were more than vague so he extended the northern border to at least include the Ohio River and its tributaries. On top of all the activity around trade the English wanted this territory for settlement. In order to facilitate this settlement the Ohio Company was formed. It was an association given a grant of 500,000 acres in the Ohio Valley by the British crown providing they could establish 100 families, build a fort and maintain a garrison there within seven years.

The French were not about to sit idly by and let the British take over the territory. Officially the British Crown complained to the French Court at Paris. Unofficially the French were about to take action to reassert their ownership of the territory that gave them unfettered access from Quebec to Louisiana. Duquesne, governor of New France, ordered a French presence in the territory backed by a series of French forts.

The French landed an expedition at P'resqu Isle, today's Erie, Pennsylvania, on the south shore of Lake Erie. It had a fine natural harbor so they build a fort here then cleared a roadway of only a few leagues to Riviere Aux Boeufs today called French Creek. They built another fort here calling it Fort Le Boeuf.

The First Nations of the territory saw an opportunity to play one European nation against the other. Although they had a trading alliance with the British they had always been more fully allied with the French. They all went out of their way to help the French move the large amount of heavy supplies to garrison two forts. The only ally the British had in the area that was fully committed to them was the Mingo. Shortly after Fort Le Boeuf was built a Mingo chief named the Half King arrived and ordered the French to leave the territory. But the French were arrogant and haughty laughing the Half King out of the fort. He was mortified and full of rage against the French. They had made an enemy that they were sure to hear from again.

In the fall of 1753 Legardeur de St. Pierre arrived to command Fort Le Boeuf. He had just settled in expecting a long and monotonous winter when a stranger arrived on horseback along with the fall rains mixed with wet snow. He was tall, young and brash a mere youth of twenty-one. He was accompanied by a much older man, several others with the pack horses backed by the Half King and several warriors. He carried a letter from Dinwiddie introducing him and containing orders for the French to leave British territory immediately. His name was George Washington.

St. Pierre afforded the young Virginian Major every courtesy and after studying the document he had presented he replied by letter to Dinwiddie that he would forward his correspondence to Duquesne for consideration. In the meantime he could only remain at his post and follow the orders of his general.

Washington struggled through extreme winter conditions to return to Virginia. He finally arrived at Williamsburg by mid-January and gave his report to Dinwiddie. It not only included St. Pierre's letter of response but the information given him by some French soldiers at a French outpost at the mouth of French Creek that the French had every intention of taking the country by force and nothing would deter them.

NEXT WEEK: Great Meadows and Fort Necessity

Great Meadows and Fort Necessity

October 19, 2010

The First Nations were just as concerned as the French about a British presence in their territory. They could see that the French were mainly interested in trade building only trading posts and a few forts scattered throughout their territories. There was only minimal clearing done around the posts for purposes of sustainability. The hunting grounds were left intact so First Nations were able to benefit from trade while maintaining their culture.

On the other hand the British were interested in expansion by homesteading thereby clearing First Nations' hunting grounds so there was no way left to support their communities. This made British expansion a dangerous proposition for all First Nation communities. So, in the spring of 1754 the council of the St. Clair Saulteaux decided to send a party of ten warriors to the Ohio to survey the situation. They would no doubt have been led by their war chief Little Thunder.

Meanwhile the French were on the move as well. Duquesne replaced St. Pierre as commandant of Fort Le Boeuf with his lieutenant, Sieur de Contrecoeur. He arrived at Fort Le Boeuf with 500 soldiers, a mix of Canadians and regulars. This bolstered the French presence in the area to 1,400 men.

At the same time Dinwiddie formed the Virginia Regiment of 300 men under the aristocrat Joshua Fry with Washington second in command. Fry kept half the regiment, all raw recruits, in Virginia shaping them up to march.

Meanwhile, Washington took the other half and made his way to the Ohio Company's storehouse at Wills creek where he set up a base camp. From there they sent a small expedition of forty backwoodsmen led by a Captain Trent over the Alleghenies to build a fort at a spot Washington had observed the previous fall. It was at the confluence of the Monongahela and Allegheny Rivers where they form the Ohio. It was indeed a strategic site as a fort there would command the Ohio country.

When they arrived they immediately started work on a small fort which the British had planned to garrison with the newly formed Virginia Regiment. But Contrecoeur moved against them with a force of 500 soldiers ousting the small band of Virginians and destroying their half completed fort. He then proceeded to build a much larger, stronger one which he named Fort Duquesne after his Governor. This fort would later become Fort Pitt and is today's Pittsburgh, Pennsylvania.

Ensign Jumonville de Villiers was sent out of the newly constructed fort as a courier carrying a letter to give to any Englishmen he might encounter ordering them to vacate French territory. He had a contingent of twenty soldiers with him and orders to evict the English by force if they did not comply with the orders of the letter.

At the same time Washington was on the Youghiogany, a branch of the Monongahela, with forty men. The Half King joined him with twelve Mingo warriors. The Mingo led him to Jumonville's camp where they took the French by surprise. There was gunfire and the French were bested. The Virginian contingent killed ten Frenchmen including the young ensign. They took the rest as prisoners. The Half King boasted that it was he that dispatched Jumonville by splitting his head open with his tomahawk.

The incident sparked an international crisis. The French were outraged. They claimed that Washington opened fire on French soldiers who were only on a courier mission. They said that Jumonville was under a white flag shouting he only had a letter to deliver when they were cut down. Of course the British denied this.

Coulon de Villiers, the brother of Jumonville, rushed from Montreal to Fort Duquesne to find 500 Frenchmen and eleven First Nation warriors there awaiting their marching orders. The eleven warriors were different from the 400 he had brought with him from Canada. He described them as people from the falls of the lake or Lake Indians. They were the Saulteaux from

Aamjiwnaang or the St. Clair region. Coulon was given the opportunity of avenging his brother's death by leading the 500 French regulars, the Saulteaux from Aamjiwnaang along with a few of the Ohio warriors as well as Mohawk, Wyandotte, Abenaki and Algonquin from Quebec, Nipissing from Superior country and Ottawa from Detroit on a mission to oust the British from Ohio country.

Washington had fallen back to a huge open prairie called Great Meadows where he hastily constructed a rather flimsy entrenchment he named Fort Necessity. He was expecting a French attack and chose this spot to make his stand because its openness made it not so susceptible to the forest style warfare First Nations were so famous for. He also called for reinforcements from Fry who he thought was still in Virginia but he had died leaving Washington first in command. Three companies did finally arrive on July 1st. A company of British Regulars also arrived from South Carolina bolstering the garrison to 400 plus the Half King's forty warriors.

Coulon de Villiers arrived on the 4th of July in a driving rain and took up position on a ridge in front of Fort Necessity and began firing down on Washington's entrenchment. This made Fort Necessity's position less than desirable because their three canons could not be fired uphill.

Coulon's warrior allies kept to the edge of the Forest as open warfare was not their first choice of battle. They took pot shots on the fort all day long. After nine hours of pouring rain the French soldiers were soaked to the bone. The Virginians were hunkered down in a sea of mud.

Coulon called for a parlay to discuss terms of surrender. Washington had no choice but to agree because what little powder he had left was wet and his guns were useless. The French wrote out the terms of surrender but Washington could read no French.

Washington relied on a Captain in his militia named Vanbraam who was a Dutchman to act as his interpreter. One clause of the surrender document read "*l'assassinat du Sieur de Jumonville*", which Vanbraam translated as the death of Sieur de

Jumonville. Washington signed the document and was allowed to return with his men unarmed to Virginia. He later disputed that he was an assassin blaming Vanbraam for the mistranslation.

The whole mission was an assorted affair. The Half King left Great Meadows in disgust saying that the French had acted as cowards and the English as fools. The other First Nation warriors fell back to Fort Duquesne where more of their own joined them in ever-increasing numbers. The young upstart Washington had killed a French ensign on a courier mission along with ten other soldiers and signed a document he could not read thereby unwittingly starting the French and Indian War!

NEXT WEEK: Braddock Arrives

The French and Indian War

Braddock Arrives

October 29, 2010

Washington led his demoralized militia back to Virginia and the French returned to Fort Duquesne. They burned Gist's settlement and the storehouse at Redstone Creek along the way. This left no British flag flying west of the Alleghenies. The First Nations returned to their respective territories to prepare for their fall hunt.

The following spring the British came to the aid of the embattled Virginian Militia. They sent two companies of 500 crack regulars each along with General Edward Braddock as their commander. Braddock was a seasoned general fresh from the battlefields of Europe. He had the reputation of being a stern disciplinarian and master tactician. An enlistment of four hundred more men bolstered his army to 1,400 soldiers.

France wasn't about to sit on their laurels. When the heard of the British movement they began making plans to counter the move. Eighteen war ships were being fitted to sail to America. They would carry six battalions of French regulars, 3,000 men in all, along with Baron Ludwig Dieskau and Marquis de Vaudreuil. Dieskau was a German born General in the French army with a reputation equal to Braddock. Vaudreuil was the son of the former governor of New France by the same name and was to replace the ailing Duquesne. The clouds of war loomed menacing on the horizon.

In the meantime Duquesne received a direct order from the King to bestow upon Sieur Charles Langlade a commission of ensign unattached to serve the troops maintained in Canada. This was the same Langlade that had such spectacular success at Pickawillany. Duquesne then asked Langlade to raise a war party of First Nations to aid in the defence of Fort Duquesne.

Ensign Langlade left Michilimackinac in the spring of 1755 with a party of Saulteaux Ojibwa warriors. He picked up more Ojibwa fighters at Saginaw and headed toward Detroit. Even more Saulteaux Ojibwa joined him from the St. Clair region. Leading war chiefs at the time were Wasson or Catfish from Saginaw, Animikeence or Little Thunder from Aamjiwnaang (Lower Lake Huron) and Sekahos or Hunter from the Thames.

The newly commissioned ensign finally arrived at his old friend Pontiac's village which was on the Detroit River opposite Fort Ponchartrain. A war council was called with the Wyandotte's leading chief Sastaresty, Pontiac and the other Ojibwa war chiefs in attendance. The conclusion was unanimous; they must come to their French 'father's' aid.

Langlade left Detroit with a war party of 637 Ojibwa, Ottawa and Wyandotte warriors including war chiefs. However the vast majority were Ojibwa. The impressive war party made their way to the southern shore of Lake Erie by way of the Bass Islands. They turned east and skirted the shore until they arrived at Presque Isle where the short portage led to the head of French Creek and Fort Le Boeuf.

French Creek was a small waterway that emptied into the Allegheny River at the Indian Town of Venago. There was an old Indian trail that skirted along the east side of the creek but at this time of the year it was quite navigable in their light bark canoes. Once they reached Venago they headed down the Allegheny to the confluence of the Monongahela and Fort Duquesne. Langlade had been travelling for about a month but was still fresh and ready for battle. They set up their camps on the west side of the Allegheny directly across from the Fort and awaited instructions.

NEXT WEEK: The Arrogance of Braddock

The Arrogance of Braddock

November 7, 2010

A council was held in the fort with the French commander Sieur de Contrecoeur. He had three captains under him, Beaujeu, Dumas and Ligneris. The commandant came up with a plan. Beaujeu would have command of the force that was to repel the British with Dumas second in command. They would meet them on the road ambushing them at the ford where the road crossed the Monongahela. Langlade and the war chiefs objected. The spot was not to their liking. The terrain was too wide and open to conduct the type of warfare they were best at. They were ignored, the plan was set and the council concluded. Returning to their camps across the Alleghany the Ojibwa and their native allies prepared for war in their usual way.

War dances were danced and war songs were sung. These were interspersed with long harangues by war chiefs and seasoned warriors containing previous great deeds done in battle. These speeches always ended with a tremendous strike at the war post with a war club or tomahawk and loud shouts of war whoops. This spectacle never ceased to send a chill through their European allies. On this occasion it was the French who watched from Fort Duquesne's ramparts along with a young English colonial who had been captured three days before.

The young Pennsylvanian James Smith had been captured by three warriors, two Delaware and one Mohawk from Caughnawaga. His companion was killed and scalped but he was brought back to the fort a prisoner. He was only 18 years of age.

When they neared the fort they gave the victory cry, a long halloo for each scalp or prisoner taken. Hundreds of warriors responded by pouring out of their wigwams shouting and screeching and firing their guns in the air. The French responded to the celebration likewise by firing off their guns including cannon from inside the fort. Smith was awed by the din and thought they must number in the thousands. What was about to come surprised him even more.

A great number of warriors began to form two columns. They were all whooping and yelling and carrying sticks. All were prepared for war with faces and bodies painted in various pigments of red, black, yellow and blue wearing nothing but breechcloths. It was a fearsome sight for the young man to behold.

One of the Delaware warriors who captured him spoke a little English and told him he must run between the two columns from one end to the other. He said to run fast, the faster the better as they were going to beat him. A shove from his advisor started him racing receiving blows all the way. As he neared the end one blow knocked him down. He tried to get up but someone threw sand in his eyes so he could not see where he was going. Beaten down again he took the warriors blows until he was rendered unconscious. Young James regained consciousness inside the fort being attended to by the post physician.

Smith was interrogated by the war chiefs after receiving medical attention. Then the Delaware warrior who spoke English came to see him. He asked his captor why the warriors treated him so badly thinking he had offended them in some way. But he was told that he did not offend but it was just an old custom they had . . . like saying, how do you do? Smith then asked if he would be permitted to stay with the French and was told he would not but after he recovered he must live with his captors and become one of them. When he could get out of bed he made his way around with the aid of a crutch.

Meanwhile, General Braddock and his army had left Williamsburg following the road cut by the Virginians the year before. They were an impressive sight to behold. A long column of British regulars, 1,750 in all, dressed in bright red tunics, white helmets and sashes with steel bayonets flashing in the sun. They were followed by 450 Virginia Militia dressed in blue. The column included cannon and howitzers, 600 pack horses and 175 wagons carrying supplies and tools all to supply the newly conquered fort and more.

The colonies were hemmed in by mountain ranges which made expansion impossible. But the British had ambitions to do just that and they had a plan. Braddock was to take Fort Duquesne and quickly move on to Fort Niagara. Sir William Johnson was to take Crown Point. William Shirley Sr., Governor of Massachusetts, was made a Major General and was to take Fort Beausejour all on the pretense that the French had invaded British territory. It seemed impossible that the plan should fail. The colonies had yet to see an army the size of Braddock's and the English had population figures on their side. The total white population of New France, from Quebec to Louisiana, was just under 80,000. The British on the other hand had a population of 1.6 million including 200,000 slaves.

So Braddock headed for Fort Duquesne with his superior army and his arrogance intact. He had little respect for the colonial militia and even less for First Nation warriors. Benjamin Franklin, who was the postmaster of Pennsylvania at the time, came to see him at Williamsburg. He spent five days with Braddock and warned him of the forest warfare practiced by the First Nations suggesting that he should consider new battle tactics. Braddock replied "These savages may, indeed, be a formidable enemy to your raw American militia, but upon the King's regular and disciplined troops, sir, it is impossible that they should make an impression." Braddock was about to get the shock of his life!

NEXT WEEK: The Rout of Braddock!

The Rout of Braddock!

November 14, 2010

Braddock's army began the long and arduous journey from Fort Cumberland to Fort Duquesne. Three hundred axe men toiled in front of the column widening the narrow trail Washington's men had cut the year before. It was hard slogging through the deep forests and over the main Alleghany mountain range. Two more mountains had to be crossed making the progress of the expedition not more than three miles a day. The vast amount of supplies being carried by 175 wagons plus pack horses, not to mention dragging heavy cannon and light artillery, made the column cumbersome and ponderous. At times it stretched out a distance of four miles.

Dysentery set in. There were also many desertions along the way so that two months after leaving Fort Cumberland the British expeditionary force had been reduced to 1,260 regulars and 200 militiamen.

The whole force was under Braddock's command. The young colonial officer, George Washington temporarily resigned his commission of Lieutenant Colonel and was assigned to Braddock's staff as aide-de-camp. The 44th and 48th regiments were under Colonel Halket and the militia under Colonel Burton. Colonel Dunbar remained at the rear with the sick, weakened horses and much of the baggage to make their way as best as they could. Braddock didn't know it but his ponderous train was being shadowed. Langlade had his scouts observe their progress from the denseness of the Pennsylvanian forest and report their intelligence back to Fort Duquesne.

Meanwhile, young James Smith was visited by the Delaware warrior who spoke a little English. He reassured him that although he must live with his captors he would be treated well by them. Smith then asked if there was any news of Braddock. He was hoping for a British victory and rescue. The warrior told him that

Braddock was advancing very close and that Langlade's warriors would surround him, take to the trees and, he said in his broken English, "shoot um down all one pigeon".

A few days later he heard quite a commotion coming from inside the Fort. He hobbled out onto the wall of the fort with the aid of his walking staff. There he observed the warriors all buzzing around the ammunition magazine helping themselves to powder, shot and flint. He then saw the war chiefs lead their warriors off in a file along with a few French regulars and some Canadians. He estimated them to be about 400 men and wondered why they would go out to meet Braddock with such a small force. In reality there were 637 warriors, 72 regulars and 146 Canadians.

Braddock's force was eight miles from Fort Duquesne and about to cross the Monongahela the second time. This was the place the French had planned their ambush but they were late getting there. Four miles from the fort the war chiefs led their warriors into the woods leaving the French on the road. They moved through the dense underbrush with deft stealth stretching themselves out behind trees, bushes and in gullies for 2,000 yards along both sides of the road. They had chosen a place for ambush more to their liking. On the north side of the road there was a large hill overlooking the trail. It soon became populated with as many First Nation warriors as there were trees or so it seemed. They settled in and waited for their prey to enter the trap.

The expedition reached the ford of the river about one o'clock in the afternoon. Lieutenant Colonel Gage had gone ahead of the main party with an advance patrol, found no sign of the enemy so he secured the far side. The main body followed each section splashing their way across the shallows.

The crossing was a spectacle to behold. Pipers, drummers and banners led announcing the advance with military music. They were followed by mounted officers, then light cavalry, the naval attachment with cannon and howitzers, the British regulars or red coats followed by the Colonial Militia dress in blue. Down the narrow road they marched followed by the supply wagons, more heavy armament, a train of pack horses and the droves of cattle.

When they were all across the river they halted to rest. Braddock wondered why the French had not protected the ford, a perfect place for ambush to his way of thinking.

After resting and refreshments the column began to move again along the restricted trail confined by dense woods, small hills and bush covered gullies. They moved further into the trap not realizing they were passing hundreds of muskets all trained on the procession. When they passed alongside the large hill on the north side they had become completely surrounded. Suddenly they observed a man ahead waving his arms. He was dress in native garb but had a French officer's gorget on his neck. It was Langlade. The gorget was a sign of his rank of Ensign and his arm waving was the signal to open fire!

The warriors gave the war-whoop and opened with the first volley. Gage turned the advance guard back toward the main body. The first regiment of red coats charged forward cheering and shouting, "God save the king!" More volleys followed in rapid succession. The warriors along the side of the large hill were firing down on their red and white targets from behind a multitude of trees.

Beaujeu arrived on the road leading his 72 marines followed by 146 Canadians. The Canadians were mere boys about the age of 15. They were cadets in the king's military and most had never tasted battle. The British regulars in the advance opened fire on the French. Many fell from the British volley and most of the Canadians panicked and fled. The rest took to the trees for cover.

For two hours the bullets rained down on Braddock. He charged back and forth on his horse, waving his sword and shouting words of encouragement. Washington did the same, but the defeat was turning into a disaster.

The advance party fell back into the lead regiment and the rear guard pressed forward crashing into it. Bodies were beginning to stack up. There was no order only chaos. The red coats formed circles and returned fire blindly into the forest. Their enemy was invisible showing only flashes of gunfire and puffs of smoke. Even the grape of the cannon fire only damaged the trees.

The militia was savvier. They had experience at this forest warfare. They broke and disappeared into the woods to take on the warriors in guerrilla style fighting. But the regulars mistook the militia's powder flashes as the enemy and opened fire on the colonials killing many. The remainder was forced to return to the main body.

Hysteria became the order of the day. Braddock was shot. Most of his officers were killed or lay wounded on the road. His men carried him to a wagon where he lay giving the order to retreat. The retreat was as disorderly as the battle. Panic stricken regulars abandoned everything, many even throwing their rifles aside racing pell-mell down the road. This sight frightened the wagon and pack-horse drivers so that many abandoned their charges and joined the soldiers in full flight. One young teamster quickly unhitched his horses, mounted one and fled as fast as his stead could carry him to the safety of his father's farm. This young man would later gain fame as the marksman and "Indian fighter" from Kentucky Daniel Boone.

The British, what was left of them, regrouped on the other side of the Monongahela. Braddock was too seriously wounded to lead. Most of his officers were dead or captured. Dunbar fled to Philadelphia leaving Washington in charge of the retreat. This would be the second time in as many years he led a defeated force on the long journey home. Braddock was heard to say from his wagon, "who would have thought it?" He drifted in and out of consciousness. During one lucid moment he muttered, "Next time we shall know better how to deal with them another time". But for General Edward Braddock there would not be "another time". He died during the retreat and was buried in the middle of the road in an unmarked grave near present day Chalk Hill, Pennsylvania. The doleful procession trampled over his final resting place obliterating any sign of it in order to prevent him being dug up and having atrocities performed on the body.

Never was there such a lop-sided victory. The French regulars took the heaviest toll on their side. Their marines had seven officers and all but four of their regulars killed or wounded. Of 637 warriors only 23 were killed or wounded.

On the other hand the British losses were staggering. Of the 1,460 officers and men only 483 were left fit for duty and many of them were wounded but not seriously. Braddock had 89 officers and 63 of them were either killed or seriously wounded. The Colonial Militia had only 30 men left alive.

They lost all they had to Langlade and his war chiefs. Wagons and supplies, horses and cattle, muskets and heavy armament, ammunition and even the coin money that was to be used to pay the king's regulars. All this booty now served as the warrior's pay.

The victorious warriors did not pursue the retreating British. There was too much loot to collect. News of the disaster reached the colonies and panicked the general populace. Dunbar's escape to Philadelphia left the colonies' only protection, Fort Cumberland, empty. The army was devastated. There was no protection and Braddock's widened road could only serve to lead a French army, or even worse, their First Nation allies into the colonies unchallenged.

NEXT WEEK: The Adoption of James Smith

The Adoption of James Smith

November 21, 2010

The afternoon of Braddock's defeat James Smith waited anxiously for word of the battle. He was sure that this would be the day of his salvation; that Braddock's army would send the warriors fleeing in retreat and Contrecoeur would surrender the fort.

While resting in his quarters he heard a great commotion inside the fort. He rose and quickly hobbled out to receive what he thought would be good news. It was not. He feared so when he observed that the excitement being exhibited by those few returning from the battlefield were exultations of joy. Although he could not understand French he did understand Dutch which one of the soldiers spoke. Hesitatingly Smith asked, "What was the news?" The soldier informed him that a runner had just arrived and told them that Braddock was certain to be defeated. He said that the warriors and French had taken to the trees and gullies, surrounded him and kept up a constant barrage of fire upon them. He said he saw the British falling in heaps and if they didn't retreat back across the river there would not be one left alive by sundown. For James Smith this was not good news!

A little later he heard the scalp halloos shouted by a number of warriors and saw them come in carrying many scalps, grenadier caps, canteens, small arms and other items issued to British regulars. Sometime after that he saw a company of near 100 warriors and a few French arrive at the fort. Almost all had a number of scalps each. Then the main body arrived with a great number of wagon-horses, captured weapons and other loot. They brought the news that Braddock was defeated. All the warriors and French kept up a constant firing of small arms while the big guns of the fort continuously thundered in victory celebrations. Intermingled in the din were shouts of hundreds of victory whoops.

About sundown Smith saw a small company of warriors coming with about a dozen English prisoners. All were stripped naked and had their hands tied behind their backs. He watched from the wall of the fort as the prisoners were taken to the west bank of the Allegheny directly across from the fort. There the prisoners were burned to death amid shouts of victory. When the first one burned began to wail in pain James Smith could watch no longer so he retired to his quarters sore and dejected.

A few days later Smith was handed over by the French to their Caughnawaga allies. He wasn't able to travel overland yet so they took him by canoe up the Allegheny to Venango where he recuperated for about three weeks. Then they moved him to a town on the west branch of the Muskingum River called Tullihas.

It was inhabited by Caughnawagas, Delaware and Mohicans. The Caughnawaga were Christian Iroquois from the Montreal area who had left there to live in Ohio and return to their old ways.

One of the Caughnawaga men began to give him the dress of a native. He began by plucking out all of the hair on his head except a small square on his crown. This he braided into three scalp locks and adorned them with feathers and silver broaches. After this they pierced his ears and nose which they fixed with ear rings and nose jewels. He was ordered to strip down and put on a breach cloth and they painted his face and body in various colors. They finished his transformation by hanging around his neck a large wampum belt and they put on his wrists and right arm silver bracelets. Since Smith had only witnessed cruel deaths perpetrated on their English captives he was sure he was being all done up for execution.

When he was ready an old chief led him by the hand out of the lodge and gave the call, coo-wigh, several times in rapid succession. The entire town came out and this old chief speaking very loudly made a long harangue. He then handed Smith over to three young women who led him waist deep into the river. He thought this was the mode of execution they had chosen for him; death by drowning.

The three young women tried to wrestle him under the water, so Smith strained with all his might trying to stay above a watery grave. The whole town was on the bank witnessing the spectacle with gales of laughter. One of the young women spoke a little English so she repeated, "No hurt you". Upon hearing these words he gave up the fight and let them submerge him completely.

After this they led him to the council house where he was given the finest of new clothes including a ruffled shirt, leggings and moccasins. They put new feathers in his scalp locks and repainted his face in various colors. They gave him a tomahawk, pipe and medicine pouch containing tobacco and dried sumac leaves. The chiefs and leading men of the town then came in and all sat in silence in a circle; all of them smoking. They were silent for a long time, and then one of the chiefs stood and made a long speech which was interpreted for him by one who spoke English.

The old chief called him his son and said that he was now bone of their bones and flesh of their flesh. That the ceremony that was done that day washed all of the white blood from his body and he was now adopted into the Caughnawaga Nation, into a mighty family and into the lodge of a great man. Again he called him son and said that he had nothing to fear because they were now under the same obligation to love and support him as they were to love and support one another. Smith was now to consider himself as one of them.

At first he did not entirely believe this speech but over the next four years while living among them he found this to be true. He would write in his memoir four decades later, ". . . from that day I never knew them to make any distinction between me and themselves in any respect whatever until I left them. If they had plenty of clothing I had plenty, if we were scarce we all shared one fate."

NEXT WEEK: Fort Oswego Falls to Montcalm

Fort Oswego Falls to Montcalm

December 5, 2010

It's been two weeks since my last post. Sorry but I'll probably be late again. December is a busy month with Christmas coming up fast and the other day we had a minor disaster here. The hose on the dishwasher broke and flooded the kitchen, down the hallway, two closets and part of the master bedroom. Everything is carpet but the kitchen. Oh well, it gives me incentive to redo the flooring anyway, something I've wanted to do for a while now.

When we last left our story Braddock was defeated, Dieskau was on his way from France with six battalions of French regulars and the Marquis de Vaudreuil the new governor. As soon as Vaudreuil replaced Duquesne as the governor-general he made a plan to attack Fort Oswego. This was a British trading post on the south shore of Lake Ontario in the midst of Iroquois territory.

However, he had to postpone that plan because Colonel William Johnson had been assigned by the British to attack Crown Point on Lake Champlain. Johnson had already started making preparations at the foot of Lac du S. Sacrament for his advance on Crown Point. He had widened the 15 mile portage from Fort Lyman on the Hudson River to the lake. When he arrived he renamed it Lake George and immediately busied himself constructing a camp from which to launch his attack. Fort Lyman would later become Fort Edward and Johnson's campsite is where the war's most famous Fort would be built, Fort William Henry.

Johnson didn't really concern himself with French movements to his north. Dieskau arrived at Crown Point in the fall to reinforce the French presence there with 3,573 men made up of French soldiers, Canadians and First Nations. Dieskau made the first move. His force moved down Lake Champlain to the headwaters of Wood Creek where a short portage brought them out at the midway point of the new road Johnson had just cut. He had a choice to make. He could either move south and take out Fort Lyman or north and take out Johnson's campsite. First Nation warriors never like to attack a position that was fortified with heavy artillery so he chose to move north.

Dieskau didn't realise that Johnson had moved three cannons to the lake and fortified his campsite with a breastwork made of logs. Dieskau attacked but was surprised by cannon fire. They were repelled time and time again. The two adversaries fought more or less to a draw but the Baron was wounded twice and taken prisoner by the Provincials. The French withdrew leaderless.

Seventeen fifty-five had not been a good year for the British so although Lake George had not been a military victory the capture and imprisonment of Baron Dieskau gave the skirmish the air of one. Great celebrations were held in New York and Colonel

Johnson was received as a great war hero. The British lavished the colonel with rewards including making him a baronet, 5,000 pounds Sterling and installing him as Superintendent of Indian Affairs. At last some good news for the English.

The following year Dieskau was replaced with a new general, the Marquis de Montcalm. He and Vaudreuil did not get along. However, they did agree on one thing. Fort Oswego should be the first campaign of 1756. Montcalm had brought two more crack regiments with him from France and he was anxious use them.

Fort Oswego was built at the mouth of the Chouagen River later to be renamed the Oswego River. It was fortified by a stockade and had two out buildings defended by earthen ramparts. It was really just a trading post so was no bastion of defence. Just as the attack started the post's commandant Colonel Mercer was cut in half by a cannon ball. The British forces defending Oswego quickly became disheartened and surrendered. Casualties were light. The British reported 50 killed and the French even less. However, 1,600 prisoners of war were taken and the plunder was exceeding for the "Praying Indians" that were with Montcalm. The news of the French victory spread through First Nation territories like wildfire.

Montcalm, Vaudreuil and the Intendant Bigot received chief after chief representing some forty First Nations. All wanted to see the great French war chief who had the reputation of being so tall his head bumped the clouds. In actuality Montcalm was a relatively short man. This caused one great war chief to state that a man's eminence is determined by his deeds not his physical stature.

Meanwhile the British had rebuilt Fort Lyman and renamed it Fort Edward. They also build Fort William Henry at the foot of Lake George. This was where British activity was the greatest. This was where the British presented the most danger. Montcalm prepared to move into the Lake Champlain area and meet the British head on.

NEXT WEEK: A Gathering of Nations

A Gathering of Nations

January 9, 2011

Well, the holiday season is over and it was busier than usual this year. I hope everyone had a joyous noel. I seemed to be running all day, every day! But things are settling down now and I can get back to writing. I don't know if I stated in a previous post or not but I am also writing a historical fiction to be published this year.

James Smith was still with the Caughnawaga Mohawks in early June of 1757 when he wrote in his journal that all the Wyandotte, Ottawa and Potawatomi towns in Ohio country were preparing for war. He also wrote that the woods were full of 'Jibewas' who had come down from the upper lakes. These would have been Little Thunder's warriors from the St. Clair and Langlade's warriors from Michilimackinac. After the war songs were sung and the war dance danced they all left the territory singing the travelling song and firing their small arms. They were off to join Montcalm and the Praying Indians at Lake Champlain.

Montcalm had gone to the Lake of Two Mountains and Sault St. Louis to take part in the same war preparation ceremonies with the Christian Iroquois or Praying Indians. He brought with him great promises of gifts and prospects of much loot and plunder. His emissaries had done the same over the previous winter with the western nations all in order to raise a huge number of First Nation warriors to compliment his army. As he was moving detachments of French regulars, Canadians and Mission Indians up Lake Champlain the Western Nations began joining them. By the end of July the whole force was gathered at Ticonderoga. A smaller force had been there since May finishing the fort and sending out war parties to set panic among the settlers along the frontier as well as to reconnoiter the strength and capacity of Fort William Henry.

While Montcalm waited for all intelligence to come in before mounting his attack upon the British fort his First Nation allies sent out sortie after sortie up and down the frontier. In the First

Nation worldview war was no game to be played on open fields between soldiers only. The enemy included the old, women and children as well as soldiers. European allies paid for scalps and neither distinguished age or sex. The frontiers of Virginia, Maryland and Pennsylvania were in a state of panic. Settlers didn't know when their turn would come to be burned out and their families killed.

The French put some normally very able officers over various groups of warriors. But these warriors were no normal military men. They looked only to their war chiefs for guidance all but ignoring their French officers. Saint-Luc de la Corne was supposedly in charge and was called the "General of the Indians". Several other officers had "charge" of the various groups. All of these Frenchmen, including interpreters, had lived most of their lives among the nations. They were well acquainted with their culture and understood their real lack of authority over them.

The so-called "Mission Indians" numbered some eight hundred chiefs and warriors and were made up of Iroquois from Caughnawaga, Two Mountains and Le Presentation as well as the Wyandotte of Detroit and Lorette. They also included Algonquin speaking nations; Nipissing from the lake by the same name, Abenaki from St. Francis, Becancour, Missisqui and Penobscot as well as Algonquin from Trois Riviere and Two Mountains. Finally there were Micmac and Malecite from Acadia. Three missionaries were assigned to the "Praying Indians". They were Abbe Picquet to the Iroquois, Father Mathevet to the Nipissing and Father Roubaud to the Abenaki.

There were also among the throng 1,000 well armed warriors from the western nations all painted for war. There were Ottawa from Michilimackinac, Saginaw and Detroit; Saulteaux Ojibwa from Lake Superior and St. Clair; Potawatomi from St. Joseph and Detroit as well as Delaware from Ohio. From further west came the Menominee, Sauk, Fox and Winnebago from Wisconsin. There were also Miami from Illinois and finally Iowa from the Des Moines. All were assigned interpreters except the Iowa because no Frenchmen spoke the language.

The size of the force at Ticonderoga numbered 8,000 men of which nearly 2,000 were First Nation warriors. When the whole force was settled they gathered in one great assembly. Their war chiefs were distinguished by the gorget that they wore to protect their necks and their civil chiefs by the large King's medal which hung around them. Montcalm spoke first explaining his plan of attack upon the British fort. Colonel Louis Antoine de Bougainville recorded the proceeding in his journal.

Pennahouel of the Ottawa and a major chief rose to speak first for the whole assembly. Stating the fact that he was the elder of all in attendance he thanked Montcalm for his words. Kikensick, chief of the Nipissing, next rose speaking for the Christian nations. He addressed the western nations thanking them for coming to help defend their territories from English encroachment. He then thanked Montcalm for coming to join the battle from across the great sea. Then he assured them all the Master of Life was with them so that only honor and glory could follow.

Montcalm responded with a speech encouraging unity followed by the presentation of a great wampum belt of 6,000 beads to seal this unity between the First Nations and the French. Pennahouel took the belt and held it up confirming the confederacy. The next day the great assembly of chiefs and warriors spread themselves out in camps along the lake and awaited the time to move on Fort William Henry.

NEXT WEEK: Fort William Henry Falls

Fort William Henry Falls

January 16, 2011

Fort William Henry was commanded by Lieutenant-Colonel Munro, a brave Scottish veteran in charge of 2,200 fighting men. His superior, General Webb, was in command of Fort Edward some 14 miles to the south-west. He had charge of 1,600 soldiers. The colonies were raising more men but this would take more time than needed to counter Montcalm's army of 8,000.

The French army had moved through the narrows on Lake George and spread themselves along the shoreline of the picturesque lake. Duc Francois de Levis was Montcalm's second in command and had moved out the day before with the First Nation warriors. They were waiting for the rest of the army at a small cove that was formed by a point of land which protected them from the line of sight of the British fort.

That night Munro sent out a small party in two boats to reconnoiter. As they passed the point they noticed something unusual on the shore of the cove. They drew near it in order to identify the object. It was an awning the Fathers had stretched over their bateaux. Sensing danger they turned and began to row as hard as they were able but it wasn't enough. Many of the warriors rushed to their canoes threw them into the water and vigorously pursued the frightened Englishmen.

Wild eyed with excitement the warriors quickly overtook them all the time shouting their terrifying war whoops. The din of a thousand shouts echoed across the placid lake magnifying the uproar tenfold. It was as if the French had unleashed an army of windigo to devour them.

Just as the spies made the eastern shore the warriors were upon them. They opened fire killing a Nipissing war chief. The fighting ceased immediately after the stand had begun. Some escaped into the blackness of the Appalachian woods, some were killed but three were taken prisoner ending up before Montcalm where he was able to extract some valuable information on the strength and position of the enemy.

The following morning Munro sent a message to Fort Edward saying the French were in sight of the lake. Nine hours later he sent another informing the General that the firing had begun. He implored Webb to send reinforcements. Webb's response was to send couriers to New England to ask for more militia. He waited out the battle 14 miles away in the safety of Fort Edward.

At the same time Munro sent his first communique the French army moved out. Levis left first with a contingent of chiefs and warriors leading the way. They made their way around the fort and positioned themselves behind it. La Corne took up a position behind Levis and the war chiefs spread their warriors across the road leading to Fort Edward.

The main body of warriors spread their canoes in a line across the lake covering it from shore to shore. They slowly moved toward the fort with slow, deliberate strokes all the while shouting war cries. Then they broke for the east and west shorelines just out of range of British cannon fire.

After the skirmishing around the fort was over Montcalm moved forward along the western shore of Lake George with five battalions. He stopped just short of the fort where he proceeded to set up siege works. He then moved in his heavy artillery and began to put Fort William Henry under siege. Munro sent a final courier to advise Webb the fort was under attack and to send reinforcements with all haste.

For several days the French inched forward all the time bombarding the fort with salvos of cannon fire. At night they laboriously dug new trenches in front of their siege works methodically plodding their artillery ever closer. Munro kept returning fire with his heavy artillery while sending out sorties to skirmish with the enemy. They were less than successful.

Finally Webb answered Munro's calls for help. He sent a courier with a message informing him that he could send no reinforcements and that he should surrender and get the best terms possible. The message never got through. A party of warriors intercepted the courier along the road, killed him and took the paper he was carrying to Montcalm. The General read it and thought it might be useful in encouraging Munro to surrender sooner so he had Bougainville deliver it personally to its intended recipient.

Fort William Henry was in deplorable condition. More than 300 had been killed or wounded. Its ramparts were blown to splinters. The walls were breached. Its artillery had been knocked out of commission except for a few small field pieces and smallpox was raging inside its walls.

Munro conferred with his officers about the dire situation. They decided to sue for peace if they could get honorable terms. Lieutenant-Colonel Young with a small escort was sent out under a white flag to Montcalm's quarters.

Montcalm's terms were more than generous. The British would be allowed to march out with the honors of war. They could carry their colors and their personal belongings under French escort to Fort Edward. In return they had to promise not serve in the military for eighteen months and all French prisoners of war held since the war began would be released. The victors would take possession of the stores, munitions and artillery.

Montcalm called the chiefs to council. He reiterated the terms of surrender and they agreed to hold their warriors back thinking the stores, munitions and artillery would be enough payment for their services. But the thinking of the warriors was that it fell far short. Dark ominous clouds hung over an otherwise sparkling victory and that could only spell disaster upon the whole enterprise!

NEXT WEEK: Montcalm's Betrayal

Montcalm's Betrayal

January 23, 2011

General Montcalm had advised Colonel Munro to dispose of the fort's supply of rum to keep it away from the warriors. But some of his men couldn't see all that good liquor going to waste. So they only broke open most of the barrels spilling the highly prized plunder on the ground.

The warriors were in a foul mood. The English were being allowed to walk away carrying their belongings including unloaded firearms. There would be neither scalps nor prisoners which the French were only too happy to turn into cash and trade goods. There would be no loot. Was this was their reward for fighting for their French allies? The First Nations felt betrayed!

The British prisoners were held in an entrenched camp just outside the fort. They were preparing for the march to Fort Edward the next day. Those who had kept back a good portion of the store's rum barrels decided to sample their wares. All this was a very bad idea but the worst was yet to come.

Some of them thought if they shared some of the rum with the warriors it would put them on their good side, just in case there was trouble ahead. Over the course of the night some of the warriors helped themselves to the liquor and they weren't shy about it. By dawn's first light they were in a state of inebriation and highly agitated over Montcalm's betrayal. The ones who didn't participate in the intoxicating spirits were just as angry and tumultuous as the ones who did. The old chiefs such as Pennahouel lost control of their young men.

The British spent an uneasy night listening to the pounding of war drums and shouting of war cries coming from the darkness that surrounded them. They became extremely nervous and at dawn gathered together anxious to move out.

Not all were ready to march. Seventeen soldiers were recuperating in the surgeon's tents too wounded to travel. The French surgeon had left them in the protection of a French guard with La Corne and other Canadian officers within sight of the tents.

For the warriors this battle was not over. They began the day by attacking the medical tents. They dragged the wounded out of their beds and killed and scalped them on the spot. The French guards looked the other way while the Canadians look on with seemingly disinterest.

The escort of 300 French regulars finally arrived and Munro complained that the terms of capitulation had been broken. They were advised to give the warriors their baggage in order to try to appease them. This turned out to be bad advice as it only served to agitate their antagonizers all the more. The warriors demanded rum and some of the British regulars in fear for their lives gave them some from their canteens. Another bad mistake!

The long procession of 2,200 prisoners finally got underway. Down the narrow road they trudged in an even narrower column stretched out too far for any kind of safety. The French escort lead the way followed by British red coats, then the women and children. The colonial militia brought up the rear.

The English being harassed all the while by individual warriors who, one at a time would grab some prized item be it a hat or canteen or unloaded musket from an unresisting soldier. If there was resistance the unfortunate one would be tomahawked on the spot and relieved of his scalp as well. The French escort did nothing to curb the harassment.

Suddenly the loud screech of an Abenaki war cry signalled an attack. The "Praying Indians" from the mission of Panaouski led the escalation in violence. They rushed upon the New Hampshire militia at the rear of the column. The militia suffered eighty killed or captured. The rear of the column pressed in on those in front. Panicked by the escalation general confusion presided and the rest of the First Nation warriors joined in attacking the long procession from all sides. The British prisoners of war were stripped to their breeches and relieved of all their possessions. Some were killed, some were taken prisoner and some were left dazed in the middle of the road. Many others escaped into the woods to make their own way to the safety of Fort Edward.

Montcalm was advised of the turmoil and he and Levis and other French officers rushed to the scene. They did try to restore order by inserting themselves in the melee calling for peace. Although brave it did little to quell the frenzied warriors.

When things did settle down the survivors were escorted back to the entrenched camp and put under extra guard until the next day. They were then marched under a stronger guard to Fort Edward where cannon fire could be heard at intervals as a signal to stragglers coming in from the previous day. Meanwhile Montcalm tried to retrieve the 200 prisoners being held in First Nations camps but it was to no avail.

The same day the survivors were marched to Fort Edward the First Nations broke camp and with prisoners in tow headed to Montreal. They were still highly agitated, upset at Montcalm's betrayal. They were determined to receive their remuneration if not from the battle then from the governor.

Governor Vaudreuil rebuked them when they arrived for breaking the terms of surrender but this was just for show. Bougainville, who was in Montreal when the First Nations arrived, thought the British prisoners should be taken from them and they should be sent home in disgrace. But Vaudreuil thought better being confronted by more than 1,000 angry warriors. Intendent Bigot wrote in a report that the warriors should be sent home satisfied at all costs.

To this end the First Nations received a ransom of two kegs of brandy for each prisoner, guns, canoes and other payment for services. They left Montreal for their homelands so distrustful of their French allies that most would not fight in their service again.

During the battle of Fort William Henry Montcalm's officers did try to alleviate the attacks of the warriors after the capitulation, but not the regulars and certainly not the Canadians. After all, they understood the time-tested arrangement for payment for First Nations support and they knew Montcalm had foolishly broken it. The French may have won the battle but it was at Fort Henry they lost the war. The First Nations held the balance of power at this time and it was here that he lost them as trusted allies.

NEXT WEEK: The Arrival of Wolfe and Amherst

The Arrival of Wolfe and Amherst

February 2, 2011

After the fall of Fort William Henry Montcalm did not advance on Fort Edward. His forces had been severely reduced by the abandonment of his First Nation allies and the Canadians who had returned to their provincial farms. He would have had to use too many of his regulars just to drag his heavy artillery down the 14 mile portage. In short, he no longer had the resources. After burning the conquered fort and levelling the ground it stood on he retreated to winter at Fort Carillon or, as the English called it, Ticonderoga.

In 1758 the British went on the offensive. After a failed attempt the previous year to take Fort Louisburg the British fleet arrived with Generals Wolfe, Amherst, Lawrence and 12,000 men. The fleet of thirty-nine ships doubled the number of fighting men.

The French stronghold was garrisoned with 3,000 regulars plus a few hundred armed citizens. First Nation support waned after Fort William Henry. The warriors that filled the Acadian forests stayed home. All that could be raised was a small band of Micmac. In the harbour there were five ships, seven frigates and another 3,000 men. The fort held out for nearly two months until it fell July 27, 1758.

In the meantime General Abercrombie with an army of 15,000 arrived at Lake George intent on taking Ticonderoga. Abercrombie was a general only because of his connections. As a military strategist he was un-inventive and single-minded. However, he plodded forward toward Ticonderoga and Montcalm.

The French fort was under garrisoned and under supplied. Vaudreuil was slow to fulfill Montcalm's requests. He had not quite 3,500 regulars, no Canadians, no warriors and only ten days' worth of supplies. But he did have his extraordinary military prowess.

After a series of military blunders by the British over two days Abercrombie lost 2,000 men trying to breach Montcalm's improvised barricades in front of the fort. Montcalm on the other hand lost only a little more than 300.

The next night the French general sent out a sortie to reconnoiter and they attacked the main British force in the dark of night. Not knowing the strength of the French attack they panicked. As they fled through the bogs the soft mud pulled the shoes right off their feet. It was a spectacular victory for Montcalm and a bitter defeat for Abercrombie.

Colonel Bradstreet who was with Abercrombie begged him for 2,000 of the 13,000 troops he had left to move north and take Fort Frontenac. It was on the north shore of Lake Ontario a French stronghold that kept the great lake under French control. Abercrombie, anxious for some semblance of a victory granted him his request.

But again Vaudreuil was lax. He had let the garrison fall to below 100 men. The fort's commandant received word of Bradstreet's advancement so he sent word to the governor to send reinforcements as quickly as possible. Vaudreuil sent one man to survey the situation and report back. Not only did he just send one man it was a one-armed man!

The woods of Eastern-Ontario were filled with Mississauga villages but they stood idly by and watched events unfold. Normally their warriors were quick to come to the aid of their French "father" Onontio but after Montcalm's betrayal at Fort William Henry they were strangely disinterested.

Bradstreet arrived to take the fort without a shot. The commandant was waiting for him with a white flag. This unbelievable victory not only gave the British command of the lake but effectively cut the French colony in two.

The previous year the British colony's frontier was racked with raiding parties by the Ohio First Nations. Delaware, Shawnee, Ottawa and Wyandotte warriors attacked settlers along the frontier with impunity. They burned farmsteads while killing or capturing pioneers. All that year they looted and ravished the countryside from Pennsylvania to Virginia. The provincials were terror-stricken.

William Pit, the new British Secretary of State, could see the source of all the First Nation malice. Fort Duquesne should be put out of commission. In the spring of 1758 a plan was being drawn up to do just that!

NEXT WEEK: The Ohio Nations Abandon Montcalm

The Ohio Nations Abandon Montcalm

By May 1758 word has spread throughout the territories that the British under General Forbes were preparing to march on Fort Duquesne with an army of 7,000 men. This included 1,200 Highlanders, a detachment of Royal Americans with the balance made up of militia from Pennsylvania, Virginia, Maryland and North Carolina.

The Three Fires Confederacy which included Ojibwa, Ottawa and Potawatomi warriors gathered at Detroit in July. The Wyandotte joined them and they all marched off to the defence of Fort Duquesne. The memory of Braddock's defeat fresh in their minds and the vast amount of plunder gotten drove the warriors on. Their design was a repeat of 1756.

The first decision was which route to take. Washington, being a loyal Virginian, favoured the road that Braddock had cut which led from Virginia. Forbes favoured a new road that would have to be cut through the Pennsylvanian wilderness. It would be a more direct route and only have to cross one range of the Alleghenies. There would be time enough to accomplish the road as Forbes planned to take his time advancing on the French fort. He knew the warriors there would tire of waiting for him and would have to abandon the field to return to their territories for their winter hunt. Thinking Washington's argument was more politically driven than sound military strategy Forbes won out. By July the advance guard under Lieutenant-Colonel Henry Bouquet was camped near Raystown the site of present day Bedford, Pennsylvania.

Governor Vaudreuil sent supplies to Fort Duquesne with reinforcements to follow. Unfortunately, the supplies were at Fort Frontenac awaiting the reinforcements when Bradstreet arrived and captured them. The reinforcements were on their way from Montreal when they got word of the fall of Fort Frontenac, so with no supplies they returned to Montreal. There would be no help for the under garrisoned Fort Duquesne except for the warriors who arrived that summer.

Meanwhile, Forbes had received word of the discontent of the Ohio First Nations. He enlisted the help of Christian John Post a Moravian missionary who knew the Delaware well, had lived among them and had married one of them. Most importantly he was well trusted by them. He arrived at the Delaware town of Kushkushkee north-west of Fort Duquesne where he met with chiefs King Beaver, Shingas and Delaware George. His message from the Governor of Pennsylvania was well received there so they took him to another town nearby.

Post got a different kind of reception there. The young warriors were in a nasty mood. Some wanted to kill him on the spot but others wanted to hear what he had to say. His message pleased them but they insisted he go with them to Fort Duquesne to deliver the message to the chiefs and warriors there. He resisted the dangerous proposal but the Delaware would accept nothing less.

When they arrived at the fort the French insisted he be turned over to them. The Delaware refused insisting that they all hear the words of the Governor of Pennsylvania. So all the First Nations and the French officers gathered outside the fort to hear what Post had to say. He informed the chiefs that General Forbes was on his way with a large army to drive the French from Ohio and that they should remain neutral in the conflict. The governor also invited them to renew the chain of friendship and peace with the British at a conference to be held at Easton, Pennsylvania. This displeased the French very much but there was nothing they could do but watch the Delaware leave with Post under their protection.

The whole Delaware nation met in council and decided that they would take hold of the peace-chain again if the invitation did not just come from Pennsylvania but from all the British provinces. This was done and the conference was held at Easton in October. The Iroquois Five Nations attended it with William Johnson along with the Delaware, Mohegan and a few other nations. The British were represented by delegates from most of their provinces. The result was that the invitation should be sent by wampum belts to all their allied nations to the west. The Moravian Post was given the task of delivering the belts. The French/First Nation alliance was beginning to disintegrate.

Post was at one of the Delaware towns meeting in council with the chiefs when a French officer from Fort Duquesne arrived. He had a belt to present them inviting them to come to the fort and help drive back Forbes. The belt was rejected with disdain. Chief Captain Peter took the French wampum string and threw it on the floor. He then took a stick and flung it across the room and the other chiefs kicked it around from one to the other. Captain Peter said that they had given their all for the French cause and had gotten nothing in return so they were determined not to help them fight the British again. He was referring to Montcalm's betrayal the previous year.

The French officer was then escorted to a Grand Council that had been called. Post delivered messages of peace from the council at Easton. They were accepted with great pleasure by everyone except the French officer. He was ridiculed by the chiefs and warriors. One called Isaac Still pointed at him and said, "There he sits! The French always deceived us!" They all began to shout whoops of agreement. The officer could take no more. He left the council to return to Fort Duquesne to give his report. The overtures of peace from the British were accepted all over Ohio as far as the Wabash River. The Delaware, Shawnee, Mingo and Miami were no longer allies with the French but were at peace with the British.

NEXT WEEK: Fort Duquesne

Fort Duquesne

February 13, 2011

In September Major Grant of the Highlanders asked Bouquet for permission to scout out the French fort and take any prisoners he might come across. Lieutenant-Colonel Bouquet consented so Grant left the advance post at Loyalhannon Creek with 800 Highlanders, Royal Americans and militia under his command.

They followed the horse trail used by Indian traders reaching their destination at about 2:00 am on the 14th. The darkness concealed their arrival. They took up position on a small hill about half a mile from the fort. This hill would be known hereafter as Grant's Hill. Below them lay Fort Duquesne housing several hundred French regulars. Outside the fort slept hundreds of warriors from Detroit all unaware the enemy was perched above them.

Grant's first plan of attack was to immediately send Major Lewis and half the Virginians to attack the sleeping warriors in front of the fort. When the warriors responded they were to feign a retreat back to the hill where the rest of the force was spread out waiting for the pursuers. Just before dawn Lewis returned to report that the plan was quite impossible as his troops had gotten lost in the thick woods because of the darkness.

So he abandoned this plan as light was upon them. He sent Lewis with 200 men two miles to the rear to guard the supplies which had been left with Captain Bullitt and a company of Virginians. Then he spread most of his force out along the tree line except for a company of Highlanders which he ordered out on the small plain between the forest and the fort. When the fog lifted he ordered the drums to play the reveille and the Highlander to play their bagpipes.

The warriors and French soldiers startled by the noise sprang into action. Soldiers poured out of the fort to attack the British positions head on. The warriors skirted along the banks of the two rivers and surrounded Grant's hill. Many of them took up position on a larger hill behind Grant's Hill and began to fire down upon Grant and the Highlanders that had stayed there.

Other warriors took to the woods and attacked Grant's men spread out along the tree line from behind. Their fierce war whoops and unseen musket fire cracked among the dense forest. This so unnerved the British that they fell into a panic. They rushed into a disorderly retreat down the horse trail toward Lewis and the supplies.

Lewis heard the gunfire so rushed to join the battle. He took a more direct route through the forest while the main force retreated pell-mell down the horse trail. Unknowingly they passed each other. Grant was horrified when he reached the supplies and found no one there while Lewis rushed headlong into a much superior force of French and warriors. Grant was taken prisoner. Then Lewis was taken prisoner. Only 540 returned safely to Loyalhannon out of 813.

When James Smith's adoptive father heard of the affair he said he was at a loss to explain the British actions. He said the art of warfare was to surprise and ambush the enemy while preventing the enemy from surprising and ambushing you. Grant had placed himself in position to do just that but instead alerted his enemy by drumming the reveille and playing on the bagpipes. He said the only way he could explain such an error was that they must have had too much brandy through the night before and had become intoxicated by dawn.

General Forbes was dismayed to say the least. He was especially disturbed that such an exercise was approved without his knowledge. However, they pressed on cutting the road as far as Loyalhannon where his whole army had gathered by November.

Meanwhile, Captain Ligneris, the commandant of Fort Duquesne had run out of supplies. He had to send most of his command back to Quebec keeping only a few hundred regulars to garrison the fort. He tried to convince the warriors from Detroit to stay on and fight one more battle but they felt it was far too late in the season and they had to rejoin their families for the winter hunt. This would be the last time the First Nations would back the French as allies in any great numbers. Fort Duquesne was left all but defenseless.

General Forbes who was very sick the whole campaign had to be carried from Raystown to Loyalhannon. The fall rain had ruined the road they had cut so far turning it to a sea of mud. Washington and Colonel Armstrong of the Pennsylvania Militia had cut the road to within a mile of the French fort but with the advance of winter and the deplorable condition of the road they decided to winter at Loyalhannon.

Then they received word from their scouts that Fort Duquesne was defenseless. They decided to press on and finish the campaign. On the night of November the 24th the advance guard camped along Turkey Creek. They were close enough to the fort that they heard the distinct rumblings of kegs of powder exploding in the distance. The explosions were coming from the direction of the fort.

The next day the whole force marched on the French fort. The advance guard was led by General Forbes being carried in a sling between two horses. They were followed by three columns. On the left Washington led the Colonial Militia and Bouquet led the Royal Americans on the right. The center column was commanded by Montgomery the new colonel of the Highlanders. When they arrived at the fort there was none. Ligneris had blown up the fortifications, burned the buildings and retreated up the Alleghany. He left nothing but a smoldering heap to conquer and no great victory to record. However, the campaign was still a great success because it gave the British the strategic ground at the confluence of the three great rivers in Pennsylvania. The following year they would construct Fort Pitt right beside the remains of Fort Duquesne and in later years it would sprawl into the important city of Pittsburgh, Pennsylvania.

NEXT WEEK: England Supplants France in North America

England Supplants France in North America

February 21, 2011

James Smith, our young captive friend, went with his adoptive father Tecaughretanego and son Nungany to Detroit for trade in

April of 1759. They stayed there until early summer then left for Caughnawaga near Montreal. While they were there he heard of a French ship that had British prisoners on it to be shipped overseas and held for exchange.

He stole away from Caughnawaga and placed himself aboard that ship. However, his plan didn't go exactly as he had hoped. General Wolfe had the St. Lawrence River blockaded and the ship could not leave Montreal. So Smith and the prisoners were transferred to prison where he was held for four months. Sometime in November of that year they were all sent to Crown Point and exchanged. He finally arrived home early in the year 1760.

Wolfe and Montcalm faced off in one of the final gasps of the war in that famous battle on the Plains of Abraham and the fall of Quebec. The Treaty of Paris was signed in 1763 transferring all French holdings in North America to England. Both generals were killed at Quebec and General Jeffery Amherst was appointed Commander-in-Chief of all the British forces in America.

Amherst epitomised the height of British 18th century arrogance. The French had a policy of present giving to the First Nations which cemented friendships and alliances. Because of this policy the First Nations allowed them to build forts as trading posts on their territories. It also gave the French safe passage to and from these posts. Amherst saw this policy as bribery. He wrote "Service must be rewarded; it has ever been a maxim with me. But to purchase the good behavior either of Indians or any others is what I do not understand"

Deputy Superintendent of Indian Affairs George Crogan wrote to Amherst that the First Nations in those parts were uneasy with the ceding of what France considered their holdings to Great Britain. They felt the French had no right to give away their land. The British had taken over all the French forts and were increasing their arms. The First Nations couldn't understand why since the French had been defeated and the war was over. Who were they arming against? All this had led to confusion on their part, so much so that it prevented them from bringing their prisoners as they had promised.

Amherst's feelings toward the First Nations were well documented. He replied to Crogan that he was sorry "the Indians should entertain such idle notions regarding the cessions made by the French Crown" and if they didn't give up their prisoners as first promised he would be forced to use "harsh measures" to make them comply.

Amherst also wrote to Colonel Bouquet, "The Post of Fort Pitt, or any of the others commanded by officers can certainly never be in danger from such a wretched enemy as the Indians are . . . I am fully convinced the only true method of treating those savages is to keep them in proper subjection and punish without exception the transgressors . . . I wish there was there was not an Indian settlement within a thousand miles of our country; for they are only fit to live with the inhabitants of the woods, being more nearly allied to the brute than the human creation."

The British traders were also far harder to deal with than the French had been. They no longer extended credit to the First Nations until after the fall hunt. Lack of credit could mean starvation. Amherst responded to First Nations complaints by extinguishing the policy of present giving. This included arms and ammunition which he said they had in abundance. This was untrue and only added to the threat of starvation.

The new policies of the British Department of Indian Affairs enacted by General Amherst only made the situation all the more fertile for hostilities. There was an Ottawa war chief from Detroit about to burst upon the scene and he brought with him the clouds of war. His name was Pontiac. Unfortunately Amherst failed to see the threat.

NEXT WEEK: Pontiac's Stratagem

Allies with the British

The Beaver War

Pontiac's Stratagem

March 15, 2011

I must apologize for being MIA the last few weeks. Tax season is upon us and I do tax returns at this time of year. Also, I hit a sort of writer's block which happens from time to time and I need to take a break and let my tank fill up again. Now, to get back to 1760's Great Lakes, we left the First Nations in the precarious position of having to deal with the arrogance of the British and the threat of starvation.

There was an Ottawa chief from Detroit that had gained prominence among the various First Nations of the Great Lakes. He earned their respect by his actions during the French and Indian War. He was at Braddock's defeat as well as other victories attributed to Montcalm. Pontiac was also among the war chiefs gathered at Fort William Henry.

In the fall of 1761 Captain Rogers of New Hampshire was sent with two hundred rangers to take possession of Fort Detroit. While camped at the present site of Cleveland, Ohio he was met by Pontiac and a few of his warriors. Pontiac asked him for what reason was he in his country. Rogers replied that he was there to take possession of Fort Detroit for the British. He told Pontiac that the French had ceded all of North America to the British and that they now had supreme command of all the territories. Pontiac, although dismayed, expressed a desire for peace then returned to his village near Detroit.

Rogers arrived at Detroit, struck the Fleur de Lei and replaced it with the Union Jack. That winter was a particularly hard one for the First Nations living in the area. The following summer the Chippewa, Ottawa, Potawatomi, Wyandotte and Seneca were invited by Pontiac to a council held on the Ecourse River just south of Detroit. Some Chippewa from the Michilimackinac area also attended as well as two Frenchmen who were travelling with them dressed in native garb. (When the area came under the sway of the British the Ojibwa became known as the Chippewa and the name Saulteaux fell out of use.) Pontiac stood in the center of the gathering and began to speak.

> It is important for us, my brothers that we exterminate from our land this nation which only seeks to kill us. You see, as well as I do, that we cannot longer get our supplies as we had them from our brothers, the French. The English sell us merchandise twice dearer than the French sold them to us, and their wares [are worth] nothing. Hardly have we bought a blanket, or something else to cover us, than we must think of having another of the kind. When we want to start for our winter quarters they will give us no credit, as our brothers, the French, did. When I go to the English chief to tell him that some of our brothers are dead, instead of weeping for the dead, as our brothers, the French, used to do he makes fun of me and of you. When I ask him for something for our sick, he refuses, and tells me that he has no need of us. You can well see by that he seeks our ruin . . .

War belts were sent out to the various Miami nations living along the Wabash River, the nations living in Ohio country as well as the Six Nations. Luc de La Corne had been propagating the rumour among the western nations that a French fleet would arrive soon to retake the country. This rumour was bolstered by Spanish and French disturbances in the New Orleans area. Most First Nations answered the call to arms, but not all. There were some chiefs who sought to deal with the British in a more peaceful manner.

Wabbicommicot, a major Mississauga chief from the Toronto area warned the British that an attack was coming the following spring. He also influenced most of the Mississauga warriors not to join Pontiac. One Miami chief had also warned the British by giving a war belt to an Ensign Robert Holmes which had been sent to him by the Shawnee. All of the unrest failed to faze Amherst. He answered it by restricting the amount of ammunition British traders could sell to the natives. He said they had plenty of ammunition which was not true. This further increased the threat of starvation.

A stratagem was devised by which plans to attack the various British western forts were assigned to individual nations. Fort Michilimackinac was appointed to the Chippewa war chief Minweweh while the Illinois were to destroy Fort St. Joseph. The forts south and east of Lake Erie were alloted to Iroquois, Ohio and Wabash nations. Fort Detroit was to be Pontiac's prize along with the Detroit and Lake Nations. The individual assaults were coordinated to happen on or about the 15th day of the Frog month or the 7th of May 1763.

NEXT WEEK: Fort Michilimackinac

Fort Michilimackinac

March 21, 2011

When the British had taken control of Fort Michilimackinac its new commandant Captain George Etherington sent dispatches throughout the territory commanding all French settlers to report to the fort. He wanted them to swear allegiance to the British Crown and for this he promised to take into consideration all of their needs as well as any complaints. The British would treat them as well as the French governor had.

Among the French in the area were Augustin de Langlade and his son Charles. This was the same Charles Langlade who had been at Pickawillany, Braddock's rout and Fort William Henry. Etherington knew well of him so when the Langlades swore allegiance to the British he gave them command of the trading post at La Baye or Green Bay, Wisconsin.

At the end of the Frog Month the principle Ojibwa war chief Minweweh and another chief named Madjeckewiss or Bad Bird gathered 400 Ojibwa warriors at Michilimackinac. Minweweh had devised a stratagem to take the fort as part of the Beaver War. They had feigned friendship with the British and offered to put on an exhibition of baggataway or lacrosse on the Queen's birthday. On June 2, 1763 they all gathered outside the fort for the spectacle. The captain and his second in command joined the Ojibwa spectators but the gates to the fort were left closed. Most of the spectators were Ojibwa women dressed in their long shawls. Little did Etherington realize that their colorful shawls concealed weapons for the warriors.

The game of lacrosse as played by the Ojibwa was a wild affair. There were little rules and the number of players on the field was only limited to the number of young men available. The ball would be struck by one side toward the opponent's goal which was a line drawn at the end of the field. The players were struck with the sticks more than the ball so there was plenty of confusion accompanied with the din of loud whooping and yelling. With all the excitement it made for an engrossing spectator sport.

The game began and several times the ball was thrown over the stockade and inside the fort where the garrison would toss the ball back over the wall and onto the playing field. Finally the captain ordered the gates opened so the players could retrieve the ball themselves. The next time the ball was thrown into the fort the players all rushed to the spectators, took hold of their weapons and then rushed into the fort. The soldiers were shocked and slow to act. The massacre was on!

Captain Etherington and his aide Lieutenant Leslie were captured immediately. The garrison of ninety soldiers fell quickly suffering seventy killed and the other twenty taken prisoner. Etherington and Leslie were to be burned at the stake so a few days later the wood was prepared and the two were lashed to the poles.

Charles Langlade was at Michilimackinac at the time of the attack to purchase supplies for the post at Green Bay. He was not only very influential with the Ojibwa but he was also an Ottawa war chief. Of course he was not taken prisoner but it all happened so fast that he was of little help to Etherington.

He had warned the commandant earlier, and several times, that he had heard rumours of treachery by the Ojibwa from his Ottawa friends at L'Arbre Croche. They were not in favor of the Beaver War, not because they liked the British so much as they were angry that Minweweh had not invited them to take part in the surprise attack. Etherington dismissed Langlade's warnings because he had called in Matchikuis, a chief of the Michilimackinac Ottawa, to ask him about the rumours. Of course he denied everything. Finally the captain ordered Langlade not to bring it up again calling the rumours "the twaddle of old women".

Langlade had left Michilimackinac the day it fell but returned with some of the Ottawa warriors from L'Arbre Croche just in time to save the two officers from the fire. When he took charge of the two officers he rebuked Etherington saying if he had listened to the "old women's stories" he would not be in the humiliating position he was in with most of his garrison wiped out. Then he negotiated with Minweweh for their safety and all twenty-two prisoners were sent under an armed guard of L'Arbre Croche Ottawa to Montreal. Fort Michilimackinac was left in Minweweh's hands.

NEXT WEEK: British Forts Fall like Autumn Leaves

British Forts Fall like Autumn Leaves

March 29, 2011

The fall of Fort Michilimackinac was a stunning success. Late spring 1763 provided other spectacular military successes for the First Nation alliance. Most of the western British forts fell under First Nation assault. The others were put under siege.

Fort Sandusky was the first to fall. Ottawa and Wyandotte warriors were let into the fort on the pretense of friendship but then opened fire on the garrison of fifteen killing them all but Commandant Ensign Pawlee who was given to one of their widows to replace a husband killed in battle.

Fort Venango capitulated much in the same way a Michilimackinac. The western Seneca, who were also known to Sir William Johnson as the Chenussios and to the Americans as the Mingo entered the fort in the guise of friendship but once inside turned on the garrison. After killing all the British soldiers there they made the commandant write the reasons down for the attack in a dispatch.

The dispatch he wrote stated that there were two reasons for the war. First, for the past two years the scarcity of powder and its price, when it was available, as well as the cost of other necessities was far too high. When they complained about this they were ill-treated and never redressed. Second, When the British began to take over the posts from the French they began to increase their military presence which made them believe the British had designs of possessing all of their lands.

The dispatch was given to a party of warriors heading toward Fort Pitt in order to have it fall into the hands of the British. The commandant of Venango was then put to death and the fort was destroyed. The Seneca also took Fort LeBoeuf and its sixteen men.

The fort at P'resqu Isle was commanded by Ensign John Christie and had twenty-seven defenders. They lined the inside of their long two-story blockhouse to reinforce it, and laid in casks of drinking water. The only door was on the first floor leading inside the fort. The only openings in the walls were long slits for their muskets and the floor between the two stories was perforated so if forced to the second floor they could shoot down upon any intruders. They abandoned the fort, locked themselves inside the blockhouse and prepared for a siege.

The Seneca, supported by some Ottawa, Chippewa and Wyandotte warriors, shot flaming arrows at the roof of the blockhouse. The soldiers worked tirelessly tearing off the burning shingles dousing the roof with their drinking water. Meanwhile, some of them dug a tunnel to the well inside the fort which was under the First Nations' control. They carried buckets of water back through the tunnel to replace their drinking water. The work was so laborious that they decided to surrender on the second day of the siege. On the 22nd of June they were taken prisoner and divided up between the four First Nations.

The Detroit Potawatomi arrived at Fort St. Joseph saying they had come to visit their relatives. They informed the commandant, Ensign Schlosser that they wished to come into the fort to wish him a good morning. They seized Schlosser and attacked the fort. Their numbers were so great that they slaughtered all but three of the garrison in about two minutes. A Mr. Winston and a Mr. Hambough hid in the house of a Frenchman named Louison Chivalie for four days before being discovered. They were taken prisoner and Hambough and a Mr. Chim were sent south to Illinois but Winston was kept at St. Joseph.

Fort Miami on the Miami River suffered the same fate as the other forts in the region. It was attacked on the 27th of May by the Miami and some Delaware. Fort Miami's commandant, Ensign Holmes, had a Miami mistress but she betrayed him by luring him outside the fort and into a trap where he was killed. They then attacked the fort killing half the garrison. The other half was taken prisoner and shipped down the Wabash River to Fort Ouiatinon to be added to the prisoners there. Not one was killed at Ouiatinon as the whole garrison of twenty men surrendered after their commandant, Lieutenant Edward Jenkins, was also lured outside the fort where he was seized and threatened with death if the garrison did not surrender. Then all the prisoners were taken to Fort Chartre on the Mississippi River. This fort was still in French hands under the command of J. Neyeon de Villiere.

The forts that were closer in proximity to the colonies were better able to withstand the First Nation onslaught. Forts Ligonier and Bedford were able to hold out against the siege tactics of the First Nations. The Delaware, who had joined the alliance in full, took over the siege from the Seneca and the Chippewa. They had even less luck.

Fort Pitt was commanded by a Swiss soldier of fortune that had joined the British army. Captain Simeon Ecuer had taken the words of General Amherst literally. Amherst, in responding to the upheaval, had said to Colonel Bouquet in June "that blankets should be infected with small pox and given to the Indians as presents." Ecuer did just that. Small pox raged through the Delaware villages that summer.

If you happened to be English "Indian County" was not the place to be in the summer of 1763. Just before the fall of Fort Miami five Frenchmen, Miny Chain, Jacques Godfrey and Messrs. Beauban, Chavin and Labadee were with a band of Ottawa and Chippewa warriors at the mouth of the Miami River. They spotted John Welch, a trader from Fort Miami, on his way to Detroit with two boats loaded down with pelts.

The warriors hid in the forest while Chain beckoned Welsh and his party to shore. When they landed they were taken prisoner and their goods divided up. Chain and Godfrey took their prisoners to Fort Miami to be added to the prisoners there. The other three returned with their share, including Welch, to Detroit. When they arrived the Ottawa seized their plunder, killed Welch, and took the goods saying that all plunder belonged to the First Nations.

King Beaver, Shingas and four other friendly Delaware chiefs came to an English trader named Calhoun who was at their town of Tuscarora. They informed him of the British forts falling like autumn leaves. They also told him that a trader named Hugh

Crawford and a boy were taken prisoner at the mouth of the Miami but six others were killed. Five English traders were also killed at Salt Lick Town on Salt Springs Creek. They warned him to remove himself and his men to a safer place as they saw tracks of a large war party heading their way.

Later they sent Daniel, one of their chiefs, and two others to escort them safely to Fort Pitt. But these three were not friendly Delaware, but had joined the alliance. They refused to let them bring their weapons with them saying the three were sufficient to escort them safely. The next day as they were crossing Beaver Creek they were attacked by a war party. The three Delaware disappeared immediately and of Calhoun's party of fourteen only Calhoun and two others escaped. Although they became lost they were eventually able to make it to Fort Pitt.

NEXT WEEK: Plans to Take Detroit

Plans to Take Detroit

April 9, 2011

Pontiac lived on Peach Island at the mouth of the Detroit River above the fort. Of the four British posts in what is today Michigan Detroit was the most important. Consequently he led the attack on Fort Detroit personally. He sent out war belts as a call to arms to the surrounding First Nations.

On May 21st Chippewa war chief Sekahos responded by arriving at Detroit with 120 warriors from the Thames River and Kettle Creek. Another Chippewa war chief, Wasson from Saginaw Bay, arrived on May 31st with 250 warriors. Other First Nations were also with Pontiac because they lived around Detroit. These included the Detroit Potawatomi and the Wyandotte led by the war chief Takay. Others from the Wabash arrived including some Miami and Kickapoo. There was even a band of Fox under Ninivois present. Pontiac had a force of 900 warriors by June.

But not all First Nations thought a war with the British was prudent. Wabbiccomicot, a very influential Mississauga chief from Toronto kept most of that Nation out of the fray. The Wyandotte were split. Most of them joined Pontiac but one band led by a chief named Teata held back.

The whole territory that surrounded Detroit was Chippewa country. As stated above the chiefs and warriors from Saginaw and the Thames answered the call of Pontiac's war belts. However, the St. Clair Chippewa was strangely absent. In fact there is no record of their major war chief Little Thunder being sent a belt. He was known to be a staunch British ally especially in his later years.

The plan Pontiac devised was much like the one used in the fall of the other British posts. It was one of stealth. On the 1st of May he came to the post with about fifty warriors saying it was his intent to dance the calumet, which was a peace dance, at the house of the commandant inside the fort. They entered the fort, made their speeches, danced their dance and then they mingled about the inside of the fort feigning friendship with all the inhabitants. In reality, this was a recognizance mission. Pontiac informed Major Gladwin that they would return in a few days with the whole Nation. They would arrive for a friendship gathering which was customary to do once each year.

Meanwhile, the commandant began to suspect something was amiss. A Mrs. St. Aubin had gone to the Ottawa village to trade her bread for sugar and grease when she noticed the warriors all filing their guns down. She asked them why they were doing this and they replied they worked better sawed off. She reported this to her cousin Mr. LaButte who was the post's interpreter who in turn told Major Gladwin.

The Ottawa also had a traitor in their midst. In one report it was a young Ottawa maiden named Catherine who had made a pair of moccasins for the commandant who planned to give them to a friend as a gift. He liked them so much he ordered another pair for himself. During the time he transacted business with her she became infatuated with him and secretly told him of the Ottawa's plans. But she was found out and when she returned to the village Pontiac beat her with a stick leaving her lying on the ground. The rest of the village called for her death but she was spared.

To convince the British there was no treachery planned the Ottawa came to the fort with an old woman in tow saying that they had heard that she was at the fort telling lies to the commandant. They said that the Ottawa only wanted peace and friendship with the English and that the old woman was evil.

In another report the traitor was an Ottawa man who did not agree with the attack on the British. Mahigama came to the fort in secret and asked to speak with the commandant as he had something very important to tell him. He was taken to Major Campbell who was being replaced by Major Gladwin. Campbell also called Gladwin to the meeting. They wanted to send for Mr. LaButte to interpret but Mahigama would not allow it. He said he could speak French well enough for Campbell to understand him.

He told them of the plan to attack the fort, on which day and how the First Nations would come into the fort for the peace gathering with all their arms including sawed-off guns hidden under their blankets. He begged the officers to keep his name secret because if his people found out they would surely kill him. It is not sure which story is true but the British did discover the details of Pontiac's plan and they did hold their source in confidence.

On the day of the planned assault the British were ready. They had 300 men under arms all with swords and pistols at the ready. They opened the gates but only let in the chiefs, Pontiac, Mukeetaa Pinaasee or The Blackbird, Neewish and Wabinema. Pontiac gave the long speech he had prepared but when he got to the part where he was to give the war-whoop and the attack was to begin he just sat down. The Ottawa plan of attack had been foiled.

They left the fort enraged rushing to an English house outside the fort which was occupied by an old woman and her family. They killed everyone in the house. Then they move on to Hogg

Island where they killed another English family that lived there. The above mentioned war belts were sent out, the Chippewa reinforcements arrived and the siege of Fort Detroit began.

NEXT WEEK: The Siege of Fort Detroit

The Siege of Fort Detroit

April 17, 2011

When the siege began Fort Detroit was quadrilateral in shape with the front facing the river. It was protected by a single palisade twenty-five feet high with blockhouses at the gates and at the corners. Its heavy armament consisted of two six-pounders, one three-pounder and three mortars. Two vessels, the Beaver and the Gladwyn, were also anchored just off the corners of the fort. They protected the fort from attack by water.

About 100 small buildings were enclosed in the fort. They were built close together on narrow streets. There was also a church, a council house and barracks for the soldiers. They were all made of wood and prone to the hazards of flaming arrows, but the cisterns were full so this didn't pose too much of a problem.

The warriors, who were made up of Ottawa, Potawatomi and Wyandotte Nations, surrounded the fort. They kept just out of reach of the heavy artillery picking off any poor soldier who happened to stick his head above the pickets or moved in front of a porthole.

Pontiac decided to try to set the roof of the church on fire as it was particularly vulnerable because it was close to the palisade. He hoped if it caught fire it would spread to the rest of the fort. The British got wind of the plan so the priest got word to Pontiac through a French settler that the Great Spirit would be angry with him if he put his plan into action. He heeded the priest's advice.

On May 10th the warriors opened fire on the fort early in the morning and kept it up until about 11 am. Then Pontiac proposed a council with the officers outside the fort. Major Campbell thought perhaps he could do some good so he agreed to go with Lieutenant McDougal. Some of the French traders advised against it but the two officers went anyway. When they arrived Pontiac changed his mind about a council to discuss terms and instead seized Campbell and McDougall as prisoners to be held for ransom.

Three days later the Wyandotte captured a trader by the name of Chapman who was coming to Detroit with five bateaux loaded with provisions. He was unaware of any hostilities and he and his men were taken prisoners. The provisions included sixteen half barrels of powder and rum. The prisoners and the booty were taken to the Wyandotte village which was on the east side of the river a short distance below the fort.

Gladwin got word of the loss and had heard that all the Wyandotte warriors were drunk on the rum. Captain Hopkins with twenty-five rangers and a few volunteers made their way to the sloop with the idea of sailing it to the village and under the cover of the ship's cannons burn the village along with the captured booty. As they were approaching the Wyandotte's village the wind shifted and they could not complete their task. The warriors open fire on the sloop as it returned to the fort but this was of little consequence. However, they did gain the intelligence that the Wyandotte warriors were not drunk but were completely on their guard.

On the 25th of May Chief Sekahos left with 150 Chippewa warriors for the mouth of Lake Erie. They had heard a large shipment of provisions from Niagara was making its way along the north shore of Lake Erie bound for Detroit. Lieutenant Cuyler had left Fort Niagara on the 14th with ninety-six men in eighteen boats. He landed at Point Pelee on the 28th to encamp but was ambushed by Sekahos and his warriors. Cuyler's men threw down their guns and ran for their boats. Five boats pushed off but only two escaped including Cuyler. The other three were captured along with a plentiful supply of provisions, arms, shot and powder.

During the first part of June seven bateaux were attacked at the mouth of the Grand River by Chief Kinisshikapoo and his party of seventy-five Mississauga warriors. Five boats were captured but two escaped. These provisions were brought to Pontiac and Kinisshikapoo and his warriors attached themselves to Sekahos' Chippewa. It was going to be a long hot summer for the British.

NEXT WEEK: The Siege Continues

The Siege Continues

April 23, 2011

By 1763 the Detroit River was dotted with French homesteads. This pioneer community had slowly grown over the previous fifty years and there had always been good relations with the surrounding First Nations. In fact most of the French families just wanted to remain neutral in this conflict. It must be remembered that Pontiac and his First Nation allies considered themselves to be at war with the British. They still considered the French to be their allies and the French settlers to be their friends.

However, when the war broke out the warriors indiscriminately began to kill their livestock and confiscate their goods. The French settlers asked for a council with Pontiac and it was granted. They complained bitterly explaining the disastrous consequences this policy had upon them and begged him to put a stop to it. He promised them he would under the condition that if the First Nations needed anything to support the continuation of the war they should give it up upon being asked to do so. They agreed. After this council the warriors ceased to trouble the settlers without the permission of their chiefs. They were allowed to continue going about their business during the week as well as go to mass on Sunday unmolested.

When the captured bataux arrived at the Ottawa encampment above the fort Pontiac secured the supplies and stowed them away. A French woman named Deriviere had been expecting a trunk to arrive for her in that shipment. It contained personal goods and clothes and she was distraught that it had been lost. She convinced the interpreter Mr. LaButte to escort her from the fort to the Ottawa camp where she told Pontiac of her dilemma. He had the confiscated goods searched and Miss Diriviere's missing trunk was found. It was returned to her with no objections.

Most of June was spent keeping the fort under siege. The warriors continually roamed near the stockade in small parties either shooting at the fort or the ship anchored in the river. The British would return fire but neither was of any consequence. Attempts were made by the warriors to set fire to both the fort and the ship but they failed.

In one instance a cart was loaded with combustibles, lit on fire and pushed full speed at the fort's pickets. The cart was let go when they reached a point just out of range of gunfire but the cart flipped over before it reached its target.

In another instance two rafts were loaded with combustibles tied together with a long length of rope and floated toward the British ship anchored in the river just off the fort. The rafts were let go about 20 rods off the ship's bow. The idea was that the current would carry the two rafts, one on each side of the ship's bow, and set the ship ablaze. But the British saw the danger approaching, raised their anchor and moved out into the river just as the two rafts floated passed a few yards off their port side.

Lieutenant McDougal made a decision to try to escape back to the safety of the fort. There were no guards at the house where he and Major Campbell were being kept but there were groups of warriors always moving about just outside the homestead. Major Campbell decided not to go with him but approved of his plan. The young lieutenant executed his plan successfully making his way back to the fort. His older superior remained Pontiac's captive at the house of Mr. Meloche.

The armed sloop Beaver was sent to Niagara for reinforcements and it returned with 300 troops and some supplies. This was the only relief Fort Detroit received. Some of the French settlers secretly sympathized with the British. They would float canoes filled with supplies downriver during the night. A lantern would be lit just as they reached the fort as a signal to the garrison to come out and retrieve the supplies. This made the strategy of starving out the garrison next to impossible.

During one of the warriors' sorties a Chippewa chief was shot and killed. The body was retrieved by a French volunteer who was fighting for the British. He desecrated the chief's body by scalping it and cutting it into pieces. The young chief happened to be the nephew of Wasson the leading war chief from Saginaw. He was livid and the rest of the Saginaw Chippewa were enraged. They raced to the house where Major Campbell was being held and demanded his life for the life of Wasson's nephew. This was in accordance with First Nations' custom. The act upon the dead chief was so grievous that Pontiac could not intervene. Campbell was turned over. He was immediately taken out, tortured by having his lips cut off, shot dead with arrows then cut into pieces. Campbell was not only a commanding officer but the cousin of his replacement Major Gladwin. This whole episode had now turned personal on both sides and could only lead to many more unnecessary deaths!

NEXT WEEK: A Royal Proclamation

A Royal Proclamation

May 8, 2011

When we last left the siege at Detroit feelings on both sides had escalated to a fever pitch. The warriors had just captured supplies sent to the fort from Niagara and were celebrating by consuming all the liquor. A nephew of Wasson, the leading war chief from Saginaw, had been killed and his body desecrated. In retaliation the Saginaw Chippewa killed and desecrated a prisoner of theirs, Major Campbell, who also happened to be the cousin of Major Gladwin.

Gladwin was in a high state of agitation over the affair so he agreed to let Captain Delyel lead a sortie of 277 men designed to surprise Pontiac's main camp which was about three and one-half miles upriver. They assumed his warriors would be either passed out or in a state of inebriation from the rum they had been celebrating with.

Delyel had very recently arrived at the fort with a company of American Royals and was eager to give the warriors a taste of British discipline. On July 31st at a quarter to three in the morning he led 247 men out of the fort and marched them up the river road toward Pontiac's camp. He was accompanied by two gunboats containing thirty men that followed them along the shoreline.

Little did they know Pontiac had a French spy inside the fort who had advised him of the British plan. All the warriors were sober and had taken up position at a place that would become known as Bloody Run. Parent's Creek ran into the Detroit River about a mile and one half up river from the fort. There was a long wooden bridge over the creek at its mouth. The Ottawa and Chippewa warriors had spread themselves out along the road on both sides of the bridge hiding themselves in the orchards, the long grass, reeds and behind fences and rows of cord wood that had been stacked by the French homesteaders who lived there.

The British arrived at the bridge just as day was breaking. Captain Delyel lead the company onto the bridge but before they reached the other side the warriors opened fire. This put the British in disarray but they soon regained composure and realized they had no choice but to retreat back to the fort. They were outnumbered two or three to one.

As they began their retreat Captain Delyel came face to face with Geeyette, Pontiac's brother-in-law. Delyel had a pistol and Geeyette motioned him to put it down. Delyel refused and the Ottawa warrior shot him dead.

The rest, with support from the two gunships, fought their way off the bridge and took up positions in several houses to try to prevent the warriors from getting between them and the fort. They stayed entrenched in the houses for nearly an hour but then left to resume the retreat. The Potawatomi and Wyandotte rushed to the sound of the gunfire and joined the battle.

The warriors who were in pursuit were hampered by fire from the gunboats and gave up the chase when they reached the range of cannon fire from the fort. The defeated company reached the safety of the fort carrying some of the dead and wounded. One wounded soldier was even carried back to the fort in a chair. Others were put into the gunboats during the battle. Only seven were left on the battlefield.

After the battle the seven dead soldiers were loaded into canoes. Pontiac ordered the French settlers to return the "English dogs" to the British fort. The British lost officers Captain Delyel and Captain Gray along with lieutenants Luke and Brown. Among the enlisted men the 35th Regiment had one Sergeant, one drummer and thirteen rank and file killed plus twenty-five wounded. The 60th had one killed and seven wounded. The 80th had two killed and three wounded and the Royal Americans had two killed and one wounded. There was also a trader's servant wounded. The total killed and wounded was sixty-one. The warriors had five killed and eleven wounded.

The battle of Bloody Run was the height of the siege. The rest of the summer was spent in small skirmishes with the French settlers friendly to the British smuggling supplies into the fort under the cover of darkness. This made the objective of starving out the British impossible.

When autumn arrived Pontiac's coalition began to fall apart. Generally speaking First Nations were unable to hold a confederacy for war together for extended periods of time. The time for the fall hunt had arrived and most warriors were anxious to abandon the war effort and begin the hunt in order the feed their people in the coming year.

Although the coalition disintegrated without realizing their impossible goal of "driving the English into the sea" the Beaver War did accomplish some great things. General Amherst was recalled to England and his Indian policy was replaced by one much friendlier, one modeled after their predecessors the French. As a footnote Major Gladwin was censured for not seizing Pontiac when he had the chance.

The King issued the Royal Proclamation of 1763 which was the first official recognition by the Europeans that land in North America was owned by the First Nations. It laid out a boundary that ran basically along the Appalachian Mountains which recognized lands west of the dividing line as "Indian Lands". These lands came under the protection of the British Crown and could not be purchased directly by a British citizen from an "Indian". British colonists were prevented from expanding onto the "Indian Lands". The colonists accused the Crown of capitulation in the Beaver War and immediately ignored the proclamation's prohibition of westward expansion. The hated proclamation helped fuel sentiments for independence a decade later. In Canada the Royal Proclamation of 1763 is still in effect and used in courts to settle modern-day land claims.

NEXT WEEK: A Decade of Turmoil

A Decade of Turmoil

May 25, 2011

After the Royal Proclamation was issued a peace council was held at Niagara in July of 1764. Some 1,500 First Nations chiefs and warriors met with Sir William Johnson, British Superintendent of Indian Affairs, who represented British interests. Conspicuously absent were Pontiac and the Ottawa of Detroit. The Potawatomi, Wyandotte and Chippewa of Saginaw also refused to attend.

Johnson presented the First Nations with two wampum belts. The first beaded belt contained two figures holding hands as well as the year of the council. Johnson proclaimed on this belt, "My children, I clothe your land, you see that Wampum before me, the body of my words, in this spirit of my words shall remain, it shall never be removed, this will be your Mat the eastern Corner of which I myself will occupy, the Indians being my adopted children their life shall never sink in poverty." Johnson was coveting with the First Nations that the British recognized their ownership of the land and that they would respect that by only occupying the eastern corner of it leaving the rest for the First Nations to live in and prosper as allies.

The second belt was called the Twenty-four Nation Wampum. It was a beaded belt that had twenty-four figures on it holding hands and pulling a large sailing ship. The English words that accompanied this belt were, "My children, see, this is my Canoe floating on the other side of the Great Waters, it shall never be exhausted but always full of the necessities of life for you my Children as long as the world shall last. Should it happen any time after this that you find the strength of your life reduced, your Indian tribes must take hold of the Vessel and pull towards you this my Canoe, and where you have brought it over on this land on which you stand, I will open my hand as it were, and you will find yourselves supplied with plenty".

To the First Nations these two wampum belts were sacred symbols that solemnized an agreement between two Nations that could not be broken unilaterally, but to the British not so much. British sentiments can be found throughout their correspondence of the day. General Thomas Gage, who had replaced Amherst, wrote to Johnson from New York on August 5th, "I wish they may be yet sincere, when the Rod is removed; and should be glad to hear that they had delivered up the Murderers agreeable to their Treaty; and to see the King of the Delawares, as He is called, and the Head Warrior of that Nation, lodged in our Hands. Till then, we ought to be upon our Guard, and put No Faith in their Speeches and Declarations." Johnson wrote to Gage on September

1st from Johnson Hall, "As to their Sincerity I believe it can be relied on whilst it's made worth their While, but I will not take upon me to say that a people who have been strongly prejudiced against us will conquer their aversion without we take steps to remove it, & whether this is necessary or not I submit to you."

The Royal Proclamation was impossible to enforce. Squatters from the colonies immediately ignored it and began to cross the Alleghenies. Both land speculators and squatters regarded the rich lands west of the Alleghenies as a prize to be had for the hard-fought victory of the French and Indian War. Land speculators like George Washington, Thomas Jefferson and Patrick Henry resented the Monarchy using the Proclamation to stifle their efforts to make a profit from "Indian lands". Washington said he thought it was only a temporary measure to settle the First Nations and would soon fall. So he advised his business associate William Crawford to scout out lands in First Nations' territories before others did. Speculators flooded the colonial government with petitions for land grants even though it was illegal.

In 1767 Indian Agent George Croghan made a trip from New York to Detroit and back to assess the state of Indian Affairs in "Indian Country". He spent two days with some chiefs and warriors of the Delaware Nation trying to ascertain the purpose of a large council of Western Nations he had heard was to be held the following spring. On the second day the chiefs told him they did not know the purpose of the council but the First Nations were generally dissatisfied with the conduct of the British. They complained that the British hounded them for every minor crime committed by them, but they ignored even the most aggrieved crimes including murder that British subjects committed against the First Nations. In short they could get no justice.

In 1768 Sir William Johnson held a council with the Six Nation Iroquois at Fort Stanwix. They agreed to cede a huge tract of land south of the Mohawk and Ohio rivers and east to the Tennessee River which was the hunting grounds of the Shawnee Nation. It covered what is now western Pennsylvania as well as most of Kentucky and West Virginia. The Iroquois claimed ownership based on conquests made in the seventeenth century but they had long since lost the territory. But none of that mattered to the Colonial Government. This gave them reason enough to openly ignore the Royal Proclamation and approve petitions for land across the Alleghenies. The land rush was on. Johnson was given a dressing down for overstepping the bounds of his government's position but the damage was already done.

The Shawnee fought back against the trespassers by killing them and/or burning them out. The nasty skirmishes continued on for the next five years. It escalated when in the spring of 1774 colonial vigilantes murdered the family of the Mingo chief Tachnedorus. The family included the chief's pregnant sister who was strung up by her wrists, sliced open and the unborn child impaled on a stake. Tachnedorus' grief was unbearable. He exacted his revenge by attacking and killing settlers in Virginia. This gave the Colonial Government a reason to declare open warfare on the Shawnee. This "war" was called Lord Dunmore's War after the Governor of Virginia.

The Shawnee sent out war belts to the other nations near them. But the British used a divide and conquer strategy. Johnson worked on the Iroquois and John Stuart, Superintendent of Indian Affairs in the South, the Cherokee. Consequently the belts were rejected and the Shawnee were left to fight the war alone.

Dunmore led an army of 1,500 volunteers down the Ohio River from Fort Pitt. General Andrew Lewis at the head of 1,100 men moved down the Kanawha River to meet Dunmore on the Ohio. The plan was to attack and destroy Shawnee towns on the Scioto River.

The Shawnee rallied their warriors but could only raise 700 men. They were hopelessly outnumbered. Their war chiefs Cornstock, Black Hoof, Black Fish, Blue Jacket and Packeshinwaw held a council. They determined the only chance for success was to meet the enemy head on in a surprise attack.

They crossed the Ohio on rafts in the night of October 9th and surprised Lewis at a place called Pleasant Point. The battle raged on all day with first the Shawnee pushing the Virginians back. Then reinforcements arrived and the Shawnee were forced to retreat and take up a position on the banks of the Ohio. Finally, with the battle lost they were forced to withdraw back to their towns on the Scioto. The only solution was to sue for peace.

Cornstock spoke for the Shawnee. He chose to deal with Lord Dunmore at Camp Charlotte. The peace was costly. The Shawnee had to give up all claim to the lands south of the Ohio and had to send four hostages to Williamsburg to be held in order to ensure future peaceful conduct. One of the hostages was Cornstock's own son Wissecapoway. Lord Dunmore's War brought a measure of peace but more storm clouds appeared as the Colonies continued to rail against Great Britain.

NEXT WEEK: Council at Fort Detroit

The American Revolution

Council at Fort Detroit

June 6, 2011

The American Revolution broke out in 1775. At first neither the British nor the colonial rebels showed any interest in drawing on any First Nations support. The First Nations around the Great Lakes basin also had little interest in getting involved. Most saw it as a "white man's" squabble. The more vocal ones advised neutrality saying "let the father chastise his rebellious son". But after the war dragged on for two years each side began to look for the help of their First Nation allies. It had become most important for the British to protect the frontier. Ohio country was crucial strategically so a tug of war arose between Colonel Henry Hamilton the British commandant at Fort Detroit and George Morgan the Colonial Indian Agent at Fort Pitt for First Nations' allegiance along the frontier.

The following spring Hamilton called a council at Detroit. Over 1600 First Nations people gathered there in June of that year. The presents flowed liberally including liquor. Of the 8,750 gallons of rum shipped to Detroit for the first six months 8,250 gallons were allocated for the "Indians".

On June 14, 1778 the council began. Both Civil and War chiefs attended from the following nations: Ottawa, Chippewa, Potawatomi, Wyandotte, Delaware, Mohawks and Seneca. Heading the list of nine war chiefs of the Chippewa was my great-

great-grandfather Little Thunder. He had been presented with a British Brigadier Generals dress and a King George III medal for service at Fort Sinclair on the St. Clair River in the late 1760's. He coveted those items and I imagine him to be an impressive sight arriving at the council in his headdress, bright red tunic and large King's medal hanging around his neck.

Simon Girty, the infamous colonial traitor, acted as one of eight interpreters. Girty "having escaped from the Virginians and having put himself under the protection of His Majesty, after giving satisfactory assurance of his fidelity" was looked upon by the British as a loyalist. One man's renegade is another man's partisan!

Chamintawaa, an Ottawa civil chief, spoke for the Three Fires Confederacy. He promised Hamilton to continue to ignore poor advice saying "bad birds come about us and whisper in our ears, that we should not listen to you, we shall always be attentive to what you say". But the bulk of his speech was directed to the Delaware.

"Listen Brethren! I am going to say a few words to our Grandfathers the Delawares in the name of all the nations here present, I speak in the name of their War Chiefs". Chamintawaa took them to task for not being wholeheartedly in unison with the other First Nations. He accused them of "breaking down branches from the trees to lay across our road, at the same hanging down your heads with tears in your eyes". He asked them to be united and "listen to our father as we all do & obey his will" and not to "take your hearts to the Virginians". Chamintawaa ended his speech with the warning, "this is the last time we intend speaking to you".

The Delaware did not answer until the conclusion of the council. War Chief Captain James said he could not speak for all the Delaware but only for his village. He said he was entirely on side and to prove his words he "sang the war song and danced the war dance" on the belt he was given. However, three Delaware chiefs who were not at the council, Captain Pipe, Captain White Eyes and John Kill Buck Jr. signed a treaty with the Revolutionary Government at Fort Pitt in September.

The British were much more adept at raising First Nations' support than the colonials. They had a well experienced Indian Department in place and had been practicing the policy of present giving for more than a decade. This had gone a long way in cementing good relations and alliances. On the other hand, the colonials had only decades of land grabbing and violent squabbles with their First Nation neighbors.

The Shawnee had become divided in 1778. The chiefs were opposed to joining the war but their warriors had become increasingly rebellious. Many ignored the prompting of their chiefs and clamoured for war. A group had already accepted a war belt from Hamilton at Detroit and joined in the raids on the frontier. By autumn the celebrated chief Cornstock had decided to accept a Delaware offer to move his village to their capital town of Coshocton for safety.

But before the move Cornstock along with chief Red Hawk and warrior Petalla visited Fort Randolph on the Kanawha River. They had made the trip to advise the Continental Army of the disposition of the Shawnee nation. Cornstock told the commander, Captain Matthew Arbuckle, that despite all his efforts to keep the Shawnee neutral the tide against the rebels was so strong that their warriors were being swept up in the current.

When Arbuckle heard this he decided to take the three hostage. Shawnee neutrality would be their ransom. After about a month in custody Cornstock's son, Elinipsico came to see what happened to his father. Just as they were visiting the body of a young frontiersman was brought in. He had been mutilated and scalped. The undisciplined militia was incensed and wanted to take revenge on the four Shawnee inside the fort. Arbuckle and visiting Colonel Charles Stewart were helpless to stop them. Cornstock and his son died in a hail of bullets while Red Hawk was gunned down trying to escape up the chimney. Petalla died in agony after being severely mauled. Needless to say this ended any hope of securing an alliance with any of the Shawnee. Nimwah, Kishanosity and Oweeconne moved Cornstock's village of seventeen families to Coshocton where many First Nations people who wished to remain neutral were gathering.

NEXT WEEK: The "Town Destroyer"

The "Town Destroyer"

June 12, 2011

In 1778 the British send 200 of Colonel John Butler's Rangers into the Wyoming Valley to evict 6,000 illegal immigrants who were squatting on "Indian lands". They had with them 300 of their First Nation allies mostly members of the Three Fires Confederacy. The Wyoming valley was situated in the middle of the Seneca's best hunting grounds and land never ceded by them.

Most of the forts the illegals had built were quickly abandoned and the inhabitants fled. Fort Forty was the lone exception. When the warriors feigned a withdrawal the colonials foolishly poured out of their fort and into an ambush. This resulted in the killing of 227 of them.

The Revolutionary government turned to propaganda releasing a series of outlandish stories of the "massacre". One such story read that it was a "mere marauding, a cruel and murderous invasion of a peaceful settlement . . . the inhabitants, men women and children were indiscriminately butchered by the 1,100 men, 900 of them being their Indian allies". In truth there were only 500 men, 300 of them being their First Nation allies. And according to an exhaustive study done by Egerton Ryerson only rebel soldiers were killed and the misinformation put out by the Congress Party was totally exaggerated and highly inflammatory.

Colonial propaganda was designed to inflame hatred among the populace toward the British's First Nation allies. However, it had the effect of inflaming hatred toward all First Nation's people due to the decades of violence along the frontier over land. The frontiersmen were convinced they had the right to push ever westward while harboring in their hearts the axiom "the only good Indian is a dead Indian".

General Washington bought into his own government's propaganda releases. In 1779 he decided to act. The Six Nation Iroquois League was divided on where their loyalties lay. Only the Oneida and Onondaga backed the rebel cause and even their loyalties were split. Washington charged General John Sullivan with a war of extermination against the Iroquois. Sullivan headed into Iroquois territory with an army of 6,500 men. His war of extermination was a failure but he did destroy forty Seneca and Cayuga towns along with burning all their crops. Although it is true that atrocities were committed by both sides those committed by the rebels were mostly forgotten. During this campaign the Iroquois dead were scalped and in one instance one was skinned from the waist down to make a pair of leggings!

The famished Iroquois fled to Niagara where they basically sat out the rest of the war. With their crops destroyed the British supplied them with the necessities putting a tremendous strain on their war effort. This expedition earned George Washington the infamous nickname of "Town Destroyer". Now not only was any hope gone of assistance from the Shawnee but also the Iroquois.

Meanwhile, in Illinois country George Rogers Clark was determined to retake Fort Sackville at Vincennes. He had captured it the year before only to lose it to Colonel Hamilton who had marched immediately from Detroit. He left Kaskaskia on February 5th marching his 170 militiamen across flooded plains and waist deep, freezing water. When he arrived at Vincennes he used the old dodge of marching his men across a small patch of tableland visible to the fort. He repeatedly marched them across this plateau giving the enemy the impression that he had many more men than he actually had. The history books claim that this had such an alarming affect on the First Nations at the fort that they were "scared off" by the ruse and the fort fell immediately.

It is true that the British were abandoned by their First Nation allies. They were members of the Three Fires Confederacy. It is not true that they were "scared off". Of the 170 militiamen with Clark some were Frenchmen from New Orleans. The French, like some of the First Nations, were also split in their allegiances. Captain Alexander McKee wrote to Captain R.B. Lernoult quite worried about news he had received regarding Three Fires support. In the letter he wrote that the Ottawa and Chippewa had sent a belt of peace to other surrounding nations saying they had been deceived by the British and the Six Nations into taking up the hatchet against the rebels. If they remained with the hatchet in their hands they would be forced to use it against their brothers the French. They reported seeing them coming with Clark and his Virginians and therefore withdrew as they still had great affection for the French. Old loyalties die hard. They were determined now to lay down the hatchet and remain quiet thus leaving the whites to fight among themselves. They were advising their brothers the Shawnee to do the same and that the tribes of the Wabash were also of like mind. This was not good news for the British.

The withdrawal of support from the Three Fires Confederacy and the sidelining of the Six Nations Iroquois that year left the British with only support from the Miami, Shawnee and some of the Delaware. There would be more atrocities to follow but still it would be another three years before the British would see any Three Fires' support.

Next Week: Massacre at Gnadenhutten

Massacre at Gnadenhutten

June 18, 2011

Hatred toward First Nations people by the rebels continued to be the norm among the general populace. Most, especially frontiersmen, failed to distinguish between their First Nation allies, their First Nation enemies and the First Nation communities that were neutral and wanting only to sit out the war in peace.

In the spring of 1782 the Moravian Delaware were living near their town of Gnadenhutten on the Muskingum River. They had been long converted to Christianity by the Moravian missionaries and had taken up western societies' ways. They were farmers. They wore European dress and had their hair cropped in European style. They lived in houses rather than lodges. They worshipped in a Christian church on Sundays. Their community functioned under the auspices of their Moravian mentors.

The Muskingum had become a dangerous war zone. They realized the danger was particularly heightened for them being "Indians". They had determined to abandon their farms and move the whole community further west to seek safe haven among the Wyandotte of Sandusky as many of their Delaware brothers who were not Christian had done already.

Before they could leave they were approached by Colonel David Williamson and 160 of his Colonial Militia. They claimed to be on a peaceful mission to provide protection and to remove them to Fort Pitt where they could sit out the war in peace. The leaders of the Gnadenhutten community encouraged their farmers to come in from the fields around Salem and take advantage of the colonel's good offer. When they arrived all were relieved of their guns and knives but told they would be returned at Fort Pitt.

As soon as they were defenseless they were all arrested and charged with being "murders, enemies and thieves" because they had in their possession dishes, tea cups, silverware and all the implements normally used by pioneers. Claims that the missionaries had purchased the items for them went unheeded. They were bound and imprisoned at Gnadenhutten where they spend the night in Christian prayer. The next day the militia massacred 29 men, 27 women and 34 children all bound and defenceless. Even pleas in excellent English on bended knees failed to save them. Two escaped by pretending to be dead and fled to Detroit where the stories of the rebels' atrocities were told.

The Virginians decided to continue the massacre at Gnadenhutten with a campaign of genocide. The plan was to take the Wyandotte and their allies at Sandusky by surprise and annihilate all of the inhabitants. They gathered a force of 478 men at Mingo Bottoms on the west side of the Ohio River. General Irvine, who had abhorred Williamson's actions at Gnadenhutten, deferred command of the expeditionary force to Colonel William Crawford.

The force left Mingo Bottoms on May 25th avoiding the main trail by making a series of forced marches through the wilderness. On the third day they observed two First Nation scouts and chased them off. These were the only warriors they saw on their 10 day march. Just before they crossed the Little Sandusky River they came unwittingly close to the Delaware chief Wingenud's camp.

Finally Crawford arrived at the Wyandotte's main village near the mouth of the Sandusky River. He assumed his covert operation had been a success and they had arrived at their objective undetected. But he was dead wrong. His Virginia Militia had been closely shadowed by First Nation scouts and reports of their progress had been forwarded to the chiefs.

War belts were sent out to neighboring Delaware, Shawnee and other Wyandotte towns and their warriors had gathered at the Half King Pomoacan's town. Alexander McKee was also on his way with 140 Shawnee warriors.

An urgent call for help had been sent to the British commandant Major Arent S. De Peyster at Detroit. He responded by sending Captain William Caldwell with 70 of his rangers. One hundred and fifty Detroit Wyandotte joined Caldwell along with 44 "lake Indians". Caldwell complained to De Peyster "The lake Indians were very tardy but they did have 44 of them in action".

These "lake Indians" were Chippewa warriors from Aamjiwnaang at the foot of Lake Huron. The Aamjiwnaang Chippewa were members of the Three Fires Confederacy and were at Vincennes when they withdrew support from the British in 1779. The fact that they only raised 44 warriors attests to the lack of their war chiefs' support. They were probably young men incensed by the stories of Gnadenhutten and acting on their own.

Crawford was dumbfounded when he arrived at the Wyandotte village and found it deserted. He and his officers held council and decided to move up river hoping to still take the Wyandotte by surprise. They didn't get far when they were met by the warriors from Pomoacan's town. They were held in check until McKee and Caldwell arrived. The battle lasted from June 4th to the 6th and resulted in a complete First Nation's victory. The rebel's expedition to annihilate the Wyandotte ended in disaster for the Virginians. It cost them 250 dead or wounded. Caldwell's Rangers suffered two killed and two wounded while the First Nations had four killed and eight wounded.

Colonel Williamson was able to lead the rebel survivors back to safety but Colonel Crawford was captured along with some of the perpetrators of the Gnadenhutten massacre. They were taken to one of the Delaware towns where they were tried and sentenced to death. Their punishment for Gnadenhutten atrocities was not an easy one.

NEXT WEEK: The Treaty of Paris

The Treaty of Paris

June 26, 2011

The massacre at Gnadenhutten seethed just below the First Nations' psyche. The Three Fires Confederacy finally re-entered the war later in 1782. British Captain Alexander McKee raised a party of 300 Lake Indians, Shawnee and Wyandotte from Detroit for an expedition into Kentucky. They left Detroit in August and after a brief and unsuccessful raid on Bryant's Station retreated to a hill at the Blue Licks on the middle fork of the Licking River.

They were being pursued by 200 militia led by Colonels Todd, Trigg and Boone as well as Majors Harlin and McGeary. The warriors chose the high ground at Blue Licks to lay an ambush. The ambush proved successful.

A short but fierce battle was fought and the rebel force was totally defeated. Casualties included 140 dead or wounded including most of their commanders. The warriors count was 10 dead and 14 wounded. Captured munitions and supplies only included 100 rifles as most were thrown in a deep part of the river during the rebel's pell-mell retreat back to their station. Colonel Boone was the same Daniel Boone that as a young man took part in another headlong, panic-stricken retreat at Braddock's rout. The Kentucky militia's reckless pursuit even cost Boone's son Israel his life.

The Revolutionary War ended the following year with the Americans emerging as the victors. The Treaty of Paris was signed between them and the British totally ignoring their First Nation allies. Boundaries were drawn that are still in effect today. The British were only too willing to give up territories that were not theirs and the Americans were only too willing to accept them. The Revolutionary War was officially over but the battle for "Indian Lands" was just beginning.

The Iroquois complained bitterly. Captain Aron, a principal chief, delivered a speech to Brigadier General Alan McLean at a General Council held at Niagara. In it he said "they never could believe that our King could pretend to cede to America what was not his own to give, or that the Americans would accept from him what he had no right to grant." Captain Aron rightly pointed out that the boundary between the First Nations and the colonies had been settled by the Treaty of Fort Stanwix (Rome, New York) in 1768 signed by Sir William Johnson. The boundary line ran from the head of Canada Creek near Fort Stanwix to the Ohio and this boundary had never been in dispute. He also reminded them "that the Indians were a free People subject to no power upon earth- That they were faithful allies of the King of England, but not his subjects, that he had no right whatever to grant away to the States of America, their right or properties without a manifest breach of all Justice and Equity".

McLean wrote in his report to General Frederick Haldimand Governor of Quebec, "I do from my soul pity these People" for "the miserable situation in which we have left these unfortunate People".

American Indian Policy was harsher than anything the First Nations had experienced before. They saw that the sale of land in their newly acquired territory could provide the necessary revenue required by the new federal government. So they took the position that the British had ceded all their lands east of the Mississippi and south of the Great Lakes to them. And because the First Nations had fought as allies of the British and the British lost the war their lands would be forfeited as well. This would include Oneida and Tuscarora lands even though they were American allies!

At the 1784 Treaty of Fort Stanwix commissioners from the new nation told the Six Nations Iroquois that they were now masters of all "Indian lands" and could do with them as they wished. They demanded large cessions of Iroquois lands. The Iroquois delegates were in no position to resist. They were still divided by the late war and they were abandoned by the British so they acquiesced. They ceded their territory in western New York, Pennsylvania as well as all of their territory west of Pennsylvania although they were not authorized to do so. When they returned to their homes their leaders were livid. They refused to ratify the treaty but the Americans carried on as if it were valid.

At the treaty of Fort MacIntosh in 1785 the Americans announced their policy of force to the Wyandotte, Delaware, Ojibwa and Ottawa. They dictated the terms for large cessions of land. The Shawnee refused to make peace and the chiefs at Fort MacIntosh returned home to prepare for war.

The Treaty of Paris made no consideration of First Nations and the new American Indian policy forced the British to provide for their Iroquois allies. To this end they purchased from the Mississauga two tracts of land for them to settle on in Canada. One tract of land contained 675,000 acres along the whole of the Grand River six miles deep on both sides. The followers of Chief Joseph Brant settled here while the followers of Mohawk Chief John Deserontyon settled on another large tract in the Bay of Quinte area. The other First Nations of Ohio and the newly designated Northwest Territories were prepared to fight on determined to hold on to their territories.

NEXT WEEK: Little Turtle's War

The Indian War of 1790-95

Little Turtle's War

July 9, 2011

United States' Indian policy grew out of the idea that because First Nations fought on the side of the British during the Revolutionary War they lost the right of ownership to their lands when Britain ceded all territory east of the Mississippi. First Nations were told that the United States now owned their territories and they could expel them if they wished to do so. This right of land entitlement by reason of conquest stemmed from their victory over the British and the hatred of "Indians" which had been seething for decades. They needed First Nation's lands northwest of the Ohio River to sell to settlers in order to raise much-needed revenue. But the impoverished new nation could not back up their new policy. So they took a different tact.

In March of 1785 Henry Knox was appointed Secretary of War and he began to institute a new policy. He proposed to Congress that there were two solutions in dealing with the First Nations. The first was to raise an army sufficient to extirpate them.

However, he reported to Washington and Congress that they didn't have the money to fund such a project. The estimated population of the First Nations east of the Mississippi and south of the Great Lakes was 76,000. The Miami War Chief Little Turtle's new "Confederation of Tribes" was quickly gaining numbers and strength and they were determined to stop American advancement at the Ohio. To try to beat them into submission not only seemed infeasible but immoral. He argued it was unethical for one people to gain by doing harm to other people and this could only harm America's reputation internationally.

The second solution, which he favored, was to return to the pre-revolutionary policy of purchasing First Nation Lands through the cession treaty process. In order to sell this idea to Washington and Congress he pointed out that the First Nations tenaciously held on to their territories and normally would not part with them for any reason. This was because being hunting societies the game on their lands supported their population. But, as proven in the past, time and again, when too many settlers moved into their territories game became scarce. Because the land was overrun by whites and ruined as a hunting territory they would always consider selling their territory and move their population further west.

In 1785 an Ordinance was passed by Congress dividing the territory north and west of the Ohio River into states to be governed as a territory. In 1787 this Ordinance was improved upon by passing the Northwest Ordinance appointing Major General Arthur St. Clair governor of the new territory. The new Ordinance covered a huge tract of land encompassing the present-day states of Ohio, Michigan, Indiana, Illinois and Wisconsin. Land would now be purchased and hostilities would cease unless "Indian" aggression were to provoke a "just war". America was determined to expand westward as its very existence depended upon it. Clearly there would be "just wars".

The first of these cession treaties was signed at Fort Harmar in 1789. This small cession did little to change the minds of the First Nations Confederacy. Hostilities continued provoking the first of the "just wars". In 1790 President Washington authorized St. Clair to raise troops to punish Little Turtle's Confederacy of Miami, Shawnee, Ottawa, Potawatomi and Ojibwa nations. He raised an army of 1,200 militia and 320 regulars and set out from Fort Washington, Cincinnati, under the command of Brigadier General Josiah Harmar.

Little Turtle retreated before Harmar's lumbering army. He led Harmar deep into enemy territory where he had set a trap in the Maumee River valley near present-day Fort Wayne, Indiana. Harmar's army was strung out in one long column. The trap was sprung and Little Turtle attacked Harmar's flank killing 183 and wounding 31. Panic set in. Harmar retreated in disarray. Little Turtle pursued intent on wiping out the American army. However, an eclipse of the moon the next night was interpreted as a bad omen so the pursuit was called off.

General Harmar claimed a victory but had to face a board of inquiry. The defeat was whitewashed but Harmar was replaced by General St. Clair who was a hero of the Revolutionary War. Little Turtle's stunning success bolstered the ranks of the Confederacy. In 1791 St. Clair raised another army of 1,400 militia and 600 regulars. He marched them out of Fort Washington and took up a position on high ground overlooking the Wabash River.

Little Turtle and his war council decided to take the Americans head on. Not their usual tactic it took St. Clair by surprise. Confederacy warriors scattered the Kentucky Militia. Other militiamen shooting wildly killed or wounded some of their own men. Bayonet charges were mowed down by fire from the surrounding woodlands. St. Clair tried to rally his troops but could not. With General Richard Butler, his commanding officer, wounded on the battlefield he ordered a retreat. It was no orderly one. Most flung their rifles aside and fled in a panic.

The American army was completely destroyed. Suffering nearly 1,000 casualties it would be the worst defeat ever suffered by the United States at the hands of the First Nations. Washington was livid. He angrily cursed St. Clair for being "worse than a murderer" and the defeat on the Wabash became known as St. Clair's Shame. On the other hand First Nations' hopes and confidence soared.

NEXT WEEK: Congress at the Glaize

Congress at the Glaize

July 24, 2011

St. Clair's Shame left the fledgling new nation in a precarious position. The First Nations had just destroyed the only army the United States had. President Washington put Major General Anthony Wayne in charge of building a new one and Congress appropriated one million dollars toward the project.

Wayne's nickname was "Mad Anthony" which he earned during the Revolution, but there was nothing "mad" about the man. He was methodical and extremely determined. Wayne set out to build the new army at Pittsburgh. It would be an army well-trained, disciplined and large enough to take care of the "Indian problem". And he would be sure to take enough time to ensure a successful campaign.

He began recruiting in June of 1792. His goal was an army of 5,120 officers, NCOs and privates whipped into the crack troops needed to defeat a formidable enemy. By the end of 1792 he had moved twenty-two miles south of Pittsburgh to Legionville where he wintered. In the spring of 1793 he moved to Hobson's Choice on the Ohio River between Cincinnati and Mill Creek. Finally, in October of 1793 he made his headquarters near Fort Hamilton.

Wayne received new recruits daily all the time relentlessly drilling them into the army he knew he needed. But all did not go well with the project. Desertion rates were extremely high. The First Nation's stunning successes on the Wabash and in the Maumee Valley had instilled terror in the hearts of ordinary pioneers and moving further toward "Indian Country" only heightened their fear. Many new recruits would desert at the first sign of trouble.

The problem had become so chronic that Wayne posted a reward for the capture and return of any deserter. After a court-martial the guilty would be severely punished usually by 100 lashes or sometimes even executed. An entry in the Orderly Book

Mss. dated August 9, 1792 reads, "Deserters have become very prevalent among our troops, at this place, particularly upon the least appearance, or rather apprehension of danger, that some men (for they are unworthy of the name of soldiers), have lost every sense of honor and duty as to desert their post as sentries, by which treacherous, base and cowardly conduct, the lives and safety of their brave companions and worthy citizens were committed to savage fury."

Meanwhile, warriors from other First Nations joined the confederacy Little Turtle and Blue Jacket had forged. In October 1792 the Shawnee hosted a congress held at the Glaize, where the Auglaize River flows into the Maumee. Delegates from the nations whose territories were being defended attended. These were Wyandotte from Sandusky, Delaware, Shawnee, Mingo, Miami, Munsee, Cherokee and Nanticoke. Also attending were other First Nations from further away but all offering support for the war effort. Some of these were Fox and Sauk from the upper Mississippi, Six Nations and Mohican from New York, Iroquois from the St. Lawrence and Wyandotte from Detroit. There were also many warriors from the Three Fires Confederacy. They were Ottawa, Potawatomi and Chippewa from Detroit as well as Chippewa from Aamjiwnaang and Saginaw. There were even some Chippewa from Michilimackinac. This was the largest First Nation congress every brought together by First Nations alone.

Even though the United States had suffered two humiliating defeats at the hands of the First Nation Confederacy they still had little respect. Henry Knox characterized them as Miami and Wabash Indians together with "a banditti, formed of Shawanese and outcast Cherokees". However, because their military was in shambles and they had a deficiency in revenue peaceful negotiations were preferable to another war.

Washington at first sent delegates to the Glaize from their First Nation allies with offers to negotiate. There were still some groups of individual First Nations friendly with the Americans despite the treatment received. The delegation of "U.S. Indians" arrived and the celebrated Seneca orator Red Jacket spoke for the U.S.

Red Jacket rose to speak to the nearly one thousand conferees. He spoke on two strings of wampum bringing the American message that even though they defeated the mighty British and now all Indian territories belonged to them by right of conquest they may be willing to compromise. They offered to consider accepting the Muskingum River as the new boundary between the United States and "Indian Country". But the Confederacy saw no need to compromise. After all they had defeated American armies not once but twice in the last two years. They insisted the boundary agreed to in the Treaty of Fort Stanwix in 1768 be adhered to. That boundary was the Ohio and they would accept no other.

The Shawnee chief Painted Pole reminded Red Jacket that while his Seneca group was in Philadelphia cozying up to the Americans the Confederacy was busy defending their lands. Now he was at the Glaize doing the Americans dirty work. He accused Red Jacket of trying to divide the Confederacy and demanded that Red Jacket speak from his heart and not from his mouth. Painted Pole then took the wampum strings that Red Jacket had spoken on and threw them at the Seneca delegation's feet. Red Jacket was sent back to the Americans with the Confederacy's answer, "there would be no new boundary line".

There was a tell-tale sign at that conference that Red Jacket's task would be difficult if not impossible. In normal negotiations the civil chiefs would sit in the front with the War Chiefs and warriors behind them. In this arrangement it would be the much easier to deal with Civil Chiefs that would negotiate. But at the Glaize the War Chiefs sat in front of the Civil Chiefs meaning that Red Jacket would be dealing with the War Chiefs.

The British sat in the wings waiting for the new republic's experiment in democracy to fail and hoping at least for an "Indian boundary state" to be formed. The Spanish at New Orleans also sat by hoping for this new "Indian State" as it would serve as a buffer state preventing American expansion into Illinois country. The British even had observers at the Great Congress at the Glaize in the person of Indian Agent Alexander McKee and some of his men. Hendrick Aupaumut, a Mohican with Red Jacket's emissaries, accused McKee of unduly influencing the conference's outcome. But the Americans were not about to be deterred so easily.

NEXT WEEK: Peace Negotiations

Peace Negotiations

August 2, 2011

The year following Red Jacket's failed negotiations President Washington appointed three Commissioners to try to negotiate a peace with the First Nations Confederacy. Benjamin Lincoln, Timothy Pickering and Beverly Randolph left Philadelphia travelling north to Niagara. John Graves Simcoe, Lieutenant-Governor of Upper Canada, afforded them British hospitalities while they waited for word on a council with the First Nation chiefs. They hoped to meet with the Confederacy at Sandusky that spring.

The Americans thought the British would be useful as an intermediary, but the British's interests were really making sure the Confederacy didn't fall apart and long-term that an "Indian barrier state" would be formed. The United States also had ulterior motives. Although they would accept a peace as long as it was on their terms they would be just as happy with failure to use as an excuse for their "just war". Simcoe had assessed the situation correctly when he wrote in his correspondence "It appears to me that there is little probability of effecting a Peace and I am inclined to believe that the Commissioners do not expect it; that General Wayne does not expect it; and that the Mission of the Commissioners is in general contemplated by the People of the United States as necessary to adjust the ceremonial of the destruction and pre-determined extirpation of the Indian

Americans". While all this was going on Wayne advanced his army to Fort Washington.

Meanwhile Washington asked the Mohawk chief Joseph Brant to travel to the Miami River where the Confederacy was in council. He was to try to persuade the Chiefs to meet the Commissioners at Sandusky. He was partially successful in that they sent a delegation of fifty to Niagara to speak to the American Commissioners in front of Simcoe.

The delegation demanded the Commissioners inform them of General Wayne's movements and they also wanted to know if they were empowered to fix a permanent boundary line. The Commissioners must have answered satisfactorily because the delegation agreed that the Chiefs would meet them in council at Sandusky.

The Commissioners travelled with a British escort along the north shoreline of Lake Erie stopping just south of Detroit. Fort Detroit had yet to be handed over to the Americans and Simcoe refused to let them enter the fort so they were put up at the house of Mathew Elliott an Irishman who had been trading with the Shawnee for many years. While they were there another delegation arrived from the Miami. The Chiefs had felt that the first delegation had not spoken forcefully enough regarding their demands that the original boundary line of the Ohio River was to be adhered to and that any white squatters be removed to south of the Ohio. They also wanted to know why, if the United States was interested in peace, Wayne's army was advancing? No answer was forthcoming. However, the Commissioners did inform this delegation that they were only authorized to offer compensation for lands and it was the United States' position that those lands were already treated away. Besides, the United States felt that it would be impossible to remove any white settlers as they had been established there for many years. The delegation returned to the Miami with the Commissioners' response which was totally unacceptable to the Chiefs.

A council was held at the foot of the Maumee rapids where Alexander McKee kept a storehouse. Both McKee and Elliott were there as British Indian Agents. Joseph Brant suggested they compromise by offering the Muskingum River as a new boundary line. The Chiefs were in no mood to compromise having just defeated the American Army not once but twice. Brant accused McKee of unduly influencing the Chiefs' position. The Delaware chief Buckongahlas indicated that Brant was right. With the Confederacy unwilling to compromise and the United States, backed by Wayne's army, standing firm things appeared to be at an impasse. The Chiefs crafted a new proposal. A third delegation carried it to the Commissioners on the Detroit.

The First Nations said money was of no value to them. Besides, they could never consider selling lands that provided sustenance to their families. Since there could be no peace as long as white squatters were living on their lands they proposed the following solution:

> We know that these settlers are poor, or they would never have ventured to live in a country that has been in continual trouble ever since they crossed the Ohio. Divide, therefore, this large sum which you have offered us, among these people; give to each, also, a proportion of what you say you would give to us annually, over and above this very large sum of money, and we are persuaded they would most readily accept of it, in lieu of that lands you sold them. If you add, also, the great sums you must expend in raising and paying armies with a view to force us to yield you our country, you will certainly have more than sufficient for the purposes of repaying these settlers for all their labours and their improvements. You have talked to us about concessions. It appears strange that you expect any from us, who have only been defending our just rights against your invasions. We want peace. Restore to us our country and we shall be enemies no longer.

The delegation also reminded the Commissioners that their only demand was "the peaceable possession of a small part of our once great country". They could retreat no further since the country behind them could only provide enough food for its inhabitants so they were forced to stay and leave their bones in the small space to which they were now confined.

The Commissioners packed up their bags and left. There would be no council at Sandusky. They returned to Philadelphia and reported to the Secretary of War, "The Indians refuse to make peace." Wayne's invasion would be "just and lawful."

Meanwhile, at the Maumee Rapids a War Feast was given and the War Song sung encouraging all the young warriors to come in defense of their country. "The whole white race is a monster who is always hungry and what he eats is land" declared Shawnee warrior Chicksika. Their English father would assist them and they pointed to Alexander McKee.

NEXT WEEK: The Battle of Fallen Timbers

The Battle of Fallen Timbers

August 15, 2011

While the United States was busy trying to relieve the First Nations of their lands peacefully and on their terms General Wayne was busy preparing for their "just" war. He moved steadily west establishing Forts Washington and Recovery along the way. They would serve his supply lines during the upcoming battles. In October 1793 he reached the southwest branch of the Great Miami River where he camped for the winter. The Confederacy made two successful raids on his supply lines that autumn then returned to the Glaize for the winter.

Meanwhile, Britain had gone to war with France in Europe. Sir Guy Carleton, Canada's new Governor, was sure that the

United States would side with France and this would mean war in North America. He met with a delegation from the Confederacy in Quebec and reiterated his feelings on a coming war with the Americans. He informed them that the boundary line "must be drawn by the Warriors." He then ordered Fort Miami to be re-established on the Maumee River just north of the Glaize as well as strengthening fortifications on a small island at its mouth.

Lieutenant-Governor Simcoe visited the Glaize in April 1794 and informed the council that Britain would soon be at war with the United States and they would reassert jurisdiction over lands south of the Great Lakes and tear up the Treaty of Fort Harmer. Several years before the Americans talked some minor chiefs and other warriors into signing that treaty turning all lands formerly held by the British over to the United States of America for a paltry $ 9,000 and no mention of an "Indian" border. Meanwhile, Indian Agents McKee and Elliott encouraged their Shawnee relatives with the likelihood of British military support. All of this was very encouraging indeed.

General Wayne had his army of well-trained and disciplined men. They numbered 3,500 including 1,500 Kentucky Militiamen. This army was not the lax group of regulars and volunteers the Confederacy had defeated at the Wabash and Maumee Valley. Neither was the Confederacy the same fighting force of three years earlier. Many warriors had left to return to their homelands in order to provide for their families.

The American Army left their winter quarters and moved toward the Glaize. Little Turtle saw the handwriting on the wall. He advised the council "do not engage 'the General that never sleeps' but instead sue for peace", but the young men would have none of it. When he could not convince them he abdicated his leadership to the Shawnee War Chief Blue Jacket and retired.

Blue Jacket moved to cut Wayne's supply lines. He had a force of 1,200 warriors when he neared Fort Recovery which was poorly defended. Half of his warriors were from the Three Fires Confederacy and they wanted to attack and destroy the fort for psychological reasons in order to give another defeat for Wayne to think about. But Blue Jacket was against this plan. The day was wasted taking pot shots at the fort and they never cut off Wayne's supply line. Blue Jacket's warriors returned to the Glaize deeply divided.

In the first week of August an American deserter arrived at the Glaize and informed Blue Jacket of Wayne's near arrival. He had moved more quickly than anticipated and had caught them off guard. Many the Confederacy's 1,500 warriors were off hunting to supplement their food supply. Others were at Fort Miami picking up supplies of food and ammunition. Blue Jacket ordered the villages at the Glaize to evacuate. Approximately 500 warriors gathered up-river to make a defense at a place known as Fallen Timbers. It was an area where a recent tornado had knocked down a great number of trees.

Out-numbered six to one the warriors fought bravely. They established a line of defence and when they were overcome by the disciplined advance of American bayonets they retreated only to establish a new line. This happened over and over until they reached the closed gates of Fort Miami where they received the shock of their lives!

The fort was commanded by Major William Campbell and he only had a small garrison under his charge. He was duty bound to protect the fort if it was attacked but not to assist the King's allies. If he opened the gates to the pleading warriors he risked not only his own life but the lives of the soldiers under him. Not only that but there would be a good chance of plunging England into a war with the United States, a war they could not afford being fully extended in Europe. He made his decision quickly. He peered over the stockade at the frantic warriors and said "I cannot let you in! You are painted too much my children!" They had no choice but to flee down the Maumee in full retreat.

It was not the defeat at Fallen Timbers that broke the confederacy. They could always regroup to fight another day. It was instead the utter betrayal of their father the British they did not know how to get over. It also established the United States as a bona fide nation because it defeated Britain's most important ally along the frontier. One chronicler wrote that it was the most important battle ever won by the United States because it was the war with the First Nations' Confederacy that would make or break the fledging nation. It also showed just how trustworthy the British could be as an ally. Years later Blue Jacket would complain "It was then that we saw that the British dealt treacherously with us".

NEXT WEEK: A Peace Treaty with Washington

A Peace Treaty with Washington

November 6, 2011

First let me apologize again for being MIA. The month of August was extremely busy for me. I did a series of literary arts workshops that took most of my time up. In the month of September I was busy putting the finishing touches on my new novel *1300 Moons.* It is now in the production phase and will be available in the next couple of weeks, but more on this later. To make things even more hectic I had to deal with three different medical emergencies in the family. Things have settled now and I can get back to posting to this blog regularly. Thanks for all your patience.

Well it's now "later". *1300 Moons* has been released and last Friday I had a successful launch. I'm also involved in a 200th anniversary War of 1812 project as a consultant. It's a graphic novel aimed at the education sector. It will also be on-line and available on DVD with hypertext links to video of various 'experts' of which I am one. The videographers are coming in a couple of weeks to Aamjiwnaang for taping. So it looks like my hectic life is to continue! However, I am determined to do a couple of posts a week if I can.

We left off with the First Nations Confederacy under Blue Jacket being defeated by General Anthony Wayne at Fallen Timbers in 1794. The following year chiefs of the various First Nations began arriving at Greenville, Ohio to negotiate a peace treaty with the United States. That summer over 1,000 First Nations people gathered around Fort Greenville. These included chiefs from the Wyandotte, Delaware, Shawnee, Ottawa, Chippewa, Potawatomi, Miami and Kickapoo.

This treaty was primarily a peace treaty between George Washington, President of the United States, and chiefs representing the above mentioned First Nations. My great-great grandfather signed as one of the seven War Chiefs of the Chippewa. But not all former combatants were represented. Among those missing and vehemently against the peace were Shawnee chiefs Tecumseh and Kekewepellethe. Rather than deal the Americans Tecumseh with his followers migrated first to Deer Creek, then to the upper Miami valley and then to eastern Indiana.

Land cessions were also included as part of the terms for peace. Article 3 dealt with a new boundary line 'between the lands of the United States and the lands of the said Indian tribes'. This effectively ceded all of eastern and southern present day Ohio and set the stage for future land grabs. Included in the United States' 'relinquishment' of all 'Indian lands northward of the River Ohio, eastward of the Mississippi, and westward and southward of the Great Lakes' were cessations of sixteen other tracks of land, several miles square, located either were U.S. forts were already established or where they wished to build towns. However, the term "lands of the said Indian tribes" had vastly different meanings to the two sides.

The First Nations wanted their own sovereign country but the United States dispelled any thought along these lines with Article 5. It defined relinquishment as meaning "The Indian tribes that have a right to those lands, are to enjoy them quietly . . . but when those tribes . . . shall be disposed to sell their lands . . . they are to be sold only to the United States". In other words we had no sovereign country but only the right to use lands already belonging to the United States of America!

The Chippewa and Ottawa also ceded from their territories a strip of land along the Detroit River from the River Raisin to Lake St. Clair. It was six miles deep and included Fort Detroit. The Chippewa also ceded a strip of land on the north shore of the Straits of Mackinaw including the two islands of Mackinaw and De Bois Blanc. The stage was now set for further U.S. expansion.

As a footnote the metaphorical language changed at the conclusion of the peace agreement. First Nations had always used familial terms when referring to First Nations and European relationships. First the French and then the British were always referred to as father. The Americans, since their beginning, were referred to as brother. This continued through the negotiations at Greenville until its conclusion at which time the reference to Americans in the person of Washington changed from bother to father.

Unfortunately because of a clash of cultures this patriarchal term held different meanings to each side. To the First Nations a father was both a friend and a provider. The Wyandotte chief Tarhe spoke for all the assembly because the Wyandotte were considered an uncle to both the Delaware and Shawnee and he was the keeper of the council fire at Brownstown. He told his 'brother Indians' that they now acknowledge 'the fifteen United States of America to now be our father and . . . you must call them brothers no more'. As children they were to be 'obedient to our father; ever listen to him when he speaks to you, and follow his advice'. The Potawatomi chief New Corn spoke after Tarhe and addressed the Americans as both father and friend. Other chiefs spoke commending themselves to their father's protection and asked him for aid. The Chippewa chief Massas admonished the assembly to 'rejoice in acquiring a new, and so good, a father'.

Tarhe eloquently defined a father for the American emissaries: 'Take care of your little ones and do not suffer them to be imposed upon. Don't show favor to one to the injury of any. An impartial father equally regards all his children, as well as those who are ordinary as those who may be more handsome; therefore, should any of your children come to you crying and in distress, have pity on them, and relieve their wants.'

Of course American arrogance stopped up their ears and they could not hear Tarhe's sage advice. Until this present day they continue to live out their understanding of the term father as a stern patriarch and one either to be obeyed or disciplined.

NEXT WEEK: A Flurry of Land Cessions

American Greed for Land

A Flurry of Land Cessions

November 10, 2011

The American 'Northwest Territories' began filling up with white settlers. The new republic clamoured for more and more land. Land speculators were greedy for profits. Legislation was being influenced by desires for statehood and statehood was dependent upon population requirements. Increases of American settlers degraded traditional hunting grounds thereby impoverishing its First Nation inhabitants. This poverty set off a spiral of more land cessions and more poverty.

Between 1802 and 1805 the new Governor of Indiana Territory concluded no less than seven treaties by which the Delaware, Miami, Potawatomi, Kickapoo, Shawnee, Sac and Fox ceded their rights to the southern part of Indiana, portions of Wisconsin and Missouri as well as most of Illinois. Huge tracts of land were dealt away for the paltry price of two cents or less per acre.

Not only was the land undervalued but it was secured by entirely fraudulent means. The Americans used such tactics as bribery, the supplying of huge amounts of liquor or the threat to withhold payments of annuities already agreed to. Treaties were negotiated with any First Nation individual that was willing to sign with no regard for his authority to speak for his people.

Thomas Jefferson was president of the United States at this time. He was a conflicted man as can be found in his writings on human rights versus his record of slavery. He admired the quality of character of the American Indian and of their culture but considered them inferior. He was of the belief that they could, however, be rehabilitated and "civilized". However, during the revolution he relished the thought of displacing the Cherokee and taking their lands and during the Indian War for the Ohio he advocated the destruction of the Shawnee. During Harrison's treaty negotiating spree Jefferson had written to him in private advising him to encourage the Indians to run up debts at the trading posts and then compel them to settle the debt by selling tribal lands. Although Jefferson tried to give the impression that America held no place for the Indian as Indian and he publicly advocated assimilation one wonders if privately he saw an America with no Indians at all.

There was a population tsunami that was happening and it continuously overwhelmed First Nation territories. In 1796 Ohio had a white population of 5,000. By 1810 it had jumped to more than 230,000. This overpowering agrarian culture would only make its way ever westward transforming pristine forests to stark farmlands. It appeared the Shawnee warrior Chiksika was right, our land was being eaten up by a windigo!

The American success in their revolution put a tremendous strain for land resources on what was left of British North America. Approximately 4% of the population of the thirteen colonies were British Empire Loyalists and left America for other British territories. Some 5,000, which was the smallest of these groups of loyalists, came to Upper Canada. Governor Haldimand also had to deal with a large influx of Iroquois refugees that had been loyal to the Crown during the revolution.

During that war the Iroquois Six Nation Confederacy's loyalties split the league. Many of the Oneida and Tuscarora backed the rebels while the Mohawk, Onondaga, Cayuga and Seneca backed the British. Chief John Deserontyon and 200 Mohawks sought refuge near Lachine in Lower Canada while Chief Joseph

Brant crossed over at Niagara. The population of these Iroquois and their allies fluctuated between 2,000 and 5,000.

In the Treaty of Paris, which ended the war, no mention was made of Iroquois lands in upstate New York. This angered the Iroquois who were now refugees from their homeland. Haldimand fearing they might take their frustrations out on the loyalist refugees ordered the Indian Agents to be extra generous in handing out supplies and presents to them.

In 1783 the Mississauga ceded two large tracts of land to the British. One ran from the Trent River to the Gananoque River. The other ran from the Gananoque to the Toniato River or present day Jones Creek near Brockville. Each tract was "as far as a man could walk in one day" deep. Out of these the British later surveyed a township called Tyendiaga on the Bay of Quinte for Chief Deserontyon and his followers.

Chief Joseph Brant preferred the Grand River area of southwestern Ontario. The Mississauga also ceded to the British the whole of the Grand River valley from its headwaters to its mouth to a depth of six miles on each side. This tract was later transferred to Brant and his followers. At the same time the Mississauga ceded a large tract at the western end of Lake Ontario including the Niagara peninsula as well as a tract of land to the west of the Grand River as far as Catfish Creek. The aggregate acreage of these land surrenders came to over 1,000,000 hectares and the total cost to the British a mere 1,180 pounds Sterling worth of trade goods.

In 1790 the First Nations commonly known as the 'Detroit Indians', the Chippewa, Ottawa, Potawatomi and Wyandotte also ceded a large tract of land from the foot of the St. Clair River to Lake Erie, east along the north shore to Catfish Creek. Reserved out of this huge tract were two small tracts on the Detroit River for the Wyandotte. The balance included all the land between the Thames River and Lake Erie and was ceded for a mere 1,200 pounds Sterling.

The British also expected an influx of First Nation refugees who were displaced from Ohio by the Treaty of Greenville. In

1796 the Chippewa ceded a tract of land on the St. Clair River to be used by the Chippewa as well as any American Indians. This tract is present day Sombra Township. At the same time they ceded a tract of land over 3,000 hectares at the forks on the Thames River and called it London. The British said they needed it to establish a new capital of Upper Canada replacing York as it would be easier to defend. Both tracts of land were not used for the purposes stated but nevertheless the Chippewa still lost the land.

NEXT WEEK: Tecumseh's Vision

Tecumseh's Vision

September 16, 2012

On November 17, 1807 another cession treaty was signed between the United States and several First Nations at Detroit. It involved a huge tract of land mostly contained in the Territory of Michigan but dipping slightly into Ohio Territory. The Treaty of Detroit was negotiated by the Governor of Michigan Territory, William Hull, and the chiefs of the Chippewa, Ottawa, Potawatomi and Wyandotte nations including Little Thunder and Walk In the Water.

The tract of land ceded included all of the south-eastern part of the lower peninsula of Michigan. Reserved out of this tract were some eight reservations scattered between the Miami River of Ohio to just north of the Huron River above Detroit. It also included six tracts of one square mile each to be located at places chosen by the "said Indians . . . and subject to the approbation of the President of the United States".

Although Hull managed to acquire a huge chunk of Michigan Territory he wasn't very visionary. The reservations laid out which, by the way coincided with First Nation villages, prevented a straight road being built between the American communities of Ohio and Detroit. So he was back the following year to negotiate right-of-ways through the reservations that blocked the soon to be built road. He managed to negotiate the Treaty of Brownstown on November 25, 1808. This treaty also included the signature of Black Hoof for the Shawnee.

However, William Hull was not as successful in dealing with the Chippewa of Saginaw. The chiefs from there had been attending conferences at Greenville with chiefs from the other nations and they formed the consensus that there should be no more land cessions. When he approached the Saginaw chiefs with a proposal they flatly refused and when he tried to insist they insisted he leave and never return.

The First Nations were becoming obstinate aggravated by the Americans gobbling up their hunting territories. Not only were they feeling cheated and abused they were angry that annuities promised from the 1805 treaty were over two years late. Of course there were still some that had always been adamant that the original boundary negotiated in 1768 between the United States and "Indian Country" should be adhered to. The premier chief of this group was of course Tecumseh. His brother Tenskwatawa was a leading holy man and strongest ally.

Tenskwatawa as a young man had become a drunk but after just a few years received a life-altering vision from the Master of Life. He abandoned his wanton ways and was received among his nation as a master shaman. He was a good orator and made a striking figure with the eye patch which he had worn since an accident had caused the loss of his right eye in his childhood.

The Potawatomi War Chief and shaman Main Poc allied himself with Tecumseh and his brother Tenskwatawa. Both Main Poc, who was noted for his spiritual powers and Tenskwatawa who was also called The Prophet were holy men. In late 1807 Main Poc suggested that The Prophet move his followers to Potawatomi territory. The following spring Tenskwatawa settled about one hundred of them near the junction of the Wabash and Tippecanoe Rivers.

Both Tenskwatawa and Tecumseh began to grow in stature. Between 1808 and 1811 The Prophet's modest village grew to over one thousand followers and the American's were calling it Prophetstown. The Prophet's vision was one of a common lifestyle where all First Nations would reject the European ways and return to their traditional way of life. This applied especially to the abstinence of alcohol. To this end he would send out his disciples to preach his message. One such disciple was Trout who was recorded at Michilimackinac preaching a return to the Indian ways and teaching that the Americans, but not other whites, were the offspring of The Evil One.

Tecumseh's vision was not as spiritual as his brother's. He envisioned a pan Indian Confederacy from the Gulf of Mexico to Lake Superior as the only way to stop American expansion. He worked tirelessly toward this goal building a coalition of warriors from various First Nations using Prophetstown as his base. Most of his warriors were from nations other than the Shawnee as most of them followed Black Hoof and his policy of assimilation acceptance.

Since 1798 the Choctaw, Cherokee, Creek and Chickasaw nations had held councils to discuss a united effort to protect their lands. They held one in 1810 and Tecumseh knew about it. There was another to be held at Tuckabatchee on the Tallapoosa River the following year. Tecumseh planned on attending to sell his vision of a pan Indian confederacy. He headed south that summer well in advance of the scheduled conference at Tuckabatchee. Tecumseh wanted to visit chiefs throughout the south and the Choctaw were the first to receive him.

The Choctaw nation had three territories each with a principal chief. The first chief he visited was Moshulatubbee head chief of the northeast. Moshulatubbee listened to Tecumseh but showed no indication of his feelings on Tecumseh's message. Instead he sent runners throughout Choctaw territory calling them to a grand council at his village of Moshulaville. While the runners were out calling the chiefs to convene Tecumseh visited many surrounding towns spreading his message.

Tecumseh's final oratory was given at the grand council called by Moshulatubbee. Many attended including the principal chief of the southern territory Pushmataha. In fact all three principal chiefs attended the August grand council but it would be Pushmataha that would be Tecumseh's nemesis.

Tecumseh passionately laid out his vision. On the second day Pushmataha spoke just as passionately against it. All three chiefs were receiving U.S. pensions and Pushmataha had received five hundred dollars for supporting the ceding of Choctaw lands in 1805. In the end Pushmataha's message of peace and friendship with the United States won out. Tecumseh's trip to Choctaw country had failed but he remained resolved to carry on. Leaving the land of the Choctaw he crossed the Tombigbee River into the country of the Creek Nation.

Next Week: Supernatural Support for Tecumseh

Supernatural Support for Tecumseh

September 29, 2012

Tecumseh left the less than enthusiastic Choctaw with his Shawnee, Kickapoo and Winnebago delegation and crossed the Tombigbee River into Creek country. Here his message would find a much friendlier reception. The two nations were tied by intermarriage. Tecumseh even had relatives of his own living in Creek towns and villages.

Big Warrior, the leading civil chief of the Upper Creek nation, was attending a major conference at the Creek town of Tuckabatchee when Tecumseh arrived. There were delegates already there from the Choctaw, Chickasaw, Cherokee and Seminole nations. Many were already familiar with The Prophet's message of return to traditionalism having traveled north to Prophetstown to hear it. This along with a ready-made audience of various nations in a country so closely related to the Shawnee afforded Tecumseh the perfect forum to deliver his own message of a pan Indian confederacy.

Something else heralded Tecumseh's coming that September. A comet appeared in the night sky. It was understood to be a sign from the spirit world pointing to the greatness of Tecumseh. After all, Tecumseh's name meant Shooting Star.

There was also another delegation at the conference. It consisted of Americans led by the Indian agent Benjamin Hawkins. He was there to proposition the Creek with the government's intention to build another road through their territory. Big Warrior was no friend of Hawkins and the Creek were still seething about a federal road being imposed upon them six years earlier. Hopoithle Mico or Tame King, the leading chief from the Upper Creek town of Tallassee, had sent a message of protest to President Madison and received the reply that his protest was unreasonable. They cut the road anyway.

Now Hawkins was here regarding a second road. The Creek resisted. Negotiations went nowhere for three weeks until finally Hawkins laid out in no uncertain terms that he wasn't there to ask them for permission but to inform them that the cutting had already begun. He laid out the terms of payment and left.

Tecumseh let Hawkins make his presentation while remaining silent about his own mission to the Creek nation. He needed a good example of American arrogance and Hawkins provided it. Now it was his turn to address the council.

The delegation from the north mesmerized the conference first with their elaborate war dance followed by Tecumseh's charismatic oratory. Many eagerly received his vision. This vision of a warrior confederacy and the Prophet's vision of a total return to traditionalism gave rise to the Red Sticks. They were a warrior society that would go on to lead the most desperate First Nation rebellion the United States would ever see.

Tecumseh left Creek territory bolstered by his success. However, there was yet to be another even more dramatic supernatural sign of his stature and his power. Shortly after his departure a series of major earth tremors occurred. Labelled the New Madrid earthquakes they would be among the severest ever felt on the North American continent. The first arrived on the night of December 16, 1811. The epicenter was in Arkansas south of the town of New Madrid, Missouri. The town was destroyed. The vibrations made steeple bells ring out in Charleston, South Carolina. They lasted until February of 1812 and for a time the Mississippi reversed course and ran backwards!

The First Nations of the south-east were terrified. A legend grew up that Tecumseh had predicted the collapse of the middle world and its recreation. Word spread that Tecumseh had prophesied that when he returned to Detroit he would stomp his foot and make the earth tremble. These great events fed warrior societies like the Red Sticks and they took ownership of the visions of Tecumseh and his brother The Prophet.

Tecumseh crossed the Mississippi in December and was in Osage country when the tremors began. The Osage were not as anti-American as some of the south-eastern First Nations. Therefore, they were not so quick to ascribe American aggression as the root cause of the quakes. Instead they believed the cause was their general falling away from traditionalism and accepting American culture. It was the Prophet who would get credit for the proper interpretation of events.

Tecumseh moved on to spread his message among his own people the Missouri Shawnee as well as the Delaware but ran into the same roadblocks as he did with the Osage. When he returned to the Mississippi he headed north through Fox country to the territory of the Santee Dakota Sioux all the time sharing his vision of a pan Indian confederation to stop American aggression. He even hinted at military aid from the British. The Dakota sent red wampum to the Sauk and Winnebago indicating their approval of Tecumseh's message and their willingness to go to war.

Tecumseh's journey was coming to an end. He retraced his footsteps down the Mississippi then turned east heading for home. He traveled through Illinois territory also speaking at Kickapoo, Ojibwa, Potawatomi, and Ottawa villages. Some chiefs were unwilling to receive his vision but many others joined the Confederacy. All-in-all the sojourn to gain adherents was a success. However, what would confront him when he arrived home at Prophetstown in late January turned satisfaction at his success to feelings of utter despair.

NEXT WEEK: Disaster at Prophetstown

The War of 1812

Disaster at Prophetstown

October 9, 2012

Tecumseh arrived back at Prophetstown in late January 1812 but there was no warm welcome awaiting him. To his bitter amazement the Shawnee town at the junction of the Tippecanoe and Wabash Rivers lay in ruins. When told the details of the disaster he was furious. He had left specific orders with his brother not to engage the Big Knives but to appease them at all cost. He had told Tenskwatawa, the Prophet that the time would come for war, but not now. It was too early. It is reported that he was so enraged that he grabbed his brother by the hair, shook him and threatened to kill him.

The summer of 1811 was one of fear and apprehension all along the frontier. The summer of unrest was caused by a few young warriors loyal to Prophetstown but nevertheless hotheads acting on their own. They had been raiding settler's farms, stealing their horses and a few had been killed.

William Henry Harrison, the governor of Indiana, met with Tecumseh at Vincennes in July. Tecumseh tried to convince him that the confederacy he was building was not for war but for peace. He was not successful. They had met in council before and although they had respect for each other they disagreed strenuously. The year before their council almost ended violently.

Winamek, a Potawatomi chief loyal to the Big Knives suggested the warriors at Vincennes raise a large war party and attack Prophetstown but Black Hoof convinced him otherwise. Black Hoof and The Wolf two Shawnee chiefs loyal to the Americans attended several councils with settlers in Ohio convincing them that they and their three hundred warriors were peaceful. Black Hoof took this opportunity to set all the blame for all the troubles at the foot of Tecumseh and Tenskwatawa.

Meanwhile, in June some of Tecumseh's entourage were busy recruiting followers from the Wyandotte of Sandusky. They encountered some resistance so they handled it by preying on the Wyandotte's fear of witchcraft. They accused their opposition of it and three were burned alive as sorcerers including the old village chief Leather Lips. American officials called for conferences with their First Nation allies at Fort Wayne and Brownstown on the Detroit River. They came from eastern Michigan, Ohio and Indiana and all denounced the Shawnee brothers. The Shawnee delegation to Brownstown was led by George Bluejacket and Tachnedorus or Captain Logan the Mingo chief. Although they affirmed their loyalty to the Big Knives they took the opportunity to visit British Agents across the river at Amherstburg.

Harrison was convinced that all the turmoil on the frontier emanated from Prophetstown. There was more trouble perpetrated by the young hot head warriors. Three of these warriors believed to be Potawatomi had stolen horses on the White and Wabash Rivers terrorizing the settlers there. While Tecumseh was on his three thousand mile sojourn building the confederacy Harrison began to assemble a large army at Vincennes. He was determined to disperse the First Nations who had congregated at Prophetstown.

Harrison made his plans public telling Black Hoof to keep his Shawnee followers in Ohio so they would not be connected to the coming conflict. He also gave the same advice to the Miami and Eel River Wea but his words did not sit well with some of the Miami. Prophetstown was situated across the boundary in Miami territory and they did not appreciate having their sovereignty impinged upon. Word of the military buildup quickly traveled up the Wabash to Prophetstown.

Tenskwatawa hurriedly call a council to decide what to do. The decision was made to send a Kickapoo delegation to Vincennes. Probably led by Pamawatam the war chief of the Illinois River Kickapoo the delegation was not successful. They had tried to negotiate that a settlement of the troubles with the settlers be sorted out in the spring.

The news they returned with was not good. Harrison had assemble an army of one thousand soldiers and they were about to march up the Wabash. The only thing that would deter them was the return of stolen horses and for those who had committed murders along the frontier to be handed over for punishment. Harrison also demanded the dispersal of Prophetstown.

The Prophet had to decide whether to comply or fight. They were not in good shape for a major battle. They needed the little lead and powder they had to get them through the upcoming winter. They were outnumbered. The congregation at Prophetstown consisted of mostly Kickapoo and Winnebago warriors that had camped there to hear Tenskwatawa preach along with a sprinkling of Potawatomi, Ottawa, Ojibwa, Piankeshaw, Wyandotte and Iroquois. There were also a small number of Shawnee followers that lived there permanently. In total they could only muster four to five hundred warriors. Tecumseh was right. The time for a fight with the Big Knives had not yet arrived.

Harrison started the long, lumbering 180 mile journey up the Wabash on the 29th of October. One third of the army he commanded were regulars from the 4th Regiment of the U.S. Infantry. The rest was made up of 400 Indiana Militia, 120 mounted Kentucky volunteers and 80 mounted Indiana riflemen. Harrison had hoped that his show of American military might would force Prophetstown to capitulate but he underestimated First Nations tenacity. The Prophet decided to disregard Tecumseh's orders and stand and fight.

Prophetstown scouts monitored Harrison's progress up the eastern side of the Wabash while the warriors prepared spiritually for the upcoming battle. Tenskwatawa pronounce the Master of Life was with them and the spirits would assist in the battle by making them invisible. He prophesied that he had the power to turn the American's powder to sand and their bullets to mud.

When Harrison's army arrived the warriors had worked themselves into a frenzy. The Americans made camp about a mile north of Prophetstown on a patch of high ground at Burnett's Creek. They sent a delegation to give The Prophet one last chance to sue for peace but the three chiefs they met with refused the offer. Harrison planned to attack the next day.

The Prophet and his council of war chiefs determined that being outnumbered 2 to 1 and low on ammunition the only real chance for success was to take the fight to Harrison that night. Before dawn about 4 a.m. on the 7th of November 1811 the warriors surrounded the American encampment. They could see the silhouettes of the sentries outlined by their campfires. Harrison and his officers were just being aroused for morning muster. The surprise attack began.

The Winnebago led by Waweapakoosa would attack from one side while Mengoatowa and his Kickapoo would strike from the other. The warriors crept stealthily into position and just as they were about to commence the assault an American sentry saw movement in the underbrush that surrounded the encampment. He raised his rifle and fired and the battle was on!

Blood curdling shrieks and war whoops filled the air accompanied by volleys of gunfire from the darkness all around. The warriors rushed forward and the American line buckled. Others scrambled to form battle lines. The volleys of musketry from the warriors were intense and some of the new recruits as well as the riflemen protecting the far left flank broke for the center. However, the main line of regulars held and the warriors were unable to break through. The right flank now came under a tremendous assault of gunfire from a grove nearby. Officer after officer, soldier after soldier was felled. The line was about to collapse when a company of mounted riflemen reinforced it.

The warrior's surprise attack was now in trouble. The American army was badly mauled but managed to hold. Ammunition was running low and daylight was breaking. The war party that had been so successful from the grove were now uprooted by a company of riflemen and were in retreat. Harrison turned from defense to offense routing the warriors who were out of ammunition. They began a full retreat back to an empty Prophetstown. When they arrived there with ammunition spent they decided to disperse.

Harrison spent the rest of the 7th and some of the 8th of November waiting for the warriors to commence a second assault. When they didn't he marched to Prophetstown only to find the town's inhabitants consisted of one wounded man and one old woman who had been left behind. They were taken prisoner but treated well. Harrison burned Prophetstown to the ground including the granary. It was going to be a long, hard winter.

Harrison and his army limped back to Vincennes where he would claim a great victory. But his badly mauled forces told another story. American casualties amounted to 188 including 68 killed. First Nation estimates range from 25 to 40 killed. The warriors had given a good account of themselves having assailed a superior force on its chosen ground and inflicting higher casualties on them.

NEXT WEEK: War Clouds on the Horizon

War Clouds on the Horizon

October 16, 2012

When the Prophetstown warriors retreated from the battlefield they carried some of their fallen with them. They quickly buried them at their town and withdrew to see what Harrison would do next.

Although the Americans held their ground during the surprise attack they were bruised and stunned. Harrison ordered them to stand at the ready expecting the warriors to mount another frontal assault. He waited all through November 7th and part way through the 8th. That attack never came. Little did he know the warriors had withdrawn due to lack of ammunition.

When the warriors failed to materialize he marched on Prophetstown burning it to the ground destroying everything that was there. The warriors watched from afar. They could see the large billows of black smoke rising from the valley. The next day their scouts informed them the Big Knives had left so they returned to see what the enemy had done. They were horrified at the sight that greeted them. Debased American soldiers had dug up the fresh graves of their brave fallen warriors. The bodies were strewn about and left to rot in the sun. They were livid. They re-interned their dead and left for their hunting grounds short of enough ammunition to get them through the winter.

Tecumseh's confederacy had been dealt a serious setback. Warriors from the several nations that had been at Prophetstown left viewing the Prophet with disdain. They declared him to be a false prophet because of the outcome of the battle. Tenskwatawa claimed the spirits deserted them because his menstruating wife had defiled the holy ground that he was drumming and chanting on during the battle. Often a reason such as this would be accepted for a failed prophecy. But not this time. The nations from the western Great Lakes that supported Tecumseh and his vision now rejected the Prophet which left them disenchanted with Tecumseh's vision as well. He had a lot of work ahead of him rebuilding the confederacy.

Harrison was basking in the glory of self-proclaimed total victory. He confidently claimed the Indians had been dispersed in total humiliation and this would put an end to their depredations upon white settlers up and down the frontier. The American press lionized him and President Madison endorsed the message in an address to congress on the 18th of December. The "Indian problem" had been dealt with or so they thought.

That congress was bristling with war hawks enraged at Great Britain mostly for impressing American merchant sailors at sea into British service in their war with France. They thought that a declaration of war on Great Britain and an attack on its colony of Upper Canada would give them an easy victory and the whole of the continent as a prize. Upper Canada was weakly defended and Great Britain's military might was stretched thin as all its resources were being used in Europe.

In 1808 Congress tripled the number of authorized enlisted men from 3,068 to 9,311. In 1811 Secretary of War, William Eustis, asked for 10,000 more regulars. Virginia Democratic Senator William Branch Giles proposed 25,000 new men. Democrats for the most part held anti-war sentiments. It was thought he upped the ante to embarrass the administration because it was generally thought that 25,000 could not be raised. However, Federalists William Henry Clay from Kentucky and Peter B. Porter of New York pushed through a bill enacting Giles' augmentation into law on the 11th of January 1812. By late spring authorized military forces had been further pushed to overwhelming numbers: 35,925 regulars, 50,000 volunteers and 100,000 militiamen.

When Tecumseh had visited Amherstburg in 1810 he made the British authorities there aware just how close the First Nations were to rebellion. Upon realizing this they adjusted their Indian Policy. Because of their weakened position they did not want to be drawn into a war with the Americans. So they informed their First Nation allies that the new policy stated that they would receive no help from the British if they attacked the United States. If they were attacked by the U.S. they should withdraw and not retaliate. Indian Agents were ordered to maintain friendly relations with First Nations and supply them with necessities but if hostilities arose then they were to do all in their power to dissuade them from war. This policy was continued by the new administrators of Upper Canada. Sir James Craig was replaced as governor-general by Sir George Prevost and Francis Gore with Isaac Brock as lieutenant-governor.

However, all the admonition to encourage peace by the British and Harrison's claim that peace on the frontier had already been achieved by his victory at Tippecanoe was for nought. The British lacked the necessary influence with the war chiefs and Harrison's proclamation was a myth. The Kickapoo and Winnebago suffered through a particularly hard winter. The snow had been unusually deep and game was scarce. The Shawnee suffered even more due to the destruction of their granary. They were forced to survive by the good charity of their Wyandotte brothers at Sandusky.

When spring arrived they were still seething at the desecration of their graves at Prophetstown. Tecumseh was travelling throughout the northwest rebuilding his confederacy. Although he preached a pan-Indian confederacy to stop American aggression his message was tempered with a plea to hold back until the time was right. But the war chiefs had trouble holding back some of their young warriors.

The melting snows turned into the worst outbreak of violence the frontier had seen in fifteen years. Thanks to governor Harrison First Nation warriors were no longer congregated in one place. Now they were spread out in a wide arc from Fort Dearborn (Chicago) to Lake Erie. They were striking everywhere at once. In January the Winnebago attacked the Mississippi lead mines. In February and March they assaulted Fort Madison killing five and blockading it for a time. In April they killed two homesteaders working their fields north of Fort Dearborn. That same month five more settlers were killed along the Maumee and Sandusky Rivers with one more on Greenville Creek in what is now Darke County.

The Kickapoo were just as busy. On the 10th of February a family by the name of O'Neil was slain at St. Charles (Missouri). Settlers in Louisiana Territory were in a state of panic. Potawatomi warriors joined in. April saw several attacks in Ohio and Indiana Territory. Near Fort Defiance three traders were tomahawked to death while they slept in their beds while other raids were made on the White River and Driftwood Creek.

On the 11th of April two young warriors named Kichekemit and Mad Sturgeon led a war party south burning a house just north of Vincennes. Six members of a family named Hutson along with their hired hand were killed. Eleven days later it is believed that the same Potawatomi party raided a homesteader's farm on the Embarras River west of Vincennes. All of the Harryman family including five children lost their lives.

The frontier was ablaze with retribution for Prophetstown and settlers were leaving the territories in droves. Governor Edwards complained that by June men available for his militia had fallen from 2,000 to 1,700. A militia was raised by each of the Northwest Territories for protection. At times American First Nation allies were caught in the middle. Two friendly Potawatomi hunters were killed near Greenville and their horses confiscated. Both Governors Edwards and Louisiana Governor Benjamin Howard called for a new campaign against their antagonizers but the Secretary of War was occupied with the clamoring for war with Great Britain and its accompanying invasion of Upper Canada.

The raids on settlers stopped as quickly as they started. By May the warriors committing the atrocities declared their anger over grave degradation at Prophetstown was spent. Tecumseh's coalition had gelled in the Northwest. In the south the Red Sticks had taken ownership of his vision and had become extremists acting on their own and not really part of his confederacy. The stage was now set for a major war. In June of 1812, while General Hull and his army of 2,000 hacked their way through the wilderness to Detroit Tecumseh sent a small party of his followers, mostly Shawnee, to Amherstburg while he traveled south to visit Fort Wayne.

NEXT WEEK: The Detroit Theater

The Detroit Theater

October 20, 2012

Tecumseh arrived at Fort Wayne on June 17, 1812. He met with the new Indian Agent Benjamin Stickney and stayed three days discussing their relations with the Americans. He laid the blame for all the unrest in the spring at the feet of the Potawatomi and informed Stickney he would travel north to Amherstburg to preach peace to the Wyandotte, Ottawa, Potawatomi there as well as the Ojibwa of Michigan. Stickney was new but no fool. He did not believe him so he told Tecumseh that a visit to Amherstburg could only be considered an act of war considering the two colonizers were so close to going to war themselves. Tecumseh left Fort Wayne on June 21st not knowing that the United States of America had declared war on Great Britain on June 18, 1812.

Earlier that spring General Hull assembled an army in Cincinnati. In May he marched them to Dayton where he added to his forces before continuing on to Urbana. Meanwhile, Governor Meigs also called for a conference at Urbana with chiefs friendly to the U.S. The purpose was to secure permission for Hull to hack a road through First Nations' land to Fort Detroit. This new road would also serve as a supply line for the American invasion force.

Tarhe spoke for the Wyandotte and Black Hoof for the Ohio Shawnee. Their speeches were followed by harangues by other chiefs including the Seneca chief Mathame and the Shawnee Captain Lewis. Captain Lewis had just returned from Washington and like the others declared their undying fidelity to Americans. They not only gained permission for the road but permission also to build blockhouses at strategic places along the way. Captain Lewis and Logan also agreed to act as interpreters and scouts for General Hull. The long and arduous trek to Michigan began.

While Hull slowly trudged through the dense forests of Ohio and Michigan the other governors of the Northwest Territories arranged for another conference at Piqua with friendly First Nations. One was planned for August 1st and included groups of Miami, Potawatomi, Ottawa and Wyandotte. The Americans assumed that when war broke out a few groups might flee to Canada and join Tecumseh's forces but the majority would remain neutral. They were expecting 3,000 First Nations people. The conference was designed to keep them neutral with the combination of presents and supplies along with an expectation that the size of Hull's forces and its reinforcement of Detroit would overawe them. But, Hull's over-extended journey left supplies short and the presents failed to arrive on schedule so the conference was postponed to August 15th. Meanwhile British agents spread the rumor that the conference was a ploy designed to get the warriors away from their villages where American militia would fall upon them killing their women and children.

Tecumseh took ten of his warriors and left for Amherstburg on June 21st. He planned to join the warriors already sent on ahead. They skirted Hull's lumbering army arriving at Fort Malden at the end of the month.

Amherstburg was a small village some seventeen miles south of the village of Sandwich on the Canadian side of the Detroit River. Located at the north end of the village was a small, dilapidated outpost called Fort Malden. It was poorly maintained and under garrisoned. Although over the previous two months it had been tripled it still only amounted to 300 regulars from the 41st Regiment of Foot and one detachment of Royal Artillery. There were also 600 Essex Militia available but they were insufficiently armed and most were without uniforms. They were mostly farm boys from the surrounding homesteads who had no real interest in fighting but only joined the militia for a Saturday night out.

The infantry was commanded by the able Scot Captain Adam Muir. Lieutenant Felix Troughton had command of the artillery. Lieutenant-Colonel Thomas Bligh St. George, who had overall command, stationed 460 militiamen along with a few regulars directly across the river from Detroit to protect the border. They settled in at the village of Sandwich to meet the invasion.

Directly in front of Amherstburg was a large heavily wooded island called Bois Blanc. There had been Wyandotte and Ottawa villages there since the founding of Detroit over 100 years earlier. The island provided a place for the numerous encampments of other warriors who had begun to gather in the area. A large main council lodge was erected opposite the island on the mainland near the village's small dock yard. The dockyard provided slips for the three British ships that commanded Lake Erie; the brig *Queen Charlotte*, the schooner *Lady Prevost* and the small ship *General Hunter.*

When Tecumseh arrived he found his warriors joining in war dances with the others. Near the council lodge warriors would give long harangues detailing their exploits in previous battles striking the war post with their war clubs and working themselves into a frenzy. The drums would begin their loud rhythmic pounding and the dancing warriors would circle their sacred fire all the while yelling their blood curdling war whoops. The garrison would respond with cannon salutes. Soldiers would shout out cheers while they fired their rifles into the air from the rigging of the three ships.

Although the din of the warrior's preparation for war was impressive their numbers were not. They were mostly Wyandotte from the Canadian side under Roundhead, his brother Splitlog and Warrow. Tecumseh was present with his thirty Shawnee. War Chief Main Poc was there with a war party of Potawatomi. The contingent of warriors also included thirty Menominee, a few Winnebago and Sioux, sent by the red headed Scottish trader Robert Dickson from Green Bay. The Munsee Philip Ignatius was also present with a few from the Goshen mission at Sandusky. The number was rounded out by a sprinkling of Ottawa, Ojibwa and Kickapoo. On July 4th a large war party of Sac arrived to bring the total warrior contingent to 350.

Canada was looking decidedly the underdog. Only 300 British regulars, 600 ill equipped militia and 350 First Nation warriors protected the Detroit frontier. Hull was approaching with an army of 2,000 and the Americans were raising another large invasion force in the east to attack at Niagara. And there would be no help arriving from England because of the war in Europe.

The general population of Upper Canada was a mere 77,000 with many of them recent American immigrants. Their loyalty was questionable. The population of the U.S. Northwest Territories was 677,000. The American Congress had approved a total allotment of over 180,000 fighting men. General Brock was looking at a war on two fronts with only 1,600 regulars and 11,000 militiamen at his disposal. Tecumseh had sent out many war belts as a call to arms but the large and powerful Three Fires Confederacy's feelings were that they should remain neutral. They saw no reason to get involved in a war with the Americans that did not look winnable. Only a few young hotheads such as Ojibwa warriors Wawanosh, Waboose or The Rabbit, Old Salt and Black Duck from the St. Clair had joined Tecumseh at Amherstburg. Canada's prospects were looking very grim!

NEXT WEEK: Hull Invades Canada!

Hull Invades Canada!

October 23, 2012

General Hull finally arrived at Detroit on July 6, 1812. He was in overall command of his forces while Lieutenant-Colonel James Miller commanded the veterans of Tippecanoe, the 4th Regiment of United States Infantry. Also with him was the 1,200 strong Ohio Militia under Lewis Cass, Duncan McArthur and James Findlay. The Michigan Militia joined him there raising his total force to over 2,000 fighting men.

This impressive show of American strength had the Canadian side of the Detroit in a panic. Canadian militiamen began deserting in droves. Their rolls quickly dropped from 600 to less than 400. Townspeople began to flee inland taking what they could with them. Some communities such as Delaware sent overtures to Hull on their own. Canadian civilians were not the only citizens to be apprehensive about the prospects of war in their own environs. Six months earlier the settlers of Michigan Territory sent a memorial to Congress pleading for protection from perceived threats from the surrounding First Nations. In it they claimed it was not the British army they feared, however they did not trust them for protection against attacks by "the savages".

The invasion came on July 12th. American troops crossed the Detroit and occupied Sandwich. The few British regulars and what was left of the Essex Militia defending the border quickly scrambled back to Fort Malden. On the 13th Hull crossed over to make his proclamation to the Canadians. He entered Canada presenting himself as a glorious liberator. All citizens who remained neutral would be treated kindly and their property respected. However, anyone found to be fighting beside and "Indian" would receive no quarter but "instant destruction would be his lot".

In an area of wetlands and tall grass prairie laid the only defensible position between Amherstburg and Sandwich. About five miles north of Fort Malden a fairly wide, slow moving stream meandered toward the Detroit. There was a single bridge which crossed the Aux Canard connecting the only road between the two villages. On July 16th it was protected by a few regulars with two pieces of artillery and about fifty warriors.

Suddenly, Lewis Cass and his Militia along with a few American regulars appeared at the bridge. Cass positioned a few marksmen on the north side of the river while he took the rest of his 280 men upstream to find a ford to cross over. Meanwhile, his riflemen picked off two British soldiers killing one. When he arrived back at the bridge on the south side of the Aux Canard he overwhelmed the warriors and their British counterparts. Shots were fired by both sides but there were few casualties. The warriors and their contingent of British regulars wheeled their artillery away and retreated back to Malden.

The Americans had tasted their first real military success at the Aux Canard as Sandwich was given up without a fight. But this victory was short lived. That night the warriors preformed a loud, boisterous war dance on Amherstburg's wharf to prepare for the expected upcoming battle. The next day Roundhead led his Wyandotte warriors north up the road to the bridge. Main Poc followed with his Potawatomi while the rest were under Tecumseh's command. To their utter amazement the Americans had abandoned the bridge and were retreating back up the road to Sandwich. They retook the bridge and moved the *Queen Charlotte* upstream to the mouth of the Aux Canard to provide cannon cover. While the soldiers ripped up the bridge except for a few planks and built a rampart on the south side of the stream the warriors hounded the Americans with wasp like sorties until they withdrew from Canada to the safety of Fort Detroit.

General Hull was a much older soldier that he had been in the American Revolution Then he had been daring and far more decisive. He had grown much more cautious and vacillating in his old age. Not only was he indecisive but he had developed an extraordinary fear of native warfare. In fact the warriors terrified him. It was him that ordered Cass to retreat much to the chagrin of his men. Now he sat day after day in war council trying to determine what to do next. But nothing was ever decided. He fretted about the security of his supply line from Ohio and he imagined far more warriors surrounding him than the few that were at Amherstburg. His men, including his officers, began to complain bitterly behind his back.

On the day after the American Invasion while Lewis Cass retreated to Detroit the small American post, Fort Michilimackinac, at the head of Lake Huron fell. It had come under attack by the British Captain Charles Roberts who had 393 warriors with him. They included 280 Ojibwa and Ottawa warriors from Superior country as well as 113 Sioux, Menominee and Winnebago braves recruited by Robert Dickson from those who had been loyal to Tecumseh and Main Poc. That most northerly fort was lightly garrisoned and ill equipped so it capitulated without a shot being fired. The warriors were on their best behavior that day attested to by Mr. Askin Jr. who wrote, "I never saw a so determined people as the Chippewas and Ottawas were. Since the capitulation they have not drunk a single drop of Liquor, nor even Killed a Fowl belonging to any person (a thing never Known before) for they generally destroy everything they meet with".

When Hull received word of the fall of Michilimackinac it only added to his anxiety. He envisioned hordes of "savages" descending on Detroit from the north. He sent dispatches back to Eustis begging for more reinforcements to be sent to provide protection from the 2,000 war-whooping, painted, feathered warriors he imagined approaching from the north.

While Hull fretted and vacillated back and forth Duncan McArthur moved his men back down the dusty road to the Aux Canard. As he advanced he kept encountering pesky bands of warriors. The warriors were so determined that they forced the Americans back. In one skirmish Main Poc was shot in the neck and had to be helped from the field. He later recovered. In another skirmish McArthur who was retreating had his men turn and fire upon the pursuing warriors. A story later sprang up that when the volley was fired the warriors all hit the ground face first except one who remained defiantly on his feet. That one was reportedly Tecumseh!

NEXT WEEK: The Invasion Stalls

The Invasion Stalls

October 27, 2012

Hull worried about his supply line from Ohio. He was also convinced he was outnumbered by fierce, unrelenting warriors. Anxious to keep "his friendly Indians" in Michigan Territory neutral he called for an all native conference to renew their pledges of neutrality. Captain Lewis, Logan and The Wolf acted as scouts for Hull when he hacked his way through the bogs of northwestern Ohio and dense forests of Michigan to Detroit. Black Hoof joined them just after their arrival. Hull assigned them the task of calling the friendly chiefs to a council at Walk-In-The-Water's Wyandotte village near Brownstown. Tecumseh, Roundhead and Main Poc were invited but declined.

On July 15th Black Hoof spoke to the council of nine nations. Chiefs from the Ojibwa, Ottawa, Potawatomi, Wyandotte, Kickapoo, Delaware, Munsee, Sac and Six Nations of the Grand attended. He brought them a message from the great American war chief who was at Detroit explaining that the Americans were obliged to go to War with Great Britain because they would not permit them to enjoy their neutral rights. Further, it was not of interest to the First Nations to concern themselves with the two government's differences. And because the British were too weak to contend with them they were enticing all the nations around to join them in their fight. It was the desire of their Great Father in Washington that they not do so but remain neutral and enjoy their peace.

Lewis and Logan followed with reminders of how the British treated them at the end of the War of Independence and how they were abandoned at Fallen Timbers. They argued that they all should let the Red Coats and the Big Knives fight their own battles and if they did they could be assured their Great Father in Washington wanted no more of their land and he would always care for their needs.

The chiefs still believing the British were fighting an unwinnable war professed their continued neutrality and on July 20th the conference ended. Black Hoof, Logan, Lewis and The Wolf left immediately for Piqua and the Conference called for on August 1st.

A week later Major James Denny moved down the Canadian shore of the Detroit to just short of the Aux Canard. He was at the head of 120 Ohio Militiamen when they came upon a small party of warriors who were out of range. They traded shots to no avail while the warriors sent for reinforcements. Denny also sent one of his men back up the road to Sandwich and their main camp. Unfortunately, he ran into another small war party of thirteen at Turkey Creek where he was tomahawked. He would be the first American soldier killed in the war.

Tecumseh and Main Poc rushed from Malden with 150 Shawnee, Ottawa and Potawatomi warriors. They skirted the road to a tall grass prairie called Petite Cote just beyond the bridge and set up an ambush. The small war party that killed the militiaman at Turkey Creek appeared and twenty militiamen gave chase down the road and past the ambush. The main body of warriors emerged from the tall sunflowers and wild carrots amid screeching war hoops and gunfire directed at Denny. He saw that he had a disaster on his hands. His troops were scattered so he broke with the main body for a wood lot on his left to set up a defensive line. The line held but the warriors moved to take possession of the road to his right. When they saw their only escape route was about to be cut off and they would be surrounded they panicked. They rushed for the road, every man for himself, with the warriors hot on their flank. They managed to reach the road safely but were in full retreat, running pell-mell back to Sandwich. The warriors hounded them all the way stopping along fence lines, orchards and behind homesteads to take pot shots at the fleeing Americans. They finally broke off the chase at Turkey Creek. Denny lost five killed, two wounded and one taken prisoner. The warriors lost one killed and three wounded.

The American captive was treated very badly because one of his comrades, William McColloch, found time during the skirmish to scalp the dead warrior. He was bound and whipped with ramrods but he did live and was ransomed by British Indian Agent Matthew Elliott.

The warriors now shifted their efforts to the other side of the Detroit. On August 3rd Tecumseh, Roundhead and Captain Adam Muir led a large force of warriors along with 100 Red Coats across the Detroit to Brownstown. They surrounded the towns of Maguaga and Brownstown and rounded up the inhabitants. Maguaga, Blue Jacket's town, was inhabited by a mix of Shawnee and Wyandotte while Walk-In-The-Water's town were all Wyandotte. The total population was approximately 300 all remaining neutral in the war.

The whole population was spirited back across the border to Bois Blanc Island where a council was held. Tecumseh and Roundhead pleaded for the Confederacy's cause. Miere or Walk-In-The-Water retorted with his intention of keeping his word to remain neutral. In the end Tecumseh won out convincing the neutral First Nations to capitulate and join his cause. This added about eighty warriors to his force.

Two days later Tecumseh left Amherstburg again. This time he crossed the river with a much smaller force of just twenty-five. Their scouts made them aware of a mail run making its way north from Frenchtown with communications from Ohio. They ambushed the unsuspecting column killing eighteen of the French volunteers and capturing the mail. Of the seven that made it back to Frenchtown two were wounded.

Tecumseh's scouts returned with more news. They had run across William McColloch, the same man that scalped the dead warrior at Petite Cote, who was with a scouting party for a mail run moving south. After learning that Major Thomas Van Horne was moving down the road from Detroit with 200 militiamen they killed all of the advance party including McColloch. Van Horne was intending to meet with the northbound mail to exchange communications. Tecumseh prepared an ambush at a most suitable spot and waited.

Van Horne approached with his mail pouches protected in the center of his column. It was preceded and flanked first by infantry then mounted militiamen. As they passed the point of ambush the trap was sprung. Mounted men and officers fell first. The militia panicked and fled. Over the next two days they straggled into Fort Detroit in a state of shock. They had lost twenty-five killed and twelve wounded. Tecumseh lost one dead and two wounded but captured both north and southbound communications. One letter from Hull to Eustis pleading for reinforcements revealed his belief that there were 2,000 unrepentant warriors about to descend on Detroit from the north, a most valuable piece of information indeed.

Hull was fraught with anxiety. His most vulnerable asset was now breached. His supplies were cut off. He failed to take the bridge on the Aux Canard or Fort Malden. He seemed to see Tecumseh's warriors everywhere. He withdrew his small advance stationed at Sandwich back to the fort and he sent a dispatch to Fort Dearborn to abandon their post and retreat either to Fort Wayne, Detroit or Michilimackinac. Now Hull gave up any notion of advancing and he assumed a defensive position inside the fort. The American invasion was over!

NEXT WEEK: The Fall of Detroit

The Fall of Detroit

November 6, 2012

Tecumseh's confederacy began to grow. Early successes against the Big Knives bolstered the First Nations around Detroit. Teyoninhokarawenor or The Snipe whose English name was John Norton arrived with seventy warriors. He was a Mohawk from the Grand River. His war party consisted of Iroquois from the Grand and some Munsee Delaware he had recruited from the Thames. Miscocomon or Red Knife joined him with a party of Ojibwa warriors also from the Thames.

The young warriors Kayotang and Yahobance, or Raccoon, from Bear Creek (Sydenham River) raised a war party and joined with war chief Waupugais and his party from the Sauble. They traveled down the eastern shore of Lake Huron to Aamjiwnaang at the mouth of the St. Clair River. They met Misquahwegezhigk or Red Sky at the mouth of the Black River. He was the war chief of the Black River band of Saulteaux Ojibwa. They were all joined by Quakegman also known as Feather a war chief of the St. Clair band across the river. The whole entourage made its way south down the St. Clair to the lake of the same name. They picked up Petahgegeeshig or Between Day as well as Quaquakebookgk or Revolution with a large group of Ojibwa warriors from the Swan Creek and Salt River bands. The whole group arrived at Amherstburg sometime in early August 1812.

Okemos, who was a nephew of Pontiac, was the chief of the Cedar River band near present day Lansing, Michigan. They were a mixed band of Ojibwa and Ottawa people. He also arrived about the same time as the Saulteaux Ojibwa. Manitocorbay also came leading a large party of Ojibwa from Saginaw. Tecumseh's coalition grew to about 600 warriors.

On the 9th of August Captain Adam Muir crossed the Detroit with just over 100 Red Coats, most of them regulars and started down the road to Bluejacket's village of Maguaga. They were joined by Tecumseh with 300 warriors. Main Poc and Walk-In-The-Water led the Potawatomi and Wyandotte bands. Just as they arrived some of their scouts came rushing down the road with news. They excitedly told their chiefs that a large party of Big Knives were arriving from Detroit.

Hull had sent out a force to re-take the road that was his supply line from Ohio. This time the size of the force he sent out was much larger and included a healthy contingent of battle hardened regulars. The allied forces picked a place conducive to the ambush style forest warfare. Muir's men flattened themselves on the ground on each side of the road while Main Poc and Walk-In-The-Water took up position ahead of the British in the woods on one side while Tecumseh covered them from the other side. There they lay, still and silent, awaiting the Americans. They didn't have to wait long.

The Big Knives appeared marching down the road in two columns one on each side of the road with a column of cavalry in between. They were led by an advance guard of infantrymen under Captain Josiah Snelling while Lieutenant-Colonel James

Miller rode at the head of the cavalry. Behind them were their baggage and heavy armament, one six-pounder and one howitzer. These were flanked by a small rear guard of regulars from the 4th U.S. Infantry. The unsuspecting Americans marched right passed the hiding enemy.

The warriors opened up fire upon the advance guard and the main column. The Red Coats joined the fire and the Big Knives broke ranks. However, they were battle tested veterans and among Hull's finest soldiers. They regrouped under Miller and quickly formed battle lines. They began to advance firing mainly upon the British as the bright red jackets made easier targets than the warriors. Their 6 pounder also joined the fray by spraying the wooded areas with grape-shot.

Then things began to go wrong for the allies. One report said that the American's forced one of the bodies of warriors to fall back and Muir's men mistook them for advancing Blue Coats and so fired upon their own allies. Another report said the Red Coats mistook a command to advance as one to retreat giving up ground to Miller's troops. Later Proctor would only record that during the battle something went amiss.

The Red Coats retired from the battlefield and retreated back to Malden. The warriors fought on for a time but were overwhelmed by superior numbers and they gave up the road to the Americans. But they didn't hold control of their supply line for very long.

Inexplicably on August the 12th the "Old Lady", that's what Hull's officers had come to call him, ordered Miller to withdraw back to the safety of Fort Detroit. Tecumseh moved back across the river and took control of the road to Urbana once again.

Tecumseh lost two warriors killed and six wounded in the Battle of Maguaga. He was slightly wounded himself. Muir lost five killed including Lieutenant Charles Sutherland, fourteen wounded and two missing. The Americans fared much worse. Miller suffered eighty-two casualties including eighteen dead. Jim Bluejacket, son of the great Shawnee Chief was also killed scouting for Miller. The Canadians lost the battle but in the end, because of Hull's trepidation, the blockade of Fort Detroit remained intact.

The Americans had also planned an invasion of Upper Canada at Niagara to coincide with Hull's arrival at Sandwich but it was delayed. This freed up the commander of the British forces Isaac Brock to personally survey the situation on the Detroit frontier. He left Long Point with 350 men skirting the north shore of Lake Erie and up the Detroit. When he arrived at Amherstburg, sometime after the sun had set on August 13th, he was greeted with a volley of gunfire. The rounds were not deadly but fired off into the air as a greeting by the warriors on Bois Blanc Island.

A meeting of the officers was hastily called. Mathew Elliot, the old Indian Agent, quickly left to fetch Tecumseh. When Tecumseh and the General met they immediately hit it off. Both men were bold warriors, decisive in deed and had the military acumen only great generals enjoy. In short they were made of the same mettle.

When Brock heard of the trembling fear General Hull had of Tecumseh's warriors he wanted to exploit that weakness. He decided to go on the offensive by attacking Fort Detroit. Colonel Proctor, who was sent to replace St. George, was against the plan as were most of the officers except for two. But Tecumseh was filled with affirmative excitement. When that meeting broke up the decision had been made to send Hull a letter giving him the chance to surrender the fort. If the offer was refused they would attack. Now Brock would replace Proctor as commander of the forces on the Detroit front.

On August 15th the letter containing Brock's offer was sent across the river to Hull. In it Brock reminded Hull "the numerous body of Indians that have attached themselves to my troops will be beyond control the moment the contest commences". He was preying on Hull's most paralyzing fear but the bluff didn't work. Hull refused to surrender. The following day British cannon fire roared across the Detroit from Sandwich. Hull returned the fire The British cannonade proved more deadly than Hull's. Several shots found their mark landing inside the fort killing several people.

Brock marched his men boldly up the road to within sight of the main gate and its gatehouse. He led 800 men who included 300 regulars and 400 Militia with some dressed in red coats to give the impression he had more regulars than he did. Norton and his seventy Mohawk and Munsee warriors also marched with Brock. When they arrived to within sight of the fort they realized they were about to be met with the deadly fire of two twenty-four-pounders and one 6 pounder loaded with grape and canister shot. Brock peeled off taking shelter in a small ravine.

Roundhead, Walk-In-The-Water, Main Poc and Splitlog led their warriors through woods in order to attack the fort from the left and rear. Tecumseh led the rest of the coalition and joined them as they faced off against Hull's militia. One story relates that during the face off Tecumseh had the 530 warriors march out of a small wood lot across an open field and into the main woods, circle around to the starting point. They filed passed the Americans again all the time screeching blood curdling war hoops in full view of the enemy. Three times the warriors showed themselves deceiving the militia and General Hull into actually believing the warriors they feared so much were there in the thousands.

While Brock had his men stationed in the ravine trying to entice Hull out of the fort he received bad news from scouts who had been patrolling the road south of the fort. They reported that a force of 350 militiamen under McArthur and Cass were approaching from the south. They had been sent two days earlier skirting through the forest to meet a supply convoy at the River Raisin. Before they reached their goal they were urgently recalled by Hull when he received Brock's letter. Now it seemed Hull had Brock and his allies hemmed in.

However, neither Brock nor the war chiefs would entertain retreat. It was a tactic only to be used as a last resort. Brock decided to abandon the ploy to entice the Americans out of the fort to fight in the open. About 10 o'clock in the morning as Brock was preparing his men for a frontal assault the big American guns stopped firing across the Detroit. To Brock's utter amazement a white flag was hung over the fort's wall. The militia facing the warriors withdrew. Not a shot was fired by either side.

Hull had fretted all morning about unrelenting "savages" overrunning the fort and committing unspeakable atrocities on the civilian populace. He especially worried about the safety of his own daughter and grandchildren who were with him. He surrendered the fort, the American army and all armament and supplies. There had been only a few cannonades exchanged across the river. Never before had First Nation warriors so overwhelmingly contributed to such an immense victory over a common enemy.

Hull's men were utterly dismayed and humiliated at being denied the chance to give account of themselves. They are said to have piled their small arms in heaps along the fort's palisade with tears in their eyes. Cass and McArthur's men had stopped to roast an ox they had caught running through the woods and were never a factor in the almost battle.

The American colors were lowered and the Union Jack hoisted above Fort Detroit to the sound of volleys of gunfire shot in the air. Sandwich returned the salute with cannon fire to celebrate the victory. The British flag had been absent from the Territory of Michigan for seventeen years. Now it had returned. The Territory of Michigan would be annexed into the Province of Upper Canada.

General Hull was taken prisoner along with 582 regulars and 1,606 militiamen. There was also 350 Michigan Militia taken into the British forces because they were not part of American federal forces. However, half of them had already defected when the engagement commenced. Hull also gave up 39 guns including 9 twenty-four pounders, 3,000 rifles, a huge quantity of ammunition and twenty-five days' worth of supplies. The spoils also included the *Adams*, a new American war ship not yet quite finished.

When Hull was returned to the U.S. he faced a court-martial charged with treason, cowardice, neglect of duty and bad conduct. The trial took place in April of 1814 where he was found not guilty of the first two charges but guilty of neglect of duty and bad conduct. He was sentenced to be shot but mercy was recommended because of his age and his exemplary war record during the Revolution. President Madison remitted his sentence and William Hull spent the rest of his life trying to defend himself and explain his conduct. He died in 1825.

NEXT WEEK: The Warrior's Offensive Falters

The Warrior's Offensive Falters

November 12, 2012

In April 1812 the simple pioneer homes of Chicago came under attack by the Potawatomi. Cannon fire from Fort Dearborn, which was adjacent to the town, scared the warriors off. The whole populace moved into the security of the fort and waited not knowing what to do next. They waited apprehensively for the next four months until Winamek; a friendly Potawatomi chief arrived on August 7th with an order from General Hull to evacuate. The chief advised against leaving and the garrison's officers agreed but the commander Captain Nathan Heald was determined to carry out Hull's order. At the same time the local Potawatomi accepted a red calumet from Main Poc who was at Fort Malden.

Billy Wells was also at the fort. He had been sent with thirty Miami warriors to escort the fort's garrison as well as the whole civilian population back to the relative safety of Fort Wayne. Wells was a conflicted man. He had been captured by the Miami as a boy and adopted into the band. He took the name of Black Snake and was raised Miami. He married Little Turtle's sister and fought with Little Turtle's confederacy when they smashed the American Armies of Generals Harmar and St. Clair.

However, confusion over his identity brought about feelings of doubt and guilt concerning the Americans he had slain in battle. He thought some could even have been his relatives! He switched sides joining General Wayne as a scout and interpreter. He fought again at Fallen Timbers, but this time on the side of the Big Knives. He went on to become the Indian Agent at Fort Wayne, a position he presently held. Both Wells and his brother-in-law were despised by Tecumseh who considered them turncoats. Although he held great sway with the First Nations friendly to the U.S. he still was not trusted by Harrison who thought he was secretly working with enemy war chiefs.

The Potawatomi were led by war chiefs Assikenack or Blackbird from Milwaukee, Tonquish of the Detroit Potawatomi and Nuscotomeg or Bad Sturgeon who came from a village at the junction of the Iroquois and Kankakee Rivers. Together, with a few Ojibwa, Kickapoo and Winnebago warriors, they commanded 600 warriors. They had the fort surrounded but Heald prepared to abandon the fort anyway. On August 14th he distributed all the goods and supplies they could not carry with them to the warriors as payment for safe passage out of the fort. The Potawatomi withdrew to the sand dunes near the road which would become Michigan Avenue.

Unfortunately Heald had destroyed all extra arms, ammunition and liquor the night before so they would not fall into the hands of the warriors. That was probably a mistake because it infuriated the Potawatomi putting them in a most foul mood. They took this action as a betrayal of their agreement thereby nullifying it so they attacked the column as they marched down the road.

The thirty Miami warriors immediately abandoned the field. Captain Heald circled the wagons then he and Wells led a charge up the dunes directly at the warriors' position. This was Heald's second mistake. After all he had only fifty-three soldiers under his command. This left the civilians cowering behind their only protection, the wagons. Heald's men were quickly overwhelmed by far superior numbers as were the civilians.

There were a total of ninety-three persons that filed out of the fort that August 15th. They got to a point three miles from the Chicago River when they were attacked. The civilians included twelve men, nine women and eighteen children. Of the military twenty-six were killed and scalped including Wells whose heart was cut out and eaten raw by the Potawatomi chiefs in order to absorb his great courage. Five more were put to death that same night. Captain Heald survived and was taken back to the fort where he found his wife who had been rescued by the friendly chief Black Partridge. The other twenty-two soldiers who survived were also taken prisoner. Of the thirty-nine civilians all of the men, two of the women and twelve of the children were killed and scalped at the wagons. The balance was also herded back to the fort as prisoners. A few were ransomed but most were split up and adopted into various bands. With the fall of Forts Michilimackinac, Dearborn and Detroit the Americans lost control of all territory north and west of the Maumee River.

After the First Nations conference at Brownstown in July Black Hoof, Logan and The Wolf hurried back to Ohio to attend the conference at Piqua. They arrived in time only to find out that the conference had been postponed until August 15th. When it finally did get underway there were only 750 First Nations people in attendance and not the 3,000 expected! Not surprisingly the attendees were the eastern Shawnee from Ohio and the White River Delaware along with a few Ottawa and Kickapoo. Tarhe's Wyandotte of Sandusky didn't arrive until September. Fearing attacks by hostile warriors they were busy moving their village to the Upper Sandusky behind American lines. Most of the missing attendees were from the Northwest and had either joined Tecumseh or were observing the war with a view to joining him.

The U.S. commissioners were Governor Meigs, Thomas Worthington and Jeremiah Morrow. In the time leading up to the conference they learned of Tecumseh's stunning successes. Just after the meetings began they received the news that Detroit had fallen and Chicago was now under Potawatomi control. The commissioners' refrain was predictable.

They tried to convince their audience that although the Americans had suffered some losses in the end they would prevail and that the United States harbored no interest in acquiring any more of their lands. If they remained neutral they would receive total protection of U.S. forces against any enemy but if they joined the hostiles that would only end in their destruction. They were preaching to the choir as all of the attendees were already committed to the U.S.

On September 6th the Potawatomi besieged Fort Wayne. Main Poc with his Detroit Potawatomi joined with their Tippecanoe and St. Joseph country men and had the Fort hemmed up. Fort Wayne was a heavily reinforced fortification. The Potawatomi had no heavy artillery with which to breach its walls. They could only hem it up taking pot shots at whatever moved while waiting for British reinforcements. Main Poc built ramparts made of logs and earth in a ruse to make the Big Knives think that British artillery had arrived. It didn't work.

On September 14th Captain Adam Muir and Roundhead left Amherstburg with a force of 1,000 to help Main Poc and Winamek take Fort Wayne. Yes, the same Winamek that was pro American, the same Winamek that brought General Hull the news of Fort Michilimackinac's capitulation in July and the same Winamek that carried Hull's evacuation order to Fort Dearborn. He had switched sides!

Governor Harrison had been given command of the western army so he relinquished his governorship and took the rank of Major General. He was ordered to raise a force of 10,000 to retake Detroit and then strike into Canada as far as possible. He was in the process of carrying out the order when the siege of Fort Wayne began. Local friendly chiefs and warriors including Captain Lewis, Logan, Bright Horn, Captain Johnny and The Wolf joined him as scouts and interpreters. Harrison marched the army of 2,000 he had raised to Fort Wayne to break the siege. Brigadier-General Winchester arrived just after him with a small contingent of Kentucky Militia. They arrived ahead of Muir and Roundhead who, when they saw they faced vastly superior numbers turned around and headed back to Fort Malden. The siege was broken and the Potawatomi assault had failed.

NEXT WEEK: The War Turns Ugly

The War Turns Ugly

November 23, 2012

September had arrived heralding autumn. Tecumseh was resting on the Wabash recuperating from his wound which had been festering since the summer when he received more bad news. Two U.S. forts had been attacked, besieged for days with much ammunition wasted and little to show for the effort. Neither fort was destroyed and only four Big Knives were killed.

On September the 5th a large party of Winnebago and Sac warriors besieged Fort Madison on the Mississippi. The siege lasted for three days and although they destroyed the trading post and other property outside the fort they failed to raze the main stockade. After running low on ammunition they abandoned the attack.

The Potawatomi put Fort Wayne under siege the same day Fort Madison was attacked. But Fort Wayne was a stronger fortification and more heavily guarded. The warriors were led by Main Poc, Winamek and a holy man named Five Medals. Like the Winnebago and Sac they destroyed everything outside Fort Wayne. They sprayed the walls of the fort with bullets shooting at every shadow that moved about but had little success. This assault lasted seven days until Harrison arrived from Piqua with a force of 2,000 and the Potawatomi dispersed.

More success was had a Fort Harrison. Shawnee, Winnebago, Kickapoo and Miami warriors from Prophetstown attacked the weakly defended fort. More than half the garrison was down with fever. Included in the fort's inhabitants were nine women and children who had abandoned their farms for the security of the fort.

During the first night of the siege one of the blockhouses caught fire. It contained the fort's supply of food along with 25,000 rations of liquor. Soldiers in the fort tried desperately to put out the fire which the whiskey had turned into a raging inferno.

The warriors took pot shots at illuminated figures trying to douse the fire with water while others ripped off combustible roofing from other nearby buildings. The din of battle, a strange mixture of gunfire, instructions being shouted by the soldiers, wailing and crying of women and children and loud shrieking of war whoops could be heard for miles. When the smoke cleared in the morning there was a twenty foot breach in the wall of the fort and all its provisions had burned. The Big Knives had lost three killed and three wounded trying to save them.

The warriors from the Wabash withdrew to employ the tactic of starving them out. Mounted detachments were sent from Vincennes. At first two smaller ones were turned back by the warriors who killed two of the horsemen. Ten days after the attack began Colonel William Russell with 1,350 men breached the warrior's lines bringing the fort much needed supplies. Another supply wagon was sent from Vincennes guarded by thirteen army regulars. The warriors ambushed it at the halfway point killing seven guardsmen and wounding one. They took the supply wagon. However, with such a large number of Big Knives now at the fort they abandoned their siege and returned to the Wabash.

Blame for the lack of success in early September can be laid squarely at the feet of the First Nations' British allies. The Americans were never more vulnerable after having their entire western army captured and Michigan Territory annexed in August. Tecumseh's Confederacy tried to take advantage of this but lacked the heavy artillery and know how needed to breach the forts' walls. The Red Coats could have supplied this but Lt. Governor-General Prevost called an armistice hoping that the repeal of the admiralty orders in council in London regarding impressment, a major source of discontent, would appease the U.S. Congress and bring the war to an end. The hope was in vain. The cease fire was called off September 8th and Proctor finally moved to support his allies September 12th but it was too little, too late.

The countryside was now mostly void of homesteaders. Most had fled to the east behind American Lines. The majority of those who stayed had either moved inside American forts or built blockhouse near their farms taking refuse there. War parties spent the early fall roaming the territory burning empty farmhouses and killing farm stock and confiscating abandoned supplies.

One small community did not take precautions and paid the price. It was called Pigeon Roost but now is Scott County, Indiana. A war party led by the Shawnee Masalemeta descended quickly upon the area destroying the community which was totally unprotected. Twenty four people lost their lives. Twenty-one of them were women and children. Upon their retreat they set up an ambush for their pursuers killing one soldier. In times of war First Nation warriors made little distinction between soldiers or civilians even women and children.

This undesirable trait was not lost on First Nation warriors. It seems to have afflicted the military as well. Even the civilian population exhibited a hatred for the enemy that would only fuel war time atrocities. The civilian population living in the east behind American lines were organizing vigilante parties sending them out to kill any First Nation people they came across and burn and destroy their property. They were indiscriminate in their raids attacking even their own First Nation allies such as the Ohio Shawnee, the White River Delaware and Sandusky Wyandotte and Mingo.

Meanwhile, Harrison was building a new western army not as a whole but in parts. The plan was send three columns via different routes to congregate at the rapids of the Maumee River. The right column made up of volunteers from Pennsylvania and Virginia was to gather at Upper Sandusky and proceed from there. General Edward Tupper was commander of the center column gathering at Urbana while General Winchester was to lead the left column from old Fort Defiance down the Maumee to the rapids. Once all three were in place at the rapids they would be in position for either a winter or spring offensive to retake Detroit. However, in order for this strategy to work Winchester's route would have to be cleared of marauding warriors.

Winchester sent out detachments of both U.S. regulars and Kentucky Militia that fall on nine separate excursions. They basically used a scorched earth policy to destroy twenty-one First Nation towns, killing livestock and burning cornfields. They even dug up graves to rob the corpses of their silver trinkets. Fortunately, only two of the towns were inhabited as the others had been abandoned when the Big Knives approached. Fifty First Nations men, women and children were either killed or captured.

On November 21st Kumskaukau, Tecumseh's younger brother, was with several of his warriors scouting high on a bluff overlooking the Winnebago town on Wild Cat Creek. They spotted one of Major-General Samuel Hopkins' scouting parties coming up the river. They set an ambush, shot one of the riders knocking him off his horse killing him. The others scrambled back down the river to the safety of their main camp.

The next day a large detachment arrived to bury the body of their slain comrade. Sixty mounted horsemen riding in three columns spotted a lone warrior riding ahead of them to their right. The right column gave a shout and peeled off to chase down the single warrior. The other two columns followed. They chased the solitary warrior for about a mile then down into a ravine and past a waiting war party crouched among the scrub brush on three sides. Before the Big Knives realized what was happening they were peppered with gunfire. They panicked retreating pell mell back down the river to their base camp leaving sixteen dead in the ravine.

Kumskaukau's party was a small one and they knew the Big Knives would return with an overwhelming force so they left the area the next day. Thus went the fall campaigns of 1812, a series of uncoordinated raids by both sides. But now winter was setting in and that was about to make things much more difficult!

NEXT WEEK: Another American Disaster!

Another American Disaster!

December 4, 2012

The Shawnee scouting for the Americans moved up the Maumee River ahead of General Winchester. They discovered that Roundhead and Muir had left the area and were headed back to Canada. However, the area was infested with pro-British warriors. On October 8th Captain Lewis, Logan and a few other scouts were attacked by Main Poc and a large party of Potawatomi. They escaped without injury beating a hasty retreat back to the American lines.

For the next two months Captain Lewis, Logan, Captain Johnny, Bright Horn, The Wolf and a few other Ohio Shawnee ranged across the region of northwestern Ohio sending intelligence back to the Big Knives. It was doubly dangerous work. They not only had to contend with roving enemy war parties but also roaming detachments of Big Knives who were carrying out Harrison's orders to clear the area of First Nations people. The Big Knives were randomly destroying all First Nations' towns they came across, burning them to the ground and destroying their winter supplies of corn. The Americans, especially the Militia, did not distinguish between enemy or friendly "Indians" but operated on the axiom "any dead Indian is a good Indian."

In the third week of November Shawnee scouts were gathering intelligence on the rapids of the Maumee when they were attacked by an enemy war party. They all managed to escape but Captain Johnny, Logan and Bright Horn became separated from the others and spent the night eluding the enemy by hiding out in the thick Ohioan forest. The three made their way back to the main American camp but their late arrival cast suspicions on them. They were accused of being captured by the enemy and had secured their safe release by providing intelligence on American troop numbers and movements.

The three left the Big Knives camp on November 22nd moving up the Maumee on foot. They intended to prove their loyalty by bringing back either a prisoner or scalps. Some distance up the river on the north bank they encountered a war party of Potawatomi and Ottawa travelling on horseback. It was led by Winamek and Alexander Elliott who was the son of the old British Indian Agent Matthew Elliott.

The American scouts tried a rouse. They pretended to be pro-British Shawnee trying to get back to Tecumseh's forces on the Wabash. Winamek and Elliott were suspicious, especially Winamek because one of the three looked strangely familiar. However, they offered to escort them to the British camp. During the trip they kept them under close guard but did not take their guns.

Along the way it dawned on Winamek who the familiar looking Shawnee was. It was Logan so he suggested to Elliott in private that they be disarmed and bound. But he was overheard and the threesome suddenly opened fire killing Winamek, Elliott and one of the Ottawa warriors and wounding another. They seized the dead men's horses and raced back down the Maumee to the Big Knives camp but they did not escape unharmed. Logan was shot in the abdomen and Bright Horn was wounded in the arm. Bright Horn would recover but on November 24th Logan succumbed to his injury.

By this time winter had set in. Winchester was inching his way down the Maumee to his ordered rendezvous point at the rapids. It was bitter cold and they were ill equipped. Many were suffering from various degrees of frost bite. Most of his Kentucky volunteers had arrived in the early fall with only summer clothing. The regulars were short of winter supplies as well. He had to deal with much complaining from the troops about the slow progress and lack of action as well as a high desertion rate. Even the threat of having to "ride the wooden horse", a most barbaric punishment, failed to discourage defectors. Deserters who were caught were made to straddle a two-by-four or small log while two soldiers shook it violently up and down causing the prisoner extreme pain. This was not exactly what the men had signed up for!

Finally on January 10, 1813 they arrived at the rapids. Harrison had suggested to Winchester that he wait and not move forward but he did not order it. On June the 13th desperate appeals arrived for help from "marauding Indians" from Frenchtown a small village on the River Raisin some forty miles up the trail towards Detroit. The British had a small garrison of men there along with one hundred or so warriors.

Winchester held a council with his officers and all agreed to act on the calls for assistance. After all, the British only had a small force there which could easily be overwhelmed and any victory over the British after the disasters of Michilimackinac, Detroit and Queenston would instantly make national heroes out of those who claimed it. Besides, their supply line back to Amherstburg or Detroit was choked with deep snow. Frenchtown was the only community south of Detroit and would make the perfect site for launching an all-out offensive across the frozen Detroit River to take Fort Malden. Winchester "seized the moment".

On January 17th Winchester sent Colonel Will Lewis forward with 350 troops hastily followed by Colonel John Allen with 110 more. They reached the Raisin on January 18th and quickly dispatched the 200 British Militia and their 400 warrior allies but at a cost of thirteen killed and fifty-four wounded. They set up camp in the midst of the village, some twenty houses set out in rows on the north bank of the frozen river. Behind the row houses were garden plots protected on three sides by a row of pickets made of split logs sharpened on the top ends. The east side of the area was open leaving a large part of the American line vulnerable. They settled in to wait for Winchester to arrive with the rest of the western branch of Harrison's army.

Winchester arrived on the 20th of January with another 350 soldiers raising the total to over 800 Kentucky Militia and 175 regulars. Winchester settled himself in at a house on the south side of the river about a quarter mile from the main bivouac and no one gave a second thought to a possible British response!

General Proctor received word that the Americans had taken Frenchtown and was amassing troops there. He had to make a decision and make it on his own. Communication lines were down because of the winter conditions. Proctor was a slow, plodding man not quick to make any hasty decisions. But this time he acted out of character. Perhaps he was inspired by his former commanding officer Isaac Brock. He called to muster every available man and crossed the frozen Detroit leaving the invitation for all First Nations warriors to join them. Roundhead sent war belts to the scattered encampments around Amherstburg. Many of the warriors that had been gathering there were Potawatomi who had been displaced by Winchester's Kentucky marauders and Miami who had suffered their depredations at Mississinewa.

Trudging through the deep snow on the 21st of January Proctor's force of 597 men and three six pounders were passed by Roundhead and Splitlog's 700 warriors on snowshoes gliding over the deep snow drifts covering Hull's road between Detroit and Frenchtown. Winchester got word of the advancing horde but chose to ignore it not believing they would attempt such a difficult trek.

The town was laid out on the east side of the road. The warriors arrived first in the early hours of January 22nd intent on retribution for the atrocities committed in the fall against their villages. Splitlog and Walk-In-The-Water left the roadway on the west side swinging around to attack from the west. Roundhead did the opposite. After positioning themselves they crouched and waited for Proctor to arrive which he did just before dawn.

The Essex Militia led by John Baptiste Askin joined Splitlog on the west side of the town. The old Shawnee war chief Bluejacket now in his sixties was with them. Proctor setup his battle line of regulars between Roundhead and Splitlog's warriors and placed his six cannons in the front. The Big Knives were now surrounded on three sides with only the frozen Raisin to their backs. The attack began at the morning's first light.

The sound of gunfire and the flash of muskets filled the air. The roar of Proctor's cannons only added to the din. Winchester arrived disheveled his uniform had been quickly pulled over his nightshirt. The American right line had crumpled under Roundhead's relentless fire. Winchester along with Allen and Lewis tried vainly to rally the troops and form a new line but they were forced back across the river's slick ice.

Suddenly panic set in. The right line had devolved in a chaotic rush for the road to the west and escape. Many cast their arms aside as they bounded through the deep snow pursued by Roundhead's screeching warriors. Many of the Big Knives were caught and shot or tomahawked on the spot. Allen did not survive. Wounded in the leg he had limped off for a couple of miles but could go no further. A Potawatomi chief, probably Blackbird, also known as Le Tourneau, noticed his officer's uniform and signaled to another warrior he wanted to take Allen prisoner but the other warrior moved in for the kill. Allen lunged at the wild eyed warrior with his sword running him through. The chief then shot Allen dead and took his scalp.

Winchester and Lewis fared better. They were captured and brought to Roundhead. The warriors demanding their payback wanted him to execute Winchester at once but Roundhead saw the value in keeping the American General alive and took both officers to Proctor.

The warriors were in a most foul mood exacting a take-no-prisoner policy. Unarmed prisoners were being shot or tomahawked then scalped one after the other in front of Winchester and Lewis. This prompted Winchester to sign a note ordering Major George Madison who was commanding the Kentucky Militia on the American left to surrender even though they were holding well and returning fire from behind the pickets. Madison would not comply unless Proctor personally agreed to protect them from the warrior's fury. He did but later broke that promise.

The fighting ended and the tallies were done. Proctor suffered heavy casualties considering the advantage he held for the whole battle. He lost 24 killed and 158 wounded. The high rate was mostly attributable to his placement of his cannons. By placing them in front of his line he opened it up to Americans firing at the big guns and the gunners were left vulnerable to their own regulars who were behind them. For this he was censured but still promoted to Brigadier-General.

American casualties were worse at 300 killed and 27 wounded. The balance of Winchester's army except for thirty-three who escaped was taken prisoner including Winchester himself. One of the escapees, a Private John J. Brice, did so by discarding his shoes so that his tracks in the snow looked like a warrior's wearing moccasins. He was the first to make it back to the Maumee and delivered the distressing news. Harrison was despondent. His entire left wing had been annihilated and his invasion plan stopped dead in its tracks.

Proctor feared an imagined approach of Harrison leading an overwhelming army. He held the American wounded in several of the town's houses under a very light guard. When he began loading Canadian casualties on sleighs for the haul back to Amherstburg the American surgeon inquired as to why the American sick and wounded were being left behind. Proctor responded that there were not enough sleighs and he must take care of his own first. So the surgeon complained about the light guard given the number of warriors there and their mood. When he complained again about the wounded being left behind with inadequate medical attention Proctor is said to have replied "the Indians make excellent doctors".

The U.S. Army surgeon was right. Proctor should have left a reasonable guard for the Kentucky wounded. Part of the booty from the victory at Frenchtown was the town's supply of liquor and a few of the young warriors drank more than their fair share. Angry and inebriated they began to go from house to house taking out their anger on the sick and wounded prisoners. Their chiefs tried to intervene but were unable to control the enraged young men.

Sometime during the night the light guard, a Major Reynolds plus three interpreters slipped away. A warrior appeared in the room of one of the wounded soldiers speaking fluent English. This could very well have been Wawanosh, a young Ojibwa from Aamjiwnaang, who was known to have an excellent command of the English language. He was asking for intelligence on Harrison's movements and strength. When he left he made the off handed remark that he was sorry but some of the more mischievous young men would be doing some bad deeds that night. It was a prelude of things to come.

By the morning the warriors were ransacking the homes for loot. They were looking especially for more whiskey. They begin to strip the sick and wounded of their clothing and in their excitement, fueled by liquor and their hatred for the Big Knives, began to shoot or tomahawk then scalp the helpless Kentuckians.

Captain Nathaniel Hart wounded, half dressed and barefoot was dragged from the home where he was being cared for. While awaiting his fate he recognized one of the warriors surrounding him as the English speaking one from the night before. He knew that he would recognize the name of William Elliott, Matthew Elliott's son. William was a captain in the Essex Militia so Hart exclaimed that William had promised to send his personal sleigh to remove him to his home at Amherstburg. The bilingual warrior replied that Elliott had lied and there would be no rescue. Hart made him an offer. Take him to Amherstburg and he would give him a horse and one hundred dollars. The warrior replied that he could not because he was too badly wounded. Then what were their intentions inquired Hart. The reply was chilling. You are all to be killed!

The massacre lasted most of the morning as the drunken, infuriated warriors moved from house to house looting and killing. When the macabre news reached the Americans it was another in a long line of interracial incidents that helped solidify their hatred of First Nations people. This particular incident gave rise to the battle call of the Kentucky Militia, "Remember the Raisin!"

NEXT WEEK: Queenston Heights

Queenston Heights

December 30, 2012

In the fall of 1812 while Harrison was using the western U.S. army to drive First Nations warriors to Tecumseh's cause the central army was trying to organize for a second invasion of Upper Canada at Niagara. They weren't doing so well. Governor Daniel D Tompkins of New York was given permission by Eustis to install a major-general of the New York militia. He chose Major General Stephen Van Rensselaer. Although Van Rensselaer was a militiaman he was without campaign experience. Tompkins was a Democrat but likely chose him because he was a staunch Federalist and he needed to gain support for the war as most of the congressmen from New York and along the St. Lawrence had voted against it. In order to compensate for his deficiencies Van Rensselaer chose his kinsman Colonel Solomon Van Rensselaer as his aide-de-camp. Solomon had held a commission in the regular army from 1792 to 1800 and had been severely wounded at Fallen Timbers.

When Stephen Van Rensselaer first inspected the troops at the end of August he found less than 1,000 stretched out along the Niagara River. They were ill-equipped, in summer dress, some even shoe-less and far in arrears in pay. There were not enough artillery or gunners to man them if there were. And tents, medicine and supplies were scarce. This militia was undisciplined, insubordinate and unreliable.

The First Nations at Niagara were Haudenosaunee or Iroquois. Those on the American side of the border had held a council and determined to remain neutral in the conflict. On the Canadian side First Nations warriors sided with the British. Wawanosh was there along with Ojibwa from Aamjiwnaang and Swan Creek. Nawahjegezhegwabe or Joseph Sawyer was there with his a band Mississauga warriors from the Credit. But the bulk of the warriors were Mohawk from the Grand River and Caughnawaga.

The warriors put themselves under the leadership of John Brant, the eighteen year old son of the celebrated late Mohawk chief Joseph Brant and John Norton, the son of a Cherokee from Kuwoki whose name was Norton and a Scottish woman named Anderson. He was adopted into the Mohawk Nation at the Grand and made an honorary chief. The older and flamboyant Norton would assume the leadership role.

By late September General Dearborn moved the Fifth and Thirteenth Regiments of the United States Infantry. Also Brigadier-General Alexander Smyth arrived at Buffalo on September 29th with a contingent of recruits. Now the American army which was stretched along the entire length of the Niagara River numbered 6,300 one half of them being militia. On the Canadian side of the river General Brock had a total of 2,200 men also stretched along the length of the river and also half of them militia. Brock had to disperse his inferior numbers so thinly because he did not know where the Americans planned to attack. He felt the invasion would most likely come from Fort Niagara so he took up a position across the river at Fort George. Norton and his 500 plus warriors concurred.

Major General Van Rensselaer planned a two-pronged attack. One division would cross the river by boats and storm Fort George from the rear. The other would cross over at Lewiston and attack Queenston and its heights. The American commanders suffered from bad intelligence estimating the British forces to be 8,500. They didn't realize the distinct advantage they had. Smyth was not happy that he had to subordinate himself to a militia commander so he successfully avoided it by insisting that an invasion point below the falls was folly. The result was that he was left out of the plan so because the assault would take place with twenty-five percent fewer troops there would be no attack on Fort George.

On October 10th the invasion force of 600 men was assembled. Colonel John Chrystie arrived that morning with 350 recruits from the Thirteenth Infantry and immediately offered his detachment for the invasion. His offer was refused because Van Rensselaer only had enough boats for his 600. Thirteen rowboats were put in charge of Lieutenant Sims but a severe storm blew through that day so they waited it out until the morning of the 11th. Now all was set but before they could get the flotilla underway Sims inexplicably pushed off in one of the boats with all of the oars. He floated down the river a ways then beached it and disappeared into the forest. Feeling along that all the necessary logistics were not in place for an invasion against what he thought was a superior force Van Rensselaer was disposed to abandon this plan. However, his officers demanded another attempt.

The invasion was rescheduled for the night of October 12th. Chrystie moved his men from Fort Niagara and was allowed to join the invasion force after agreeing to put himself under the command of Solomon Van Rensselaer. Late in the afternoon of the 12th Lieutenant-Colonel Winfield Scott arrived with the Second Artillery and placed his cannon to fire on the heights across the river. Now all was in place.

Under the cover of darkness 4,000 troops amassed on the American side of the river. They still only had thirteen rowboats so the plan called for seven crossings for each one. The river was 200 yards wide with a swift current and the heights on the other side towered 345 feet above the Niagara. Colonel Van Rensselaer stepped into one of the first boats to cross as did Lieutenant-Colonel Chrystie but Chrystie's boat became lost and was swept downstream with two others. The remaining ten boats ferried 300 men across successfully over the next quarter-hour.

The British opened fire on the first of the invasion force. This threw the beachhead into disarray and Colonel Van Rensselaer was severely wounded. Scott's cannon opened fire on British muzzle flashes forcing the British to retreat to the top of the heights chased by young Captain John F. Wool. The British who were reinforced by local troops returned fire and forced Wool back to the river bank where he took shelter and hung on to the beach head.

General Brock heard the gunfire as did Norton and the warriors. Brock charged out of Fort George at a full gallop toward Queenston some five miles away. He arrived at the British battery near the top of the hill as dawn broke. Wool had launched another assault. Brock had the artillery spiked and they made their escape just in time. Now Wool was above them on the hill and Brock gathered a force of 100 but they were beaten back. Brock added another 200 stragglers and made another attempt. Up the heights they charged with Brock leading the way, all six-foot four of him and all decked out in his General's uniform. The easy target was hit directly in the chest and fell instantly. The death of Isaac Brock was a most serious blow to Upper Canada's cause. Brock was by far the best military leader the British had.

More senior leaders than Wool began arriving on the Canadian side including Major General Van Rensselaer, Brigadier General William Wadsworth of the New York Militia and Lieutenant-Colonel Winfield Scott, United States Second Artillery. Overall Command was given to Scott and the U.S. force now stood at 350 regulars and 250 militiamen. Van Rensselaer recrossed the river to bring the balance of the invasion force over.

There had been a lull in the action until early afternoon. But now Major General Sir Roger Sheaffe who had received Brock's order to come with reinforcements posthumously was now marching down the road from Fort George with 800 men. Scott and Wadsworth were not too concerned because they were expecting Van Rensselaer to arrive with many more reinforcements.

Norton arrived ahead of them and attacked the Americans from the surrounding woods. This threw the regulars into a state of confusion and terrified the militia but after about an hour they managed to beat the warriors back into the woods. At this point Chrystie had found his way to the battlefield and joined Scott. Meanwhile, Sheaffe swung behind the heights and was now on the south side where he picked up a detachment marching north from Chippewa.

The warriors kept the Americans occupied with harassing, lightning-like sorties from the woods. This also kept them disorganized while Sheaffe formed his battle lines. The loud, screeching war whoops of Norton's warriors could be heard across the river. This terrified the volunteers who refused to cross over. They stood on their right as a militia not to serve except voluntarily on foreign soil. This was not the only problem the officers had with the reinforcements. The crossing was in a direct line of British cannon fire from Vrooman's Point so the boat owners refused to let them use their boats claiming it was too dangerous. There would be no reinforcements arriving on the Canadian side to support Scott.

The warriors now attacked head on placing themselves between British and American lines. At first Scott's line held but then wavered, and then it broke. The route was on. The Americans reached the river's bluffs some tumbling over, some setting up to make a stand. Scott and his officers decided that a quick surrender would be the only thing that would save their men from being massacred by the warriors. But how could they get word to Sheaffe? They sent two separate couriers with white flags but the warriors killed them. Scott determined to go himself. He left dressed in his officer's uniform and carrying his sword with a white scarf tied to its point but only managed to get himself captured by Brant and another warrior, but luck was with him that day. Two York militiamen happened to arrive while the warriors were trying to decide what to do with such a highly prized prisoner. John Beverley Robinson and Samuel Jarvis intervened to take charge of the prisoner and escort him to Sheaffe.

Sheaffe accepted Scott's surrender and the ceasefire was sounded by the British bugler. But the warriors paid no attention to the order. They were enraged by the loss of two of their chiefs in the battle and were intent on annihilating all of the Americans pressed against the river. Sir Roger was so appalled by the carnage wrought by the warriors on the battlefield that he insisted that his men stop Norton and Brant from continuing the battle. They succeeded and finally it ended.

Queenston Heights turned into another American debacle. The second invasion of Upper Canada was also a second dismal failure. Van Rensselaer's American army suffered 958 captured. Far more militia crossed over than Scott and Wadsworth had realized. Besides this they suffered 90 killed and 100 wounded. By contrast and thanks to Norton's Mohawks the British suffered only fourteen killed, eighty-four wounded and fifteen missing, but by far the most detrimental loss suffered by the British was the death of Isaac Brock.

NEXT WEEK: Beaver Dams

Beaver Dams

February 5, 2013

In the spring of 1813 the Americans made another attempt at invading Canada. This time they enjoyed more success. General Dearborn left Sackett's Harbor on April 25th with a flotilla carrying 1,700 men. Although Dearborn was on board he gave the field command to Brigadier General Pike. They managed to establish a beachhead just west of the town of York. It was a small town with a population of only 625 but was the capital of Upper Canada. They fought their way to the town where General Sheaffe was commanding. Seeing he was about to be overpowered he withdrew to Kingston taking his regulars with him. However, before the fall of York a main magazine blew up with a tremendous force exacting a heavy toll on the American forces and killing Pike.

General Dearborn assumed command and headed west with all his forces toward Fort George, but not before some general looting and burning down the Government House. Dearborn arrived on the 8th of May at the mouth of Four Mile Creek just four miles east of Fort Niagara where he established a base camp. By May 25th Commodore Isaac Chauncey had arrived from Sackett's harbor with Brigadier General John Chandler and 1,450 reinforcements. They began to bombard Fort George with seventy cannon while Brigadier General John Vincent, commander of Fort

George, could only answer with twenty. Vincent had 1,900 troops in the fort but most of them were unreliable militia.

Dearborn was too ill to participate and watched the battle through his spyglass from the deck of the *Madison*. Major General Morgan Lewis was tactical commander but the actual battle was directed by Lieutenant Colonel Winfield Scott and Major Benjamin Forsyth. With the fort about to be overwhelmed General Vincent ordered the canon spiked and abandoned the fort Meanwhile, Chauncey who had received word that Sackett's was under attack sailed away to assist taking 2,000 men with him.

Now with the town of Newark in their control and the capture of Fort George the Americans finally have a firm foothold on Canadian soil. On the 1st of June Lewis began his advance on Vincent by sending out Brigadier Generals William Winder and John Chandler. The pursuit of Vincent did not go well. The Americans made camp on June 4th along Stoney Creek. Vincent's forces were camped seven miles away and Lieutenant Colonel John Harvey convinced Vincent that the American's position was vulnerable. Vincent allowed a night attack where Harvey employed the ruse of using the loud and terrifying war whoops of feared Mohawk warriors. The results were devastating. Both American generals were captured along with large piles of stores. The result of the Battle of Stoney Creek was the Americans were now penned up in Fort George.

The men in the fort had to be supplied with provisions from the lake head. Captain James Lucas Yeo of the British navy was having great success intercepting American supply boats capturing up to fifteen at a time. British patrols were also having the same kind of success bushwhacking American patrols. So Dearborn ordered Lieutenant Colonel Boerstler to take a detachment and clear out Lieutenant James Fitzgibbon who had a company of rangers trained in forest warfare.

Fitzgibbon had appropriated the two-story house of John Cew, a militia captain to serve as his headquarters. The house was near Beaver Dams on Twelve Mile Creek. After nightfall on June 23rd Boerstler left Fort George with 570 men, two canon and two four-horse wagons headed for Fitzgibbon's headquarters. As they marched through Queenston civilians who were loyal to the crown realized where the Americans were headed. Someone had to rush on ahead and warn Fitzgibbon. That duty fell to a woman, one Laura Secord who made her way across country. She didn't get too far when she fell into the hands of some Caughnawaga warriors. She was able to communicate her mission well enough to them that they escorted her to their leader.

Dominique Ducharme, a captain in the Indian Department, was camped near De Cew's house between Fitzgibbon and the advancing Boerstler. Ducharme commanded some 500 Caughnawaga Mohawk warriors from Lower Canada. So Ducharme was the first to receive Secord's warning and while she continued on to the De Cew house the warriors headed out to prepare an ambush.

By dawn the warriors had taken up their position hidden among a thick stand of beech trees just east of their main camp. Between 8:00 A.M. and 9:00 A.M. the head of Boerstler's column entered the cool shade of the beechwood. When the whole column was strung out along the narrow path the warriors opened fire. There was little room for maneuvering and the first volley knocked all twenty of the advance point off their horses sending the whole column into a state of confusion.

Boerstler got control of his men and they fought their way out of the woods and into the open. They took up a position at the top of a hill which they held for about two hours. Meanwhile eighty British regulars and about 200 militiamen had joined the skirmish. Fitzgibbon arrived late as did Norton and his Grand River Mohawks. Fitzgibbon called a ceasefire to parlay with Boerstler. He managed to convince him he was hopelessly outnumbered and Boerstler, seeing no way to escape, surrendered. The Americans began to lay down their arms and the Grand River warriors rushed in to collect the booty. The Caughnawaga warriors were incensed leaving the Niagara area for Quebec.

The Battle of Beaver Dams cost the Americans dearly. The Caughnawaga warriors neutralized almost 600 men and the

British captured two cannon and the Grand River warriors looted the supply wagons. Later Norton would write of the battle that the Caughnawaga warriors did the fighting, the Grand River warriors got the booty and Fitzgibbon got the credit.

NEXT WEEK: Fort Meigs

Fort Meigs

February 13, 2013

Meanwhile, in the Detroit Theater General Harrison was laying plans for his second attempt at a Canadian invasion. In February 1813 he set Captain Wood busy improving Fort Meigs' fortifications. The fort was vital to his plans as he wanted to use it as a springboard for his invasion. Wood worked feverishly and by spring the improvements were almost complete. The fort was a potato shaped structure near the mouth of the Maumee River just south of the old British Fort Miami but on the opposite bank. Wood had added a twelve-foot palisade fronted by huge mounds of earth.

On April 1st the six month tour of duty was up for the Virginia and Pennsylvania militias and all but 250 men left the fort for home. The 250 men that remained only planned to stay another two weeks. Tecumseh's scouts had the fort under surveillance and reported the departure to him immediately. Tecumseh told General Proctor the time to attack Fort Meigs had come and Proctor agreed but bad weather held him up at Amherstburg until April 23rd. Proctor arrived at the mouth of the Maumee on April 26th with 450 regulars and 475 militiamen. Tecumseh joined him with 600 warriors and then Roundhead arrived with another 600.

Harrison who had heard of the British plans to advance on Fort Meigs rushed forward from his winter quarters at Cincinnati. He managed to arrive at Fort Meigs before Proctor and his First

Nation allies. All he could do now was take shelter in the fort along with the few troops left there and their Shawnee scouts. They anxiously awaited reinforcements who were on their way from Kentucky.

By May 1st the British had built reinforced blockhouses across the river and were firing on the fort. However, their cannonballs sunk uselessly into the soft mud of the earthen ramparts. Meanwhile, hidden among the woods the warriors busied themselves by taking pot shots at any slight movement behind the stockade. The siege continued for four days during which General Green Clay made his way down the Maumee with 1,200 Kentucky Militiamen.

Most of the Shawnee scouts loyal to the Americans were hold-up in the fort but a few others were leading Clay's forces. These Shawnee were rather reluctant participants. They had preferred to remain neutral in the conflict but were enlisted by the Indian agent John Johnston after he put them under considerable pressure. Among these reluctant warriors was Black Fish the son of a Shawnee war chief.

Black Fish and three militiamen traveling ahead of the main force in a canoe reached a point within sight of the fort. There they ran into a hostile party of Potawatomie. They turned and fled back up the river but two of the Kentuckians were captured. However, Black Fish and the other man who was wounded in the encounter escaped. Clay kept coming.

On May 1st they landed just south of the fort on the American side of the river. Clay, acting upon Harrison's orders, split his forces in two. He sent 800 militiamen under Colonel William Dudley along with all his Shawnee warriors across the river with orders to capture and spike the British cannon then recross the river to the fort as quickly as possible. Meanwhile, he and the other 400 fought their way to the fort.

Dudley was successful. The warriors who were fighting Clay outside the fort realized what Dudley was up to and quickly swam the river to engage him. Dudley's men were raw recruits with no military experience and they became over exuberant at their victory. Tecumseh's warriors arrived and lured the militia deeper and deeper into the woods. When the Shawnee, who were adverse to the adventure in the first place, saw what was happening surrendered to the British immediately. Tecumseh and Roundhead sprung their trap and the militia panicked and fled back toward British lines to surrender. Dudley was killed and many were cut down. Many more were captured. Of Dudley's 800 Kentucky Militia fewer than 150 made it back to the fort.

The prisoners were escorted to old Fort Miami where they were held under a small British guard. The warriors were in a highly excitable state and began tormenting the Americans by making them run the gauntlet. Suddenly one was tomahawked and scalped on the spot. Things were getting out of hand. The British soldiers in charge tried to control the situation but one of them was killed so they backed off and sent for help.

Help quickly arrived in the form of one very recognizable warrior riding into the ruins that was once a British fort brandishing a tomahawk and yelling orders to cease and desist. It was Tecumseh and he quickly took control. He reamed out the leaders of the agitated warriors by threatening death to the next one to disturb any of the prisoners. He didn't want another massacre like Frenchtown laid at the feet of his confederacy.

Black Fish insisted he and his warriors had been coerced into service by the Americans. In fact he told Proctor that all the Shawnee in Ohio had British sentiments but were being held prisoner in their villages at Wapakoneta and Lewistown. Upon hearing this Proctor made an offer to Harrison; the return of all American prisoners if they would allow any loyal Shawnee to remove to Canada. However, this British offer only served to cast suspicion on the Shawnee at Wapakoneta loyal to the Americans. They came under attack again by militia and settlers alike. Black Hoof complained so Johnston intervened managing to settle things down.

The warriors collected all the booty from the battlefield. One by one individual war parties withdrew following their chiefs back to their villages as was their custom after a great military victory.

This left Proctor and Harrison stalemated so Proctor withdrew. The weather had been bad the whole time so he blamed his failure to take Fort Meigs on it. He also blamed his commanding officer, General DeRottenburg for not adequately supplying the mission.

NEXT WEEK: Fort Stephenson

Fort Stephenson

February 16, 2013

Robert Dickson, a tall Scotsman with flaming red hair, had been appointed Indian Agent for the First Nations of the far North West Territories. He had traded with them for some time with the reputation of being always honest and fair. The Sioux called him Mascotopah or The Red-Haired Man and he was married to one of their own, a Yanktonais woman. In short he was well liked. It was only natural that he was tasked by the British Indian Department to recruit warriors for the cause. Dickson had great success. Sioux war chiefs Little Crow, Itasappa and Red Thunder joined him easily as they had already been plied by Tecumseh and The Prophet a few years earlier.

Tecumseh's warriors began amassing at Amherstburg again in July. Main Poc returned from Illinois Territory where he had been recruiting with the help of fellow Potawatomi chiefs White Hair and White Pigeon. At the same time a large group of warriors from the North West Territories, flags flying, all decked out in their finest war regalia paddled out of Lake St. Clair and into the Detroit River. In the lead canoe was the red-headed man Dickson. His entourage included Ojibwa, Sioux, Menominee, Potawatomi, and Winnebago warriors all recruited from his base at Le Bay or Green Bay. Their arrival at Amherstburg bolstered Tecumseh's forces to 2,500.

Tecumseh pressured Proctor to invade Ohio again. Captain Barclay warned Proctor of the fleet being built at the U.S. Naval Yards at Presque Isle. But Proctor was short on supplies for his heavy artillery so he postponed an attack on the ship yards. However, he did have 2,500 men to add to Tecumseh's 2,500 which he felt was more than enough to mount an invasion. Tecumseh wanted to return to Fort Meigs but Proctor wanted to attack Fort Stephenson a much weaker fort on the Sandusky River. To take Fort Stephenson would have cut the supply line to Fort Meigs but Tecumseh was insistent so he left Amherstburg in the middle of July bound for Fort Meigs. Proctor followed on July 19, 1813.

General Harrison had left Fort Meigs in the command of General Green Clay while he moved to the Lower Sandusky. Tecumseh's warriors arrived first at the mouth of the Maumee so Clay called for reinforcements from Harrison. He sent none convinced Fort Meigs with its current garrison was strong enough to withstand any assault. Instead Harrison withdrew up the Sandusky to Old Seneca Town leaving Fort Stephenson under the command of Major George Croghan. From this vantage point he could either move on Fort Stephenson or Fort Meigs wherever he was needed. This was good strategy the only hindrance being he would have to contend with the Black Swamp which lay between them.

Proctor settled in for a siege of the fort and began pounding the stockade with cannon fire. But his guns were not heavy enough. He had come with only three six-pounders and two howitzers. The warriors spread out among the thickets surrounding the fort taking pot shots at the men inside whenever they popped up to fire through the loopholes. Tecumseh complained it was too difficult fighting these Americans who were acting like groundhogs instead of coming out and fighting like men.

He came up with a plan to lure them out. The warriors moved to the road that led to Fort Stephenson just out of Clay's sight. They began firing their rifles and hollering loud war whoops increasing in intensity. This ruse was intended to convince Clay they were engaging a relief force sent by Harrison. But Clay had already received word from Harrison that he would not send reinforcements unless he received the call from Clay and he had sent no such message. Although he had trouble convincing his officers it was a trap he did manage to hold them back. Tecumseh's plan failed.

The siege of Fort Meigs was also a failure. A few hundred of Dickson's warriors from the west drifted away since there was no plunder to be had. Proctor packed up his cannon and sailed to the mouth of the Sandusky and up the river to within a mile of Fort Stephenson. It was a much smaller post than Fort Meigs and although it was an impressive looking fort it was in truth weakly defended. It had a stockade of sixteen foot pickets and was surrounded by an eight foot wide moat. Each picket had a bayonet thrust horizontally through its tip. However, it only had one heavy gun, an old six-pounder left over from the Revolution affectionately referred to as "old Betsy".

Tecumseh had moved his warriors up the Sandusky between Fort Stephenson and Old Seneca Town to cut off any retreat or prevent any reinforcements arriving. Okemos was a redoubtable Ojibwa war chief from Cedar River and also a nephew of the renowned war chief Pontiac. He and his cousin Manitocorbway from Saginaw were further upriver scouting for any signs of Harrison coming to Croghan's aid. They ran into one of Harrison's patrols and Okemos was severely wounded in the skirmish. Meanwhile, the seven hundred warriors with Proctor settled in among the surrounding woods as spectators. A frontal assault facing cannon fire out in the open was not their style of warfare.

Proctor decided to storm the fort. He was in the habit of becoming unsure of himself when patience and resolve was required. His men were unprepared to storm the garrison. They didn't have the ladders to scale the palisade which was higher than they thought. Their axes were dull from lack of use. The moat was deeper than they realized. Proctor's men became bogged down in the moat and "old Betsy" raked them lengthwise with grape-shot. They lost 150 men either killed or wounded. Proctor made no second attempt to take the fort but withdrew limping back to Amherstburg.

The Americans had a clear and decisive victory at last. And they had a national hero in Major Croghan a mere youth just turned twenty-one, who had defeated the British General in command of their western army and a force five times his size. Proctor had to explain himself to his superiors. He openly admitted he ordered the disastrous assault on Fort Stephenson under the threat of First Nations withdrawal from the war. General Prevost retorted he never should have committed any part of his valuable force due to the clamoring of "the Indian warriors". To Tecumseh the failure to take either fort may have been a sign that the tide of the war was turning but he was resolved to fight on.

NEXT WEEK: Retreat up the Thames

Retreat up the Thames

February 19, 2013

The Americans continued their shipbuilding efforts at Presque Isle (Erie, Pennsylvania) unabated. Proctor wanted to use a naval attack to destroy the fruits of their labors but he was just not ready. All summer long they waited for supplies and ammunition to arrive. The supplies included sail and guns for the brig *Detroit* which was still under construction. There were few trained seamen at Amherstburg to sail the other three war ships anchored there. On June 3rd 1813 Captain Robert Heriot Barclay arrived at Amherstburg with nineteen sailors and the schooners *Lady Prevost* and *Chippewa*. These two brought the British fleet to six ships. Barclay had arrived from England that spring fresh from naval action in the Napoleonic wars. He had lost an arm at Trafalgar.

In charge of the American Lake Erie fleet was Master Commandant Oliver Hazard Perry. He was in charge of the shipbuilding at Presque Isle when Barclay arrived at Amherstburg. He also had to oversee the transfer of five ships built at Black Rock which, with the ships built and under construction at Presque Isle would consolidate his Erie fleet there. During the third week of June while Barclay was cruising the lake trying to catch the transfer Perry slipped the five vessels into the harbor at Presque Isle under the cover of fog. Barclay missed them. The American fleet was now consolidated and the construction phase was nearing completion. But the British fleet was still not ready so Barclay advised Proctor to attack the U.S. shipyards by land. Proctor had 500 regulars and Tecumseh 1,000 warriors at Amherstburg but he vacillated saying that he needed to wait for reinforcements to bolster his regiment the 41st Foot.

By August 10th Perry was out on the lake with his fleet of nine war ships. They included the brigs *Lawrence* 20 guns, *Niagara* 20, *Caledonia* 3, schooner *Ariel* 4, schooner *Scorpion* 2, sloop *Trippe* 1 and schooners *Tigress*, *Porcupine* and Ohio 1 each. His plan was to attack Barclay's fleet at Amherstburg before the *Detroit* could be completed but he became gravely ill along with 270 of his sailors with lake fever and had to postpone.

The British were now in a desperate situation. Supplies were held up at Long Point because Perry now controlled the lake. DeRottenburg had to impress wagons from the general populace and haul them to the Thames where they could be barged down river to Proctor. On September 5th some supplies along with thirty-six more sailors arrived at Amherstburg. Still not enough but Prevost and DeRottenburg both pressed Proctor to take action. Proctor gave in and stripped Fort Malden of its guns to outfit *Detroit.*

On September 14th Barclay sailed out of the Detroit River and into Lake Erie woefully out manned and out gunned. His fleet consisted of H.M.S. *Detroit* 21 guns, H.M.S. *Queen Charlotte* 18, schooners *Lady Prevost* 14 and *Chippewa* 1, the brig *Hunter* 10 and the sloop *Little Belt* 3. He could only supply each ship with ten experienced sailors. The balance of the compliment of 440 men was made up of infantrymen supplied by the 41st.

They engaged Perry off the Bass Islands. For two hours the roar of the ship's big guns could be heard back at Amherstburg but could not be seen. Then silence. It would be two days before Proctor got word of Barclay's total defeat. In the meantime Harrison was moving north toward Detroit with 2,500 regulars, 3,000 Kentucky Militia and 150 Pennsylvania Militia. Proctor's situation had gone from being desperate to hopeless. He planned to evacuate the fort and retreat up the Thames but kept his decision to himself for three days.

Tecumseh wanted to cross back into Michigan and ambush Harrison at the Huron River. But some men were seen dismantling Fort Malden and Tecumseh and the other chiefs demanded a conference with Proctor. Ojibwa war chiefs Naiwash and Nahdee were with him but his closest ally and staunchest supporter Roundhead was not. He had died unexpectedly of natural causes earlier that summer. Finally, after several days they met in council. Tecumseh spoke for the chiefs:

> Listen! When war was declared, our Father stood up and gave us the tomahawk, and told us he was now ready to strike the Americans; that he wanted our assistance; and that he certainly would get us our lands back which the Americans had taken from us. Listen! You told us at that time to bring forward our families to this place. We did so, and you promised to take care of them, and that they should want for nothing while the men would go and fight the enemy . . . When we last went to the rapids [Fort Meigs] it is true we gave you little assistance. It is hard to fight people who live like groundhogs. Father, listen! We know that our fleet has gone out. We know they have fought. We had heard the great guns, but know nothing of what has happened to Our Father with One Arm . . . We are astonished to see our Father tying up everything and preparing to run . . . without letting his red children know what his intentions are . . . and we are sorry to see our Father

> doing so without seeing the enemy . . . Listen Father! The Americans have not yet defeated us by land; neither are we sure they have done so by water. We, therefore, wish to remain here and fight our enemy should they make their appearance. Father! You have got the arms and ammunition, which our Great Father [the King] sent for his red children. If you have an idea of going away, give them to us, and you may go . . . Our lives are in the hands of the Great Spirit. We are determined to defend our lands, and if it is his will, we wish to leave our bones upon them.

Proctor was embarrassed by Tecumseh's speech so promised his answer in two days. Again they met in council but this time Proctor was more forthcoming. With a map of the Detroit area laid out on a table he explained that both his supply lines were now cut off. Fort Malden was now defenseless having lost her guns along with the brig *Detroit.* Not only did Perry control Lake Erie but he could sail right past the fort into Lake St. Clair to stop supplies arriving via the Thames. Proctor saw no other option but to retreat up the Thames and make a stand near Chatham. Tecumseh reluctantly agreed but Main Poc left with his Potawatomi warriors crossing back into Michigan determined to harass Harrison's advance.

Harrison crossed into Canada occupying Amherstburg unopposed seventeen days after the battle of Lake Erie. Proctor and Tecumseh left Sandwich about the same time heading for the Thames. Twelve miles upriver they passed the great burial mound left over from the Iroquois War more than a century earlier. They passed Chatham deciding instead to make a stand at the Delaware village of Moraviantown. Harrison left Brigadier General Duncan McArthur with 700 men to defend Detroit and pursued Proctor and Tecumseh up the Thames. On October 3rd Tecumseh decided to test the Americans. He had 1,500 warriors and he prepared an ambush after destroying the two bridges over McGregor's Creek. One they burnt but the other was too wet so they tore up the planks. Harrison had over 3,000 men and the skirmish lasted for over two hours. Tecumseh's lines finally broke and he retreated back to Moraviantown. Seeing the strength of the Harrison's forces many of his warriors drifted away and he was left with only 500.

On the morning of October 5th Proctor formed a line three and one half miles west of the village of Moraviantown. It ran north from the river for 500 yards to a large swamp. That line was held by 540 men of the 41st Foot Regiment and 290 men of the Royal Newfoundland Regiment. The warriors took up positions in the swamp and they waited.

Harrison arrived at eight o'clock in the morning with 1,000 Mounted Kentucky Riflemen, 2,300 Kentucky Volunteers and 140 regulars. The mounted riflemen were unusually well-trained by Colonel Richard M. Johnson. Each carried a tomahawk, a scalping knife and a long rifle and Johnson had drilled them over and over again in a highly unusual maneuver Instead of charging a defensive line then dismounting and continuing the fight on foot they rode right through the line then dismounted attacking from the rear. This took the British by surprise and they surrendered almost immediately. When Proctor saw this he fled in his carriage.

Tecumseh fought on. Johnson's tactic could not be employed because of the swamp. So they dismounted and advanced on foot. The warriors would wait until the Kentuckians were almost upon them then shower them with a hail of bullets. The Kentuckians kept coming screeching cries of "Remember the Raisin". Then the great leader fell and the warriors broke away. The British suffered 12 killed, twenty-two wounded and 600 captured. The Americans lost seven killed and twenty-two wounded. The warriors' casualties are unknown except for the incalculable loss of their august Shawnee leader Tecumseh.

NEXT WEEK: Beginning of the End

Beginning of the End

February 21, 2013

The distinguished Shawnee chief from Ohio was gone. For years after the war great controversy arose over who had killed him and what happened to his body. Much credence was at first given to Colonel Johnson as being the one to fire the fatal shot. The only thing that seems certain is that he did shoot a warrior at close range. By 1830 he was a senator for Kentucky and was being touted as a candidate for president and did rise to vice president in 1837. During this time many so-called witnesses who backed Johnson came forward to corroborate the story. Those who opposed him produced many more deniers. Credit for slaying the great chief had become valuable political capital but he had always resisted never claiming to have done the deed. After all he had never seen the great chief in person. Finally he succumbed to temptation in 1843 by affirming that indeed it was him that shot Tecumseh dead, but there is no definitive proof.

Just as many stories swirled about as to where his body was put to rest. Many of the fallen warriors were scalped and mutilated at the end of the battle. Some were skinned for such things as souvenirs and to make items like razor straps. Harrison was shown one body the day after the battle as it lay mutilated on the field. He was told it was Tecumseh but it was so badly abused and the face so swollen that he could not recognize him. One story has the body given to the Canadians who took it back to Sandwich for burial. Another has him buried at the site of the battlefield. Mythical stories arose of his closest companions spiriting the body away to be buried in a secret place. There is a monument at Bkejwanong (Walpole Island, ON) that claims him to be resting on the island. Another possibility, if the story of him being carried away by his comrades is true, is that he may have been interred at the great burial mound west of Chatham. Other great war chiefs were taken there for burial as it was a great honor to be laid to rest with other fallen warriors.

The Battle of Moraviantown and especially the loss of Tecumseh effectively broke his confederacy. Many of the warriors who drifted away never came back. Ojibwa chief Naiwash of Saugeen complained the following year saying "perhaps the Master of Life would give us more luck if we would stick together as we formerly did . . . and we probably might go back and tread upon our own lands. Chiefs and warriors, since our great chief Tecumtha has been killed we do not listen to one another. We do not rise together. We hurt ourselves by it. It is our own fault . . . We do not go to war, rise together, but we go one or two, and the rest say they will go tomorrow." But there were those who carried on like Wawanosh from Aamjiwnaang who fought at Lundy's Lane and Megish, a Shawnee who was living at Little Bear Creek (North Sydenham River) in Upper Canada, who also was killed at Lundy's Lane. And of course the Caughnawaga Mohawks continued in the east at battles such as Chateauguay.

The War of 1812 ended with the Treaty of Ghent in 1814. Nothing changed. The U.S./Canada border remained the same. First Nations were left out of the treaty process altogether. The war became a textbook example of how not to conduct a war. Like most wars it consisted of a series of blunders made by one side then the other. One thing it did do was usher in a new era for First Nations. This was the last time they would be looked upon as allies. The future did not bode well for Tecumseh's people.

In the fall of 1818 the Saulteaux Ojibwa of the St. Clair region were invited to an "Indian Council" at Amherstburg to treat with the British Indian Department for a large tract of land known as the Huron Tract. The Napoleonic Wars were over in Europe and there had been a great influx of immigration to Upper Canada. The Colonial Government of Upper Canada needed more land for the newly arrived settlers. On October 16th the council was convened. In attendance were twenty-seven chiefs and principal men of the bands as Chenaille Escarte, St. Clair, Sable and Thames Rivers as well as Bear Creek. The colonial government was represented by John Askin, Superintendent of Indian Affairs. Lieutenant Colonel Evans recorded the minutes and J Bth Cadot served as interpreter.

The minutes record that it was the desire of the government to purchase all of the lands north of the Thames River owned by them and asked what their terms were for the tract's disposal.

The chiefs responded affirmatively by saying a most curious thing. According to the minutes they replied they "were willing to sell our lands . . . that is our wish that he [the Lieutenant Governor of the Province] set the valuation on the tract required". The seller was asking the buyer to set the selling price!

We have here members from two different cultures not communicating. To understand the Ojibwa's strange request one must also understand their culture. Various nations had always traded with each other but it was not like the trade Europeans conducted. For example when these Ojibwa lived on the north shore of Georgian Bay they traded with their Huron neighbors to the south. The Ojibwa were hunters and fishers while the Huron were more agrarian. Extra produce was exchanged each year but it was done in a spirit of sharing rather than one of negotiations. Commerce for this culture was a system of sharing and if one suffered some calamity such as drought and had no surplus the other shared theirs anyway.

This system flowed out of the Ojibwa worldview where human beings as in the Western creation story were created last. But the stories are diverse from there. In the Western story humans are presented as the pinnacle of God's creation and placed on the top of creation's hierarchy even over and above their environment. The Creator instructs them to subdue and have dominion over it. In this culture any surplus was held back for the best price and if that could not be met the surplus goods could even be let go to waste.

In the Ojibwa story human beings were made weak and vulnerable. Their place on the hierarchy of creation was on the bottom. They were so vulnerable that the Creator called a council with all of creation. He asks the animals, birds, fish, and plants if they would give themselves as sustenance for humanity's survival.

They agreed. So all of nature provided for their sustenance making all things a gift from the Great Mystery. To hold any surplus back would be an affront to him so negotiations were unheard of. The word for this system of sharing was daawed.

Daawed was translated into English variably as sell, purchase, price or trade as understood in Western Society's terms of commerce. The British understood the treaty to mean land title transfer but the Ojibwa understood daawed to mean a sharing of surpluses. They knew because of a great decrease in their population due to war and disease they had a surplus of land but they had no way of knowing what the government had in the way of a surplus to offer them. So they asked and daawed was translated here as valuation. All treaties with the Crown have such misunderstandings embedded in them and unfortunately these historic documents are still misunderstood today.

For the Ojibwa the treaty was set that day but for the British the treaty would undergo two more revisions and not be completed until nine years later. Treaty No. 29 would see the title for 2.2 million acres transferred to the Colonial Government of Upper Canada and the creation of four reserves containing less than 20,000 acres. From there it would be all downhill. For example, Canada would see the infamous Indian Act enacted in 1876. It is a stifling paternalistic, monumental piece of legislation designed to control every aspect of First Nations lives. It is still in effect today. In 1887 the U.S. Congress would adopt the Dawes Act. This piece of legislation was designed to relieve First Nations of more of what little land they had left. Today, in Canada, First Nations are calling for the treaty relationship with the Government of Canada to be reset to a nation to nation basis. One of equal partnership sharing the land and its resources as the original treaties called for. At this time the struggle continues.